THE
TEACHING LIFE

PROFESSIONAL LEARNING
AND CAREER PROGRESSION

KATE JONES AND
ROBIN MACPHERSON

First published 2021

by John Catt Educational Ltd,
15 Riduna Park, Station Road,
Melton, Woodbridge IP12 1QT

Tel: +44 (0) 1394 389850
Fax: +44 (0) 1394 386893
Email: enquiries@johncatt.com
Website: www.johncatt.com

ISBN: 978 1 913622 89 3

Set and designed by John Catt Educational Limited

PRAISE FOR THE BOOK

For a field that is rife with superficial and ill-informed thinking, it's rare to read something about professional development that is so considered, so insightful and so based on evidence as this book is. I can think of no better guide for school leaders looking to create a dynamic culture of development for their staff. An indispensable guide.

Dr Carl Hendrick, Wellington College. @C_Hendrick

Rarely does one read a book that captures not only the essence of its time, but also makes such a distinct and valuable contribution in its field. Full of practical advice on, for example, great professional learning, applying for jobs, working abroad, and gaining qualifications, I have no doubt this book will be a faithful companion to teachers right across the UK and beyond. Kate and Robin are honest and pragmatic about the challenges for our profession but optimistic and bullish about what can be achieved. It draws on a wonderfully diverse range of teachers and leaders to offer educationalists a rich range of perspectives, all grounded in reality, yet rooted in achieving the best for the next generation. Highly recommended!

Andy Buck, Founder – Leadership Matters, Creator –
The BASIC Coaching Method, CEO – Andy Buck Leadership Services
and author of Leadership Matters. @Andy__Buck

The Teaching Life is terrific. Two young, yet widely experienced professionals with a lens informed by working in a number of different jurisdictions have written the book that would have been so helpful to me earlier in my career. Kate and Robin have grounded *The Teaching Life* in insights from research, practice, and conversations with individuals. This serves to make it a lively and really helpful resource and reference for teachers considering how to make the most of their talents and time in this marvellous profession.

Mary Myatt, Education consultant, founder of Myatt and Co and author.
@MaryMyatt

The Teaching Life is a fantastic read. The interplay of evidence and experiences brought to the table by Kate and Robin ensures that teachers and leaders at any stage of their career can both relate to this book and draw out clear ideas to further their own professional development. It is fluid, research rich yet also offers highly relatable practical examples and oceans of advice. An absolute must read.

Sam Strickland, Principal of The Duston School and author of
Education Exposed. *@Strickomaster*

In this book, Kate and Robin have tackled the broad and vitally important challenge of teacher professional learning. Being a successful teacher, as they have recognised, is about much more than just *becoming* a teacher – it's also about what you do after that point. There are so many different ways that today's professionals can engage with learning opportunities, and *The Teaching Life* provides a very engaging and useful guide to these. I was particularly pleased to see the focus that the book places on engagement with research, and on sharing and networking. If we are to have a high-quality teacher profession, we need teachers to understand the opportunities that are available for them to develop and to grow their skills and knowledge. Kate and Robin – both inspiring educators themselves, as well as talented authors – are perfectly placed to guide readers to better understand these opportunities. *The Teaching Life* is highly recommended.

Jonathan Firth, author and Teaching Fellow, School of Education,
University of Strathclyde. @JW_Firth

Teaching can be challenging and arduous, but it can also be uniquely inspiring and influential for the lives of young people. Kate and Robin offer a personal and powerful account of the joy of teaching, along with lots of practical advice on how to navigate your way through a flourishing career. From accessing good quality professional development, to accessing evidence, and taking your next steps in your career, it offers a clear, helpful window on a successful teaching life.

Alex Quigley is National Content Manager at the Education
Endowment Foundation, and author of Closing the Reading Gap
and other books for teachers. @AlexJQuigley

Where does your life as a teacher stop and the rest of your life start? Where does your life as learner stop and the rest of your life start? Much as having boundaries is vital to preserving teacher wellbeing, the opportunities for those who work in education to flip tradition and find opportunities for professional learning in new places and formats are exciting and liberating. *The Teaching Life* is a superb book that explores these themes and provides a menu of options that will provide something of value to EVERY teacher, no matter how much prior experience, time or budget they have. This is a massively important contribution to the world of teacher education from Robin and Kate.

Lena Carter, Deputy Head Teacher of 2 to 18 Pupil Support in Scotland, WomenEdScotland Lead, Teacherhug Radio Presenter (Wellbeing Team). @lenabellina

A highly accessible and informative book for teachers (new, experienced and those returning to teaching) as well as school leaders to assist them negotiate between the demands of the everyday while retaining a thirst for knowledge and personal growth. Drawing from vignettes from a range of teachers and school leaders from across the UK and internationally, the book provides ideas on how to engage with transformative professional learning, to engage in learning that is cognitively demanding and reflexive and to consider what might be needed at different stages of the career journey.

Professor Emerita Rowena Arshad CBE, FEIS Chair in Multicultural and Anti-Racist Education. @rowenaarshad

In *The Teaching Life*, Kate and Robin have produced a book for every teacher, for every stage of their career. It covers a plethora of topics from classroom to career and places the enhancement of teachers' experiences of the profession at the heart of the book. What is exceptional is the diverse range of voices, case studies, and robust questions that provide a pathway for further deeper professional discussions. From Early Career Teacher to those in leadership, there is something for you in this book and I get the sense that once you have read it, it will leave you with a sense of optimism about your own teaching life.

Sonia Thompson, Headteacher at St Matthew's Research and Support School. @son1bun

CONTENTS

FOREWORD BY DAME ALISON PEACOCK

To teach is to learn.

This powerful book celebrates the importance of professional learning as a necessary precursor to career development. When I began my teaching career many years ago, the process of actively planning a career path was uncommon. Often promotion was achieved with a lack of transparency – through a 'tap on the shoulder' or as a matter of expediency. Opportunities appeared (or didn't) with a degree of randomness. The professional learning menu offered in these pages shows how much progress has been achieved: you can now discover a wealth of opportunities to grow your career and build the professional capacity which will enable you to transform children's lives for the better.

My own career developed because I was fortunate enough to be able to afford to study for a master's degree while taking a career-break with our two children. I found time to read a great deal and as I was studying Early Years I also had two little developing case-studies at my fingertips. I taught part-time at a local village school and carried out a mini-research study of a child with additional needs for my thesis. Upon my return to full-time teaching, I was approached by one of my tutors to participate in some research with our students and subsequently was recruited to join the Learning without Limits project as one of the nine teachers across England whose inclusive classroom practice was studied. So began a period of twelve years when my teaching and then my leadership was scrutinised, critiqued and ultimately written about by academics. I was actively involved in the process of review and reflection through a form of coaching and enquiry where others would observe my work and then hold up a mirror, genuinely interested in my response to their analysis.

I realise that being the subject of research as a teacher and carrying out the role of headteacher/ insider-researcher as we studied at my school, was a rare privilege, and I will always be grateful for this. Essentially, I was given the opportunity to deeply consider the principles that underpinned my teaching and leadership.

I was called upon to study and explain the unconscious decision-making processes which occur multiple times during any lesson. Through this greater knowledge of self, and through a sense of openness, it became easier to lead and to maintain a vision driven by clear values and dispositions.

The central premise of this book is that teachers grow and develop their practice, their efficacy and their purpose, when they are enabled to flourish. The developing role of the teacher is too important to leave to chance. My decision to leave headship to establish the Chartered College of Teaching was based entirely on the same premise. I am convinced that professional learning and enhanced expertise have the capacity to transform not only classrooms but entire schools and collaboratives. We have a collective responsibility to build cultures of ambitious professional learning and growth on behalf of every child or young person who attends school. Thank you for choosing this book, I wish you every success in this collective endeavour as we seek to build schools and colleges full of inspired, knowledgeable, fulfilled colleagues.

Professor Dame Alison Peacock
Chief Executive Officer of the Chartered College of Teaching

#THETEACHINGLIFE

INTRODUCTION

ROBIN

If there is one person I have consciously modelled myself on as a teacher, it's my father's cousin Archie Bevan. Here's why.

Archie was born in 1925 in Lewisham, London, but tragedy struck when his father died before his birth. His mother moved with her children to be with her sister in Stromness, Orkney, and Archie grew up helping in the family bakery. In 1938, Archie went to the Empire Exhibition in Glasgow, which clearly had a profound effect on him; he later wrote about this experience in a book, *Westward Ho*. In 1942 he enlisted in the Royal Artillery and served in India, and was still there in 1947 to witness the human catastrophe of partition.

After his military service he read English at Edinburgh University, and qualified as a teacher at Moray House, the School of Education. He moved back to Orkney to become a teacher, and in 1952 he married Elizabeth Cromarty, who would become his lifelong friend and collaborator. They had three children together, and many grand (and great-grand) children. He went on to be Head of English at Stromness Academy, and then Deputy Rector ('deputy head') until his retirement in 1988.

This would have been a busy enough life just as it stands, but Archie's civic efforts were phenomenal. He was politically active as a convinced socialist; he was involved in the Campaign for Nuclear Disarmament and campaigned in general elections. He hosted a show for Radio Orkney, was an officer in the Boys' Brigade, a member of the Hoy Trust and the Orkney Regional Health Board. In 1968, he was a founding member of the Orkney Heritage Society, of which he was chairman for many years.

Perhaps his most significant collaboration came from his friendship with two of the greats of British culture in the 20th century. The poet and author, and fellow Orcadian, George Mackay Brown was a trusted friend and made Archie his literary executor when he died. Archie curated the poet's unpublished works and brought them into print, and he co-edited the *Collected Poems* in 2005. He was made an honorary fellow of the Association of Literary Studies in 2012.

Archie met the composer Peter Maxwell Davies when the latter was on his first visit to Orkney. Max (as he was known to his friends) took the ferry to Hoy, clutching his newly purchased book by George Mackay Brown which had mesmerised him. Another passenger, Kulgin Duval, noticing the book, approached him saying he was about to see the author who was staying with friends in Rackwick, so would he like to tag along? This visit, on a dull rainy day brightened by Archie and Elizabeth's curry and home brew, fostered a lifelong friendship between composer, poet and teacher which saw them establishing, largely over the Bevan kitchen table, the internationally renowned St Magnus Festival in 1977. It is still going today.

Archie was recognised for his efforts with an MBE in 2000, and sadly passed away in 2015. It is fair to say that his impact on culture and education extended far beyond his beloved home community in Orkney. When I went to visit his grave, I couldn't help but notice something. How could you possibly sum up such a rich and vibrant life? There was one word that Archie wanted to be remembered for, and had it carved on his tombstone. It reads:

ARCHIE – TEACHER

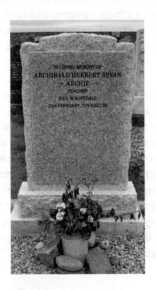

This book is therefore for everyone who is proud to call themselves a teacher, and who wants to do the job to the best of their ability. It is about learning as much as you can about the craft of the profession, and how to plan your career so you make the most of it. It is written by two people who simply love what they do and want to help others feel the same way about teaching. I will spend the rest of my career (and my life) trying to make the same level of contribution to society that Archie Bevan did. I doubt I will get anywhere close to his remarkable list of accomplishments, but I will keep trying all the same. That, in essence, is what drives the best teachers out there.

KATE

In the second year of my teaching career my line manager asked when I would be applying for a Head of Department role. I was told about upcoming opportunities in the local area and was encouraged to start looking. I was very taken aback by this as I had struggled through my NQT (Newly Qualified Teacher) year and felt I had so much more to learn before even thinking about leadership. I had not yet taken a cohort through a full two-year examination course, and I lacked confidence in many areas, from behaviour management to subject knowledge.

My line manager had no intention of leaving at that point so a promotion to Head of Department would have meant leaving the school. I loved the school. I enjoyed working with the students and staff, I felt I was finally getting to know people and understand the different systems and routines in place. I didn't feel ready for leadership and I didn't want to leave the school I was at. This traditional model of leadership and career progression was suggested early in my teaching career, so I felt it was the natural route to follow.

I took my time to develop as a teacher, and in terms of learning and trying to improve as a classroom teacher, I am still doing so a decade later. I have led without a title, time and money. I didn't realise leading without a title was actually providing me with great experiences and useful opportunities that would support me later in my career but there is a time limit to leading without any formal recognition and support. I have been rejected from pastoral leadership positions because I have been told my strengths lie with academic teaching and learning. I expressed that I wanted to develop in other areas and not be confined to one aspect, albeit an important aspect, of education. I have also experienced a lot of success in my career so far, which has left me feeling fulfilled, happy and proud.

I have held a number of middle leadership roles, but my career has taken a quite unexpected turn which I could not have planned for or predicted when I first started teaching, mainly because lots of the things I now do linked to education did not exist (or weren't mainstream) in 2010 when I qualified. In terms of career progression, I have experienced a lot of failures, disappointments and frustrations and no doubt more failures lie ahead, and likely more success and exciting opportunities too.

Teaching has taken me all over the world; teaching in a wonderful British curriculum school in Abu Dhabi, visiting a school in Sri Lanka and presenting at an educational conference in Hong Kong to name just a few highlights. I have a global network of educators, from classroom teachers based in the UK to leading academics in Australia. Reflecting on my teaching practice has led to me becoming a writer; for my own blog, various educational magazines and for this, my sixth book with John Catt Publishing. Talking about teaching has resulted in me having my own podcast and being a host on a radio network dedicated to teachers. Teaching has opened so many doors for me, but the door to the classroom is always my favourite door to walk through. My teacher life has been, and still is, incredible and highly enjoyable but not without its challenges.

Robin and I have had many discussions about the changing and exciting nature of education and what it means to be a teacher today. Being a teacher and school leader can be difficult, demanding and at times exhausting. Being a teacher and school leader can be immensely rewarding, fulfilling and unique. Each teacher has their own path to follow, and we need to recognise and respect this in our profession. We all have our own aims, ambitions, goals and limits, but regardless of yours we hope this book will help you reflect on your teaching career thus far and support you with further career development and progression whatever door you choose to open.

#THETEACHINGLIFE

ACKNOWLEDGEMENTS

Juggling a full-time job in teaching and your personal life is tough at the best of times, so adding a book to the mix would lead many to question our sanity. However, there are key people that a) are to blame for inspiring us and b) are owed thanks for supporting us through the whole process.

KATE

I don't come from a family of teachers, yet they are the first people to congratulate me, celebrate me and pre-order my books with support and love in abundance! My Gran Hazel is my biggest champion and I adore her. Mum and Dad, Heather and Andre are the kindest people I know. My family Emily, Paul, Jessica, Joanne, Ella and Isla – thank you and I love you.

A huge thank you to all my colleagues at The British School Al Khubairat in Abu Dhabi and my former colleagues at Elfed High School in North Wales; for the inspiration, support and teaching me so much throughout my teaching life. My best friend Tom Rogers; we all need a teacher friend we can turn to in our teaching life, to share the highs and lows and for that I have Tom. Finally, Hannah Bellis, my (non-teacher) best friend, and just like my family, despite not being involved in education, Hannah supports me with everything I do.

ROBIN

First and foremost, my amazing wife Hossa. She continues to be my best friend and biggest supporter. She patiently bears my ridiculous enthusiasm for every exciting project that comes my way, and my general inability to turn them down. She is without doubt an angel, and has brought two more little angels into the world who I adore. *Dostet dorum Hossa jan.*

My Dad – a fabulous teacher, and much missed by all who had the privilege of meeting him – will always be a great source of inspiration to me, and he would have been the first person to offer to read the draft manuscript and give feedback. I miss you, Dad. My wonderful Mum Mary and courageous sister Lorna are perpetual sources of support and encouragement, and this book will no doubt have pride of place on their coffee tables at home. And Gerald, I am very proud of you for joining me in becoming an author! Your love and counsel over the years mean everything.

This kind of project is absolutely impossible without a strong network of friends and colleagues who are every bit as passionate about education as we are. I couldn't list them all, but you know who you are. The section on sponsors is based on my great fortune to have worked with Andrew Hunter, Robin Silk, Sir Anthony Seldon, Robin Dyer, and David Knapman. Chris Caves was my first mentor as a trainee, and I totally hit the jackpot. Jill Berry continues to be my mentor in headship and without her advice and wisdom I would be in the professional wilderness.

And finally, to everyone at Robert Gordon's College who stoically puts up with me (especially you, Jennifer Stewart!) I want to thank you for having me in your wonderful community. I thank my lucky stars every day that I work with you. To be a Gordonian is a beautiful thing, and I am tremendously proud that my children will be able to say that.

#THETEACHINGLIFE

PROFESSIONAL LEARNING

The first section of this book is dedicated to professional learning. Schools are an embodiment of learning, and this shouldn't just apply to the students, but to all the teachers and leaders too. We believe professional learning is at the heart of the teaching life.

Professional learning has transformed in many ways over recent years, with elements of it proving popular now which did not exist or were not even possible as recently as just ten years ago. However, there are many long standing components of professional learning which have always been relevant and will continue to be so; for example learning from our colleagues and observing others teach. The first section of our book will focus on elements of change and continuity within professional learning. Regardless of your role or experience, we strongly believe that professional learning can and should be highly effective, empowering and enjoyable.

IS IT A GOLDEN AGE OF PROFESSIONAL LEARNING?

Teacher and author Carl Hendrick (@C_Hendrick)[1] tweeted about professional learning in September 2020:

When I think back to when I started teaching, it's amazing just how narrow CPD was. It took me years to discover stuff. Now there's a wealth of opportunity for teachers to become informed about their profession. We're living in a golden age of professional development.

---

1. Whenever we cite an educator in the book who uses Twitter, we add their handle immediately after their name so you can follow them. Using social media for professional learning is a major theme of the book, so we've tried to make it easy for you to connect with people we respect.

We both agree with Hendrick and can relate to his previous experiences, struggling and muddling our way through professional learning. In the early years of our careers professional learning or CPD (continuing professional development) was infrequent, high cost and closely linked to ticking boxes as opposed to promoting ongoing and meaningful review, reflection and effective development and dialogue.

Teachers would be set a specific target or targets for a term or year, sometimes with no input or involvement in what those targets would be; then once that box was ticked that particular door would be closed permanently, only for another to be temporarily opened. Professional learning felt disjointed and not always productive or helpful, when in fact it should be the exact opposite. Professional learning should develop the individual but also link with departmental, phase and whole school priorities.

The abundance of materials and opportunities now available can be a blessing and a curse. There is a wealth of professional learning content, and this is ultimately a good thing, but the sheer volume and variety can be overwhelming and even intimidating. It can feel challenging to attempt to keep up with emerging trends, developments and reading all the latest blogs or books because, quite simply, we can't. It is worth noting here that not all that glitters is gold. There is an issue with quality assurance, and unfortunately professional learning content (whether that be events, webinars or books) is not all high quality and can leave teachers feeling irritated instead of informed. Professor Becky Allen has explored this issue, writing:

> We consistently see that it is secondary school classroom teachers that are the most negative about their experiences of CPD, perhaps because so little is subject specific. For example, 40% of them feel that CPD has had little or NO impact on their classroom practice. Many classroom teachers also report that abandoning INSET days would have no effect on their teaching![2]

Allen further adds the importance of getting professional development right; 'I think that supporting teachers in getting better at teaching is critical to teacher morale and the long-term health of the schooling system.'

---

2. Allen, R. (2019, January 16) If CPD is so important, then why is so much of it so bad? *Musings on education policy.* https://rebeccaallen.co.uk/2019/01/16/if-cpd-is-so-important-then-why-is-so-much-of-it-so-bad/

We suggest taking time to carefully consider all the professional learning you are thinking about undertaking: is the juice worth the squeeze? Even if the content is free, there is a time cost. Is that time better spent elsewhere? Conversations with other teachers and leaders about professional learning should be taking place regularly. If a book has been helpful or beneficial then it can be useful to share that with those around you and online. The same can apply for events and courses; if you would or wouldn't recommend it then be vocal about that with others, although what might help one teacher in a specific context might not be as relevant to another teacher in a different one.

Professional development was once confined to one-off Inset days at a hotel venue with potential networking opportunities, but those days are slowly disappearing. We both believe that the biggest transformation to happen in terms of professional learning has been teachers and leaders taking ownership and control of when and what they choose to focus on. Professional learning is now more varied, frequent, accessible and can be low cost with a high impact, so a key factor to consider is choice. There is a wealth of books, blogs, articles, events, webinars, qualifications and so on. We simply cannot attend, view, read or access them all. Some do complain about the professional learning market becoming saturated, but they forget that we have a choice, and that choice is powerful.

We can choose what we spend our time and energy (and money) on; agency is important. Teachers and leaders have control over the choice of the professional learning decisions they make; for example, you chose to read this book and others chose not to. There will be times, perhaps during a whole school Inset, where choice isn't an option, for instance with compulsory safeguarding training, but for the majority of the time we have choices.

The professional learning gap

Although this has likely always existed in schools, it is becoming clearer and more evident that there is a professional learning gap in our profession. There is a well-known and widely shared quote from Dylan Wiliam about professional learning:

If we accept that every teacher needs to improve, not because they are not good enough, but because they can be even better, professional development becomes welcome – it is just the way we become better.[3]

---

3.   Wiliam, D. (2019) Teaching not a research-based profession. *TES*, 30 May 2019. https://www.tes.com/news/dylan-wiliam-teaching-not-research-based-profession

It promotes a very important message, and we wholeheartedly agree with the sentiment. Regardless of the years in the classroom or role within a school, each individual can and should continually aim to improve. Professional learning should be consistent from initial teacher training to the end of a teacher's career. The needs will change and evolve as we progress throughout our career, but the desire to grow and refine our skills should remain.

The 'professional learning gap' refers to the clear distinction between those teachers and leaders who embrace professional learning and those who reject it. This is commonplace in schools around the world and poses problems for school leaders. Ultimately, the people that suffer will be the children taught by those teachers who do not have a desire to learn, develop and improve their practice. A vast number of teachers are very knowledgeable about the latest developments in education and actively take ownership of their professional learning. There are many different methods – some of which are explored in this section – to help educators stay informed as the profession moves forward, but the challenge for school leaders is to try to get all staff in a school engaged and excited about professional learning. How can this be achieved?

Schools have a responsibility to support their staff with professional learning; mainly in terms of time and finance (although there are other factors to consider), and school leaders at all levels must lead by example in terms of embracing professional learning. We believe all great teachers have one key element in common; **they never stop learning**. We also believe that all great schools have one thing in common; **they never stop improving**. A great teacher will flourish at a school that encourages them to keep learning. A great school will only be able to improve with teachers that never stop learning. Teacher development and school improvement go hand in hand.

When teachers and leaders are reluctant to engage and develop professionally or have perhaps plateaued, with no interest or responsibility for their own professional learning, it is very disappointing. We have empathy with those who struggle to find the time to engage with research or reading, and that issue does need to be addressed and resolved with support. What frustrates us more is the attitude of those who think they don't really need to keep learning and developing once they have got a few years of experience; the CPD they do is statutory and done under sufferance, but other than that they feel there is no need to keep working on pedagogy or keep abreast of new insights gleaned from research. Treating deeper learning about what we do with cynicism is not the right attitude, and definitely not one we should model to our colleagues and students. Having said that, there are teachers who do engage with research and evidence yet feel frustrated because senior leaders at their schools are not doing the same. Conversely, there are the senior and middle leaders who are leading by example, using evidence-informed practice and methods, but who struggle to motivate their colleagues to do the same.

We don't claim to have all the answers, but we do aim to provide a wealth of helpful suggestions and practical advice in this section for effective and evidence-informed professional learning. It is likely the professional learning gap will always exist, as it probably does in other professions, but the fact that you are reading this book shows you are dedicating time to develop your professional learning. And remember, you can also play an important role in the professional development of others, from colleagues around you to those you may lead.

THE CHANGING ECONOMICS OF PROFESSIONAL LEARNING

In this section we will explore low cost, high impact methods of professional learning that have become popular and highly accessible in recent years. We also look at a range of qualifications and courses that are costly. We consider all of these in terms of both their impact and the required investment of time, effort and finance.

The Education Policy Institute (EPI) published a report in July 2021 entitled *The cost of high-quality professional development for teachers in England* which discussed the potential benefits of investing in professional development for teachers. It will always be difficult to assess how much schools spend on professional learning for staff, and what value they get for that expenditure, as there are many variables. A school may choose to focus on in-house CPD, therefore not spending the same amount of money as they would on inviting an external speaker or consultant, but we cannot measure effectiveness simply by how much money is spent. The EPI report investigated how much schools spend on professional learning:

- *The current cost of teacher professional development differs significantly among schools. It also encompasses not just the direct spending on the CPD training itself, but also the costs to staff time from their participation.*
- *Taking this into account, on average, schools in England spend around £3,000 per teacher per year on professional development.*
- *The average spending on CPD per teacher is slightly higher for academies than for local authority-maintained schools, with academies spending around £3,050 per teacher per year, compared to around £2,850 for local authority-maintained schools.*

- *The vast majority of schools (around 80%) spend just under 3% of their total school budget on teacher CPD each year, which is higher than previous estimates.*

The key findings from the report stated the following:

- *EPI research has shown that introducing a formal entitlement for teachers in England to 35 hours of high quality CPD a year would boost pupil attainment by an extra two-thirds of a GCSE grade – which in turn translates to extra lifetime earnings of over £6,000 per pupil.*
- *In the short term, a policy of CPD entitlement could also significantly improve retention, leading to an estimated 12,000 extra teachers remaining in the profession a year.*
- *Despite these benefits, secondary school teachers in England spend fewer hours a year on CPD compared to other OECD nations, while it is also likely that the majority of CPD currently being provided in England does not meet the criteria for high-quality CPD.*

Any data and financial figures published do not take into account the fact that teachers and school leaders also spend their own money on professional learning. This can include buying books, attending paid events (and expenses such as travel), attaining qualifications and more. Where do we draw the line? Should teachers and school leaders as professionals spend their own money? Many are happy to do so and consider it a personal investment as well as a professional one, and find it enjoyable and interesting. However, there is no denying that schools also have a significant role to play in the economics of professional learning.

There is often a tension when authoring a book; whether to focus on breadth or depth? We aim to do both, but we also recognise that inclusion of a wide breadth of areas can result in a lack of depth at times. Professional learning is relevant to everyone involved in education, although there will be parts within this section of the book that are more relevant than others to different educators. We are hopeful that every teacher and leader, regardless of their position or experience, will be provided with plenty of food for thought and we have added challenge questions at the end of each chapter to help you reflect further. Our main goal is that ultimately this book will act as a valuable method of professional learning for teachers and school leaders at all levels.

#THETEACHINGLIFE

CHAPTER 1:

EVIDENCE-INFORMED
PROFESSIONAL LEARNING

Purpose of this chapter: To explain the benefits of becoming evidence-informed and how this can be achieved.

There is an appetite among the teaching profession to learn more about how research – and specifically evidence from research – can support classroom practice. Teachers and school leaders are keen to become evidence-informed in their approach to professional learning and development. Wiliam has stated that 'Every teacher needs to get better at the things that the best available evidence shows have the biggest impact on student achievement.'[4]

As mentioned in the introduction to this section, some methods of professional development for teachers and school leaders are radically different and unrecognisable from those used in previous years. In an ever changing and digital world we need to embrace these changes. We need to ensure that new technologies, strategies and methods do not negatively add to teacher workload but instead enhance and support teacher development and ongoing learning to ultimately have a positive impact on our students.

Before we explore the benefits, potential barriers and other issues related to evidence-informed professional learning and practice, it is important to clearly establish what we mean when we refer to evidence-informed practice. There are myths and misconceptions around the term 'evidence-informed' in education. It does not mean blindly following and accepting any research or evidence presented to us. Being evidence-informed involves carefully combining the best

---

4. Wiliam, D. (2018) 2 simple changes to create the schools our children need. *Teachwire*, 22 October. https://www.teachwire.net/news/2-simple-changes-to-create-the-schools-our-children-need

evidential findings from the available research with our professional judgment, expertise and experience, and applying that within our own unique classroom context. Wiliam writes:

> *Classrooms are just too complicated for research ever to tell teachers exactly what to do. Teachers need to know about research, so that they can make smarter decisions about where to invest their time, but teachers, and school leaders need to become critical consumers of research – using research evidence where it is available and relevant, but also recognising that there are many things teachers need to make decisions about where there is no research evidence, and also realising that sometimes the research that is available may not be applicable in a particular context.[5]*

Evidence is only one aspect of being evidence-informed in education. This graphic, created by the Chartered College of Teaching (CCT),[6] clearly and simply illustrates what it means to be an evidence-informed practitioner.

Figue 1: Evidence-informed practice

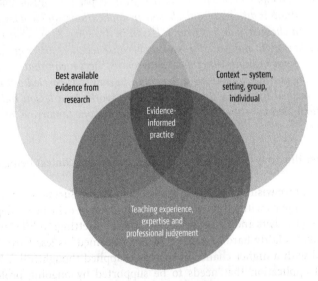

Best available evidence from research

Context – system, setting, group, individual

Evidence-informed practice

Teaching experience, expertise and professional judgement

---

5.   Wiliam, D. (2019) Teaching not a research-based profession. *TES*, 30 May 2019. https://www.tes.com/news/dylan-wiliam-teaching-not-research-based-profession

6.   Stefanini, L. and Griffiths, J. (2020) Addressing the challenges of using evidence in education. *Impact,* September 2020. https://impact.chartered.college/article/addressing-the-challenges-using-evidence-education/

Leading academics Paul A. Kirschner and Tim Surma[7] also provide a useful explanation to distinguish between the terms evidence-based and evidence-informed. They write:

> There is an, albeit sometimes subtle, distinction between evidence-based and evidence-informed in terms of practice in education. An evidence-based practice is an approach to practice that focuses practitioner attention on sound empirical evidence in professional decision making and action. Evidence-informed practice is still based on empirical evidence, but acknowledges the fact that it's harder for real classroom practice to determine what works for who under which circumstances. What seems to work in one classroom does not always work in another classroom.

Hence why evidence alone is simply not enough. Kirschner and Surma further add:

> Five-year-olds are different from fifteen-year-olds both with respect to their cognitive development and their knowledge and expertise, a lesson on concepts and definitions is different from a lesson on applications, and to a lesser extent a lesson in chemistry differs from a lesson in drawing. Also, what works for one teacher might not work for another because teachers differ qualitatively; subtle and not so subtle differences between teachers mean that the way that they carry out the same thing differs both in how it is carried out and how it is perceived by their students. Also, what works in a lesson today won't necessarily work in the same lesson this afternoon, tomorrow, or in three months.

This further illustrates the points regarding nuance and context being key.

Another point we wish to highlight from Kirschner and Surma is that evidence does not provide us with all the answers. Application of evidence is dependent on classroom teachers and school leaders within their setting: 'While "evidence-based" provides fairly hard results, "evidence-informed" is less hard, but still very useful with a higher chance of success if applied thoughtfully'. It is this thoughtful application that needs to be supported by ongoing professional learning in order to be evidence-informed.

---

7.   Kirschner, P. and Surma, T. (2020) Evidence-informed pedagogy. *Impact*, September 2020. https://impact.chartered.college/article/evidence-informed-pedagogy/

DIFFERENT TYPES OF EVIDENCE

Discussing the 'evidence' element of evidence-informed practice can raise a lot of questions, for example where is the evidence from? How reliable is the evidence? How secure is the evidence base? Below is a summary of the different types of research that can elicit evidence linked to education. Some methods and approaches are regarded as more rigorous, reliable or accessible than others and each have their advantages and disadvantages.

Action research

This refers to research undertaken in a school environment in order to address a problem, answer a question or make a significant impact on an area of school improvement at a whole school or classroom level. This can be completed as part of a qualification such as an MA in Education or a Doctorate (you can read more about this in Chapter 5). Action research is often on a smaller scale and less formal than research carried out by academics; examples include lesson study and practitioner enquiry. The key factor of action research is that it is carried out by teachers and leaders within schools, which means it can focus on a precise issue in a specific context, involving the teachers and students that can benefit directly from the research findings. A problem with this approach is that it is carried out by teachers and leaders, many of whom are very busy with the daily demands of their roles and are perhaps not trained in the art and science of conducting and analysing research studies and experiments.

The School of Education at the University of Bristol describes action research in their course as the following:

> The start of the process is usually an issue or situation that, as a teacher, you want to change. You will be supported in turning this 'interesting problem' into a 'researchable question' and then developing actions to try out. You will draw on the findings of other researchers to help develop actions and interpret the consequences. As an action researcher, or teacher-researcher, you will generate research. Enquiring into your practice will inevitably lead you to question the assumptions and values that are often overlooked during the course of normal school life. Assuming the habit of inquiry can become an ongoing commitment to learning and developing as a practitioner. As a teacher-researcher you assume the responsibility for being the agent and source of change.[8]

---

8. University of Bristol (2021) *Action Research*. http://www.bris.ac.uk/education/study/continuing-professional-development-cpd/actionresearch/

Research

It can be commonplace to hear the phrase 'The research tells us ...' but that should immediately elicit a response such as 'What research? Where is this research from? Has it been peer reviewed? Has the research study or experiment been replicated? Under what conditions and context was the research carried out?' Research can lead to more questions than answers. Research refers to the collection of evidence, data and information which is collected and published. In education there are many variables to consider with research and the conditions in which it is carried out, which can vary from a classroom to a laboratory. While we need to take care and exercise caution when engaging with research we should do so with an open mind and a desire to improve while also fully understanding that although most research can help us, no single research paper, journal or study will provide all the answers we are looking for.

Bradley Busch, a psychologist from Inner Drive, has wisely phrased it that, 'On our own, we are all separately bumbling around lost in the dark to our own experiences. With research, we at least have a lamp and a map to help guide us.'[9] Research can provide us with insight, guidance and support but as Kate has previously written in *Love to Teach*, research is only one piece of a complex puzzle when it comes to teaching and learning in schools.

Wiliam points out that:

> A further difference between teaching and other professions is the role of research, and who creates it. Very few teachers are involved in academic research, and the vast bulk of published research in education is produced by academics in universities who are rarely involved in teaching the students that are the focus of their research. In other professions, much of the published research is done by those who are still practicing.[10]

This can account for the skepticism or reluctance of some teachers to engage with academic research findings, which can be seen as being far removed from the classroom.

9. Jones, K. (2021) *Becoming evidence-informed*. Webinar. 27 May 2021.
10. Wiliam, D. (2019) Teaching not a research-based profession. *TES*, 30 May 2019.
    https://www.tes.com/news/dylan-wiliam-teaching-not-research-based-profession

Meta-analysis

A meta-analysis does not refer to research but rather to a collection of research and evidence findings which have been grouped together for analysis, thus combining research with an explanation of the wider picture. An example of meta-analysis is the Education Endowment Foundation (EEF) and their published findings and various toolkits. The EEF writes on their website:

The nature of a meta-analysis is that it aggregates a number of different effect sizes from different studies into a single effect size. It is, therefore, unlikely that any effect size we get from meta-analysis would not differ from any of the individual 'sources'. To address this, we look at the extent of variation among the individual effect sizes to determine how reliable the overall effect size will be. This is one of the factors we use when assessing the 'security' rating for each strand, a five point padlock scale which is presented next to the effect size (months of additional progress) for each Toolkit strand.[11]

Meta-synthesis

A meta-synthesis collects various meta-analyses so is therefore a meta-meta-analysis. Meta-synthesis is most associated with the work of Professor John Hattie, although aspects of his work and meta-synthesis have been critiqued and challenged by fellow academics.[12]

The *Visible Learning* website states the following:

John Hattie developed a way of synthesizing various influences in different meta-analyses according to their effect size (Cohen's d). In his ground-breaking study 'Visible Learning' he ranked 138 influences that are related to learning outcomes from very positive effects to very negative effects. Hattie found that the average effect size of all the interventions he studied was 0.40. Therefore he decided to judge the success of influences relative to this 'hinge point', in order to find an answer to the question 'What works best in education?'... His research is now based on nearly 1200 meta-analyses – up from the 800 when 'Visible Learning' came out in 2009. According to Hattie the story underlying the data has hardly changed over time even though some effect sizes were

---

11. EEF (2017, March 10) Our Teaching and Learning Toolkit – what are the risks and how do we address them? Education Endowment Foundation.
https://educationendowmentfoundation.org.uk/news/the-teaching-and-learning-toolkit-what-are-the-risks-and-how-do-we-address/#closeSignup

12. Slavin, R. (2018, June 21) John Hattie is Wrong. *Robert Slavin's Blog.*
https://robertslavinsblog.wordpress.com/2018/06/21/john-hattie-is-wrong/

updated and we have some new entries at the top, at the middle, and at the end of the list.[13]

You can find more about the work of Hattie and his effect sizes by scanning the QR code at the end of this chapter.

BENEFITS OF BECOMING EVIDENCE-INFORMED

We are both advocates for promoting an evidence-informed approach to teaching, learning and leadership as we have experienced and observed many of the benefits of doing so. While there are many advantages to becoming evidence-informed at an individual, departmental and whole school level, we have chosen to focus on three specific areas that we believe will benefit all teachers, school leaders and students: motivation, confidence and impact.

Motivation

Interest in educational research and its evidence findings have invigorated the teaching profession. Not everyone shares the same enthusiasm towards the evidence-informed movement but those that have taken an interest are highly motivated to find out more, ask more questions and seek more answers as to how we can all improve, and support students to progress and learn.

We believe that being evidence-informed is highly enjoyable and rewarding. It motivates us to continue to learn and develop, rather than plateau. Professor Daniel Mujis, former Head of Research at Ofsted and Dean of the School of Education and Society at Academica University of Applied Sciences, has stated that 'the growth of the evidence-based movement is the best thing to happen to education in decades and has led to genuine change for the better in our schools. The most exciting part of this is that it has been a bottom-up movement, led by the profession,'[14] and we fully agree.

---

13. Visible Learning (2018) *Hattie Ranking: 252 influences and effect sizes related to student achievement.* https://visible-learning.org/hattie-ranking-influences-effect-sizes-learning-achievement/

14. Muijs, D. (2021, April 29) The problem with toolkits. *Education ruminations.* https://educationruminations.com/2021/04/29/the-problem-with-toolkits/

Confidence

Kate has written about this extensively, with a particular focus on strategies supported by cognitive psychology, such as retrieval practice. Becoming evidence-informed has boosted her confidence as both a teacher and middle leader, and she firmly believes this has had a knock-on effect; boosting the confidence of her students and their families. Confidence is an incredibly important element of thriving as a teacher. All aspects of professional learning should ultimately increase teacher confidence; whether that is domain specific, teaching and learning centred or indeed any aspect linked to education.

Primary school teacher and leader Jon Hutchinson is also an advocate for taking an evidence-informed approach to teaching and learning:

> In primary classrooms we have the privilege and huge advantage of teaching children all day. Using that time as effectively as possible to help them to develop academically, socially, emotionally and physically is a huge responsibility and one that no teacher takes lightly. Making sure that our decisions of how to deliver lessons are in line with the most recent evidence is, therefore, a moral imperative. Happily, many of the most evidence-informed strategies (such as building on prior knowledge, or interleaving a spacing practice) are much easier when you know the class and what they are learning so well.[15]

Knowledge of our classes, the content being taught, and evidence-informed strategies all combine to boost teacher confidence in the classroom.

Impact

This should be a central and ongoing aim of all professional learning; to have a positive impact on student learning and outcomes. Is there an immediate or short-term impact? What will the long-term impact be? This is where reflection, evaluation and analysis are key in order to assess and measure the impact. This is a message that Hattie regularly promotes and shares with teachers; know thy impact.

---

15. Jones, K. (2021) *Becoming evidence-informed*. Webinar. 27 May 2021.

BECOMING EVIDENCE-INFORMED CAN HELP YOU CHALLENGE, CONFIRM AND BECOME INFORMED

Challenge

When current practices in education are challenged (or even 'debunked') by research, two possible responses are that it can either be difficult to accept or warmly welcomed. A well known example of research challenging a previous fad in education is that of 'learning styles', which suggests that individuals learn better based on their preferred style of learning. Cognitive scientist and author Daniel T. Willingham, among many others, has been very vocal in dispelling the learning styles myth, which has been found to be untrue.[16] The concept of learning styles was initially believed to be supported by research, and many teachers were told to plan lessons to cater for different learning styles. This illustrates the importance of engaging with research through a critical lens and asking questions about how the evidence collected – and the actions that evidence informs – improves and impacts our classroom practice.

Confirm

Not all evidence from research will challenge our classroom practice; it might actually confirm that what we are doing in the classroom is effective and we should keep doing it. Teachers could potentially roll their eyes at research that simply confirms good practice, but we should not dismiss this evidence just because we already knew something or were already doing it in our classroom. Instead, this should be welcomed as it shows that evidence and our experiences are in alignment.

Inform

Research can challenge or confirm our existing classroom practices and strategies, or it can provide us with new and insightful information which can help us to better understand how students learn and how we can support them in the classroom. If we take for example research around cognitive psychology, it would probably be fair to suggest that teachers have always used quizzing in lessons as a teaching and learning strategy (although perhaps more so for assessment purposes). However, what is clear is that as a profession we did not always possess the knowledge and understanding of the mechanics of memory, learning and forgetting that we have now thanks to the research which has informed us and shaped our practice. Understanding the psychology of memory helps us to refine the approaches we take to quizzing, thus maximising the impact it can have on pupil learning.

---

16. Willingham, D. (ND) *Learning styles don't exist*. www.youtube.com/watch?v=sIv9rz2NTUk

Evidence from research can provide us with answers, suggestions, solutions and plentiful information that can help us develop and learn as classroom practitioners and leaders. Engaging with evidence linked to education is something that everyone in the profession should do; and whether that is to embrace or question the evidence provided, the key element is that we are discussing, sharing and reflecting on the evidence presented to us.

BARRIERS TO BECOMING EVIDENCE-INFORMED, AND HOW TO OVERCOME THEM

There are various issues, complications and problems that can prevent teachers becoming as evidence-informed as they would like to be. Below are some of the most common barriers faced when attempting to engage with research, as well as solutions as to how these barriers can be overcome.

Problem: Access to research. There has been a wealth of research and evidence linked to learning and memory for decades, but it has only become accessible to teachers in recent years. Why is this the case? Previously, studies were mainly carried out in a laboratory at a university or research centre and the findings were published, but they were generally shared across the academic community and not with the teaching profession. If teachers wanted to access this information the main problem was finding it. Research papers and journals were (and some still are) hidden behind a paywall, making them difficult or costly to access.

Solution: Research summaries. The gap between the academic and teaching communities is certainly closing. There are plenty of websites, presentations and research summaries that can be freely accessed and downloaded. The beauty with research summaries is that not only are they easily available, but they are a condensed version and summary of the key research findings, which are often written for teachers so avoid academic jargon and are easier to digest and understand. The organisation researchEd, founded by Tom Bennett and Hélène Galdin-O'Shea, has also done a remarkable job closing the gap between academic research and classroom practitioners (more information about researchEd can be found in Chapter 3).

If you do wish to access and read research material in full, we recommend joining the Chartered College of Teaching (CCT). Members have access to a huge database of research (as well as other benefits), and membership is a much cheaper alternative to purchasing research journals behind various pay walls, as well as making the process of identifying and searching for relevant information much easier and quicker.

Problem: Time. Teaching is universally a demanding job. There are lessons to plan, work to be assessed, administrative tasks such as writing reports, pastoral responsibilities and much more. The idea of engaging with research isn't – for many – the issue, but rather finding the time to do so. Teacher and Senior Leader Jennifer Webb wrote 'Most classroom teachers do not have the time or inclination to wade through reams of academic writing – teaching is intricate and time consuming enough already.'[17] Time is precious, and is a significant barrier in terms of accessing and engaging with all elements of professional learning.

Solution: Professional learning support and time provided by schools. Research summaries also provide a solution here, as a five-page document will take a fraction of the time to read in comparison to a lengthy and in-depth research study. The Education Endowment Foundation (EEF) published a report in 2021 entitled *Cognitive Science Approaches in the Classroom*, and although the full report was 372 pages, the summary was still 50 pages, which still represents a considerable investment of time to read and digest. If school leaders want staff to take an evidence-informed approach they must be willing to provide the time to support staff to do it. This time can be found during Inset or twilight sessions or departmental or phase meetings. Webb argues that school leaders play a key role in disseminating research to teachers:

> *Good leadership of evidence-informed teaching and learning recognises that teachers need to engage with research in a way which is purposeful, appropriate for their context, and so that there is a clear link between theory and practice.*[18]

Problem: Application in the classroom. In 2017, Robin co-authored a book with Carl Hendrick entitled *What does this look like in the classroom? Bridging the gap between research and practice.* This is a key question that teachers engaging with research will continually ask: what does this look like in the classroom? More specifically, what does this look like in my classroom with my students? A laboratory in North America with college undergraduate students is very different to a Year 9 class taught in a small rural school in the UK.

Solution: Teachers reflecting and sharing practice. There are many teachers online who are sharing their reflections and experiences of engaging with research. This can be seen – and engaged with – on social media, through

---

17. Webb, J. (2021) *The Metacognition Handbook: A Practical Guide for Teachers and School Leaders.* Woodbridge: John Catt.

18. Ibid.

blogs and by teachers speaking at events, but we also see it in our schools, with colleagues sharing, reflecting and learning from each another.

As teachers we have a shared understanding of the experiences that can take place in a classroom environment, so when we do reflect on the application of evidence-informed practice we are doing so from a classroom perspective. Academics play an incredibly important role in carrying out and sharing research studies and findings, but teacher voice is also an essential element of evidence-informed practice.

Problem: Academic jargon. Research papers, journals and literature reviews are not often written with teachers as the intended audience, and there can be terminology used which is unfamiliar and difficult to comprehend. This can be very off-putting, and trying to decipher the content of the research material can add even more time to the process.

Solution: Evidence-informed glossary and (again) research summaries. Many academics have realised that teachers don't have the time, technical comprehension or inclination to read their lengthy academic papers. So once again research summaries are useful as not only are they a much shorter, condensed version focusing on the key points and messages, they are also a lot easier to understand and grasp. In terms of the terminology, Kate has created an in-depth evidence-informed glossary which can be found at the back of this book and referred to when engaging with academic research and evidence findings.

THE TPACCK MODEL (2018) FOR PROFESSIONAL LEARNING

Kate has written and spoken about the TPACCK model since first publishing it in her book *Love to Teach* in 2018. It has evolved as school leaders have embraced the model to design their own evidence-informed approaches to professional learning. The origins of the TPACCK model lie with the PCK model developed by American educational psychologist Lee S. Shulman in 1986. Shulman has written extensively about the importance of teachers possessing strong and confident knowledge of content and pedagogy,[19] posing the following questions:

> *Whether in the spirit of the 1870s, when pedagogy was essentially ignored, or in the 1980s when content is conspicuously absent, has there always been a*

---

19. Shulman, L. S. (1986) Those who understand: knowledge growth in teaching. *Educational Researcher*, 15(2), 4-14.

cleavage between the two? Has it always been asserted that one either knows content and pedagogy is secondary and unimportant, or that one knows pedagogy and is not held to account for content?

Shulman provided an overview of previous testing and examinations that teachers had to complete which found these focused on one aspect; either content or pedagogy, with the shift from one to the other occurring during the 1980s. There was a failure to recognise the importance of both content knowledge and pedagogical methods. Shulman became frustrated with the literature focusing on certain aspects of teaching such as classroom management, activities and planning lessons but which neglected the content of the lessons taught and quality of explanations.

PCK – Pedagogical Content Knowledge

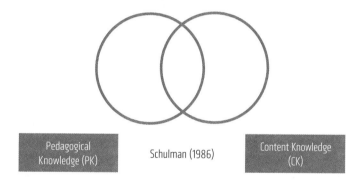

Shulman and his colleagues wanted to redress this imbalance, which he referred to as the 'missing paradigm'. Shulman worked on the assumption that teachers would have both studied to achieve a requisite level of subject knowledge, and studied to obtain the necessary qualifications to enter the profession, but he was concerned about the transition of teachers from being expert learners to novice teachers. He stressed the importance of blending content with different elements of the teaching process.

The TPACK model took this idea of balance further, introducing the third element – technology – and focusing on the combination of 'Technological, Pedagogical and Content Knowledge'. In 2006 an article was published by Matthew J. Koehler and Punya Mishra, titled *Technological, Pedagogical Content Knowledge: A new framework for teacher knowledge*. This article explained that TPACK is a conceptual framework which claims that the successful integration of technology to support students' learning requires a teacher to have the following:

- Strong content knowledge of the specific subject being taught.
- Solid understanding of effective pedagogy.
- Knowledge and experience of different methods of teaching and learning.
- A good grasp of the technology that could be used. Koehler and Mishra write, 'At the heart of good teaching with technology are three core components: content, pedagogy and technology, plus the relationships among and between them.'

A teacher can use their experience and knowledge of effective teaching methods to consider how to incorporate technology into those methods. If the teacher lacks the knowledge and understanding of how that technology works, this will undoubtedly cause problems and end up being a barrier to learning. Technology has the potential to hinder rather than help in the classroom, so it is important we get this right. If a teacher knows how to use technology and has a good comprehension of teaching and learning approaches, but their subject knowledge is weak this can also have a negative impact on learning. Knowing subject material but having a lack of knowledge on how to communicate that information through pedagogy will also result in poor outcomes.

TPACK – Technological, Pedagogical and Content Knowledge

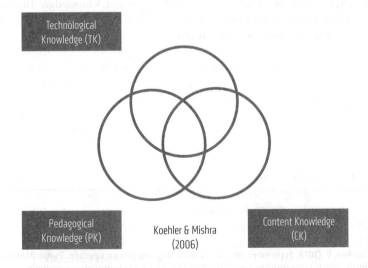

Technological Knowledge (TK)

Pedagogical Knowledge (PK)

Koehler & Mishra (2006)

Content Knowledge (CK)

When using technology, all three aspects of the TPACK framework are important and need to complement one another. If a teacher has deep subject knowledge, is able to use effective pedagogical strategies, and has a good understanding of the technology being used, this combination can lead to greater success in the classroom. It is also important to recognise that this is not about using technology more. A key factor of the technological element is that it is down to the professional choice of teachers whether or not to use technology. Koehler and Mishra write, 'TPACK is truly meaningful, deeply skilled teaching with or without (because sometimes this can be the best choice) technology.' However, many teachers have been forced to drastically upscale their skills to use technology for teaching and learning since the outbreak of the pandemic, making this model more relevant now than when it was originally proposed.

In September 2018 the TPACK diagram was updated once more. Mishra revealed an extended version of TPACK which included a new focus on contextual knowledge.[20] Mishra writes: 'Contextual knowledge would be everything from a teacher's awareness of the kind of technologies available for them and their students; to their knowledge of the school, district and state policies that they have to function within.'

This is clearly all-encompassing and takes into consideration a wide range of factors teachers must consider when integrating technology successfully into the classroom. Koehler and Mishra did not want to add another CK for contextual knowledge as the original CK represented content knowledge. Instead, the new revised model has an outer circle or section that is referred to as XK for Contextual Knowledge, as shown below:

TPACK – Technological, Pedagogical and Content Knowledge

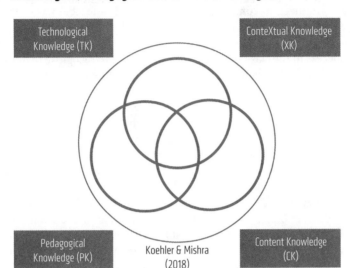

Technological Knowledge (TK)

ConteXtual Knowledge (XK)

Pedagogical Knowledge (PK)

Koehler & Mishra (2018)

Content Knowledge (CK)

THE TPACCK MODEL

Kate added cognitive knowledge and understanding to the model and diagram, explaining that we should combine our content and pedagogical knowledge with our understanding of cognitive science and psychology when using technology.

For example, we know that quizzing is a great strategy to support retrieval practice and there are lots of great digital tools we can use to do this. To create a challenging and appropriate quiz for students to complete requires subject knowledge. Using quizzing as a method to support learning is a pedagogical strategy and demonstrates our understanding of cognitive psychology and the benefits of retrieval practice. Finally, we are using technology efficiently to create, deliver and record quizzes.

TPACCK – Technological, Pedagogical, Cognitive and Content Knowledge

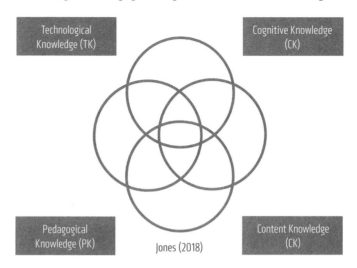

Jones (2018)

Without the subject knowledge, we would be unable to write questions that cover a wide breadth and depth of content with an appropriate level of challenge. Without pedagogical knowledge, we would not consider effective techniques such as quizzes at the start of a lesson as part of a firmly embedded classroom routine. Being unaware of the impact of retrieval practice for supporting learning would mean that we would only use quizzing as an assessment tool instead of a learning tool. Attempting to use technology but failing to understand how to create a quiz online or instruct students how to respond and engage with the quiz would also cause problems. So, a successful quiz using technology requires the teacher to have a solid knowledge of all the factors involved in the learning process and task design. This does not just apply to quizzes, but is relevant to all teaching and learning tasks.

It could be argued that cognitive psychology should be considered as part of our pedagogical knowledge (PK) or as part of the new addition of contextual knowledge (XK) as it focuses on how memory works and how we can use this information to support learning. Since the TPACK model was introduced however, our understanding of cognitive psychology has developed, and its relevance has been acknowledged, respected and included in the debate to help move it forward. It is important that we embrace the findings of this important field of research and think carefully about how we choose to use technology based upon what we know about what works.

There are still many questions unanswered in the field of cognitive psychology, and particularly in the complex area of how children learn, so there is much progress to be made. Just as technology will continue to advance and teachers will continue to need support to improve their technological knowledge, the same can be said of cognitive psychology – we will never stop learning. Teachers embody life-long learning, and as new research develops explaining what does and does not work, or what works best, teachers need to stay informed and apply this new learning to their practice.

The TPACCK model will encourage teachers to carefully consider how different aspects, such as technology, can impact teaching and learning, as well as enabling them to recognise the value and importance of cognitive psychology. TPACK supports the integration of technology, but TPACCK focuses on how effective that integration of technology is on learning. Naturally, teachers will have areas of the TPACCK model that they are more drawn to and interested in; from subject development to cognitive science or the use of technology, but it is important that we have a good grasp and confident knowledge and understanding of all the elements. It is vital to stress that we can focus professional learning on combining all the factors of the TPACCK model, without one aspect dominating and others being neglected.

It is important to remember that the TPACCK model only focuses on elements of teaching and learning and does not include other important aspects such as behaviour, pastoral issues, safeguarding, or SEND, although these can be incorporated into different elements of the model, and can all be evidence-informed.

CHALLENGE QUESTIONS

- Do you consider yourself and your practice to be evidence-informed?
- What barriers or challenges have you faced to becoming evidence-informed?
- What benefits have you experienced as a result of becoming evidence-informed?
- Does the school you work at promote an evidence-informed culture?
- Does the department or phase you work in promote an evidence-informed culture?
- What has the impact of becoming evidence-informed been on your students' progress and outcomes?
- Have you engaged with any online professional development linked to evidence-informed practice, such as researchEd Home presentations on YouTube?

QR CODES FOR FURTHER READING AND INFORMATION

Education Endowment Foundation (EEF)
https://educationendowmentfoundation.org.uk

Visible Learning
https://visible-learning.org

Evidence Based Education
https://evidencebased.education

Innerdrive.co.uk
https://www.innerdrive.co.uk

Learning Scientists
https://www.learningscientists.org

The Chartered College of Teaching (CCT)
https://chartered.college

CHAPTER 2

EARLY CAREER TEACHERS: ADVICE TO SUCCEED AND TO SUPPORT

Purpose of this chapter: To offer advice and guidance to teachers in the early years of their careers. To help all teachers and leaders understand their role in – and the importance of – supporting early career teachers.

You may or may not be a teacher in the early years of your career, but we have written this chapter with a focus on providing advice for teachers entering the profession to help them succeed. It is also written with experienced teachers and leaders in mind, so they can effectively support early career teachers. Please do not skip this chapter if you're an experienced teacher or leader, as we firmly believe that regardless of role or responsibilities, every teacher has a duty to support colleagues who are in the early stages of their careers.

While our experiences and challenges may vary, there is much more that unites us than divides us in this profession, and we have all be in the same position of being a newly qualified teacher just starting out. The early years of being a teacher are crucial to establishing the firm foundations for a long, happy and fulfilled career. In this chapter we aim to provide an overview of the latest changes, frameworks and policies in place as well as providing advice and guidance which we hope will ultimately keep teachers in the profession.

The 2021 House of Commons Library briefing paper *Teacher recruitment and retention* in England revealed that:

> *Since 2011 the overall number of teachers has in general not kept pace with increasing pupil numbers. This means the ratio of qualified teachers to pupils has increased from 17.8 in 2011 to 19.1 in 2019* [sic]. *In addition, the number*

of full-time teacher vacancies and temporarily filled posts have both risen over this period.[21]

The paper further reported that '22% of newly qualified entrants to the sector in 2015 were not recorded as working in the state sector two years later'.

There have been numerous alarming reports sharing data and statistics about teacher retention and recruitment, their findings illustrate the importance of training, support and professional learning in the early years of a teacher's career. A 2019 article entitled *Supporting newly-qualified teachers' professional development and perseverance in secondary education: On the role of informal learning* stated that 'High percentages of newly qualified teachers (NQTs) drop out during their first five years in the classroom. Often, formal support systems are put in place to overcome practice shock.'[22] This practice shock, referring to the shock element of being fully in control of classes, planning and other responsibilities, can be overcome by avoiding a 'throw them in the deep end' attitude and mentality and instead using support, guidance and kindness.

Between us we have taught in Wales, England, Scotland and internationally, so we are well aware of the differences and nuances between countries in terms of approaches, policies and even the terminology used in education. Taking this into consideration we will not focus solely on any single approach or document but instead aim to provide a wide spectrum of advice and guidance which can be applied in different countries, contexts and classrooms. We will provide an overview of the framework and guidance reports in place across the UK, but will not go into specific detail and depth as we have included links for further information and reading at the end of this chapter.

We believe it is important to have an awareness of the educational landscape across the UK and hopefully the summaries below and links to further reading will be insightful for all. If you are a teacher searching for employment for your first, second or even third teaching year, having an overview of the different levels of support and approaches might inform your decision as to where to teach and begin your career. It is also important to have an awareness of the different

21. Foster, D., Long, R. and Danechi, S. (2021) *Teacher recruitment and retention in England.* House of Commons Library, Research Briefing. https://commonslibrary.parliament.uk/research-briefings/cbp-7222/

22. Colognesi, S., Van Nieuwenhoven, C. and Beausaert, S. (2020) Supporting ewly-qualified teachers' professional development and perseverance in secondary education: On the role of informal learning. *European Journal of Teacher Education, 43*(2), 258-276. https://www.tandfonline.com/doi/full/10.1080/02619768.2019.1681963

education systems in the home nations, as teachers can move throughout the UK, sometimes unaware of the impact this can have on their professional learning and progress in the early years of their career, not to mention the varying approaches to mentoring and support they may experience.

THE EARLY CAREER FRAMEWORK IN ENGLAND

The Department for Education (DfE) published the Early Career Framework (ECF) in January 2019, with the aim of rolling out the framework in schools in England from September 2021, although some trial schools had been following the ECF prior to this. You can access this framework, if you have not already done so, by scanning the QR code at the end of this chapter.

The DfE write on their website:

> *The early career framework (ECF) reforms will create a step change in support for early career teachers, providing a funded entitlement to a structured two-year package of high-quality professional development. The reforms are part of the government's teacher recruitment and retention strategy, which aims to improve the training and development opportunities available to teachers.*

> *The early career framework is the evidence base which underpins this new entitlement for early career teachers' professional development. It sets out what all early career teachers should learn about, and learn how to do, during the first two years of their careers.*

> *Before September 2021, schools should:*
>
> - *read the updated statutory guidance*
> - *choose a delivery approach in order to meet the new requirements*
> - *set up their programme through the DfE's online service if they want to use an approved funded provider, or deliver the accredited materials themselves.*

The ECF was created by teachers and leaders from across primary and secondary phases, along with leading voices in education, referred to as the Expert Advisory Group. There was also collaboration and involvement from a range of organisations linked to education including The Chartered College of Teaching, Teach First, UCL Institute of Education and the Teacher Development Trust to name but a few (all are fully credited in the original document). In addition to this the DfE stated that the 'content of the framework and its underpinning evidence has been independently assessed and endorsed by the Education Endowment Foundation (EEF).'

The ECF illustrates the shift the profession has taken towards becoming evidence-informed (as discussed in Chapter 1) which is also reflected by Ofsted in their 2019 framework (there is a QR code to access this document too). The ECF demonstrates that there needs to be ongoing support in place for teachers which extends beyond the initial year in the classroom as a Newly Qualified Teacher (NQT) and into the second year within the classroom, therefore NQT and RQT (Recently Qualified Teacher) have been replaced by ECT in England. The ECF states, 'Teachers deserve high-quality support throughout their careers, particularly in those first years of teaching when the learning curve is steepest.' We agree with this statement and believe that focusing solely on the NQT year rather than longer term support was a short-sighted mistake.

The ECF emphasises the importance of supporting teachers early in their career in order to promote recruitment and retention within the profession, and to do this ECTs will continue to receive a ten percent reduction in their teaching timetable in their first year and a five percent reduction in their second. Mentors will also be provided with funding to enable them to have the time to support ECTs within their school for both the first and second year and receive training themselves from accredited providers, which will ensure they are able to draw on the best evidence to support ECTs properly.

Time really is crucial to any form of professional learning and the ECF has identified the importance of this:

> Too often, new teachers have not enjoyed the support they need to thrive, nor have they had adequate time to devote to their professional development. The Early Career Framework (ECF) underpins an entitlement to a fully-funded, two-year package of structured training and support for early career teachers linked to the best available research evidence. The package of reforms will ensure new teachers have dedicated time set aside to focus on their development.

While the ECF is specific to England we do think it is a document that schools outside of England should read as it contains very useful guidance, references and clear advice as to what teachers early in their careers should be focusing on and be aware of. The framework covers five fundamental areas of practice: pedagogy, curriculum, assessment, behaviour and professional behaviours.

These are mapped against the Teacher Standards, as ECTs will be assessed on their progress against these, not the framework itself. This structure also means there is a clear congruence with the Core Content Framework they will be familiar with from their time in ITE. This aims to promote consistency across the country in terms of the priorities and areas of professional learning for ECTs.

Generally, the reaction to the ECF has been very positive among the teaching profession. Ambition Institute Trust have described the ECF as:

> *One of the most significant reforms to the teaching profession in a generation, aimed at providing extended, evidence-based development that will produce better-trained teachers who are more likely to stay in the profession.*[23]

Further time will tell if the ECF does have the intended positive impact it has set out to achieve; recruiting, retaining and supporting teachers to stay within the profession and become evidence-informed. The ECF has also been designed to support teachers beyond their initial two years in the profession, as it will be linked to the career-long programme of National Professional Qualifications (NPQs) which are discussed in Chapter 5.

There has been criticism of the ECF. The most notable critique has been linked to the broad nature of the framework, as there is one single framework to be applied across all different subjects and across different ages and phases. There is considerable difference between teaching different subjects and different age ranges, so this is where schools and subject or phase leaders will have to support teachers with specific guidance, advice and support. The ECF could not be all encompassing, nothing ever would be, but it is clear that it aims to support the professional learning of those entering the profession with time, funding and evidence-informed approaches.

Our advice for getting the most out of the ECF:

- Don't do what people often do with policy documents; print them off and consign them to a desk drawer or shelf where they will simply collect dust. You need to revisit and refer to it again and again.
- Do visit the references cited for further reading in the ECF.

---

23. Ambition Institute (2021, March 1) *Six ways NQTs and mentors will get quality support from the Early Career Framework.* https://www.ambition.org.uk/blog/six-ways-nqts-and-mentors-will-get-quality-support-early-career-framework/

- It should not be viewed as a tick box activity, when a teacher feels confident in one area, such as behaviour management, it does not mean it has been mastered. Reflection and professional learning linked to behaviour management should be ongoing. This is important for ECTs and mentors to continually keep in mind.
- The ECF should not be viewed or used as a device to assess or formally grade teachers. This is stated clearly in the DfE guidance. There is potential for the ECF to be lethally mutated (as other aspects in education sadly have) into a laborious task of collecting reams of evidence and data, when that is not necessary or helpful for ECTs or mentors.
- The ECF shouldn't be viewed as restrictive. It is a great guide for ECTs and mentors but there are many educational blogs, articles, books and resources that aren't referenced by the ECF that are interesting, informative and helpful. It's important that ECTs and mentors don't feel shackled to the framework.

THE INDUCTION FOR NQTS IN WALES

Wales will be keeping the focus on the initial year with NQTs. The Welsh government has stated that every school should be NQT-ready. From September 2021, every school in Wales should have an induction mentor (IM), a role which previously existed but the roles and responsibilities have now been made clearer.

The IM is responsible for the following:

- Providing high-quality day to day mentoring support for each NQT.
- Setting targets and approving professional learning experiences.
- Observing the NQT teaching.
- Completing the three required profile reviews.
- Working closely alongside the external verifier (EV).

Every NQT at a school in Wales is entitled to mentoring support, including those on a temporary contract or short-term supply. Again, there is a clear emphasis on support but there are obvious issues that schools will have to address. For example, the IM may lack the subject or phase-specific expertise to support the NQTs within their school. Therefore it is essential that middle leaders and line managers are also involved, but then there is the issue of time being provided for all those responsible for supporting NQTs.

All schools in Wales are expected to release the NQT for eight days over the course of the induction period (generally an academic year) so they can attend or engage with professional learning. This includes a three-day national programme specifically designed for NQTs, while further opportunities will be offered and shared in different regions across Wales. How this time is spent is incredibly important: as we have stressed, time is precious, especially with professional learning.

Time and professional development are also provided for mentors across Wales, and each mentor is expected to attend four sessions of a National Professional Learning Programme to gain insight and up to date knowledge about the process and develop their skills as a supportive mentor. The aim of this programme is to prepare teachers across Wales to effectively deliver the 'Curriculum for Wales'. NQTs must demonstrate they have made progress against the Welsh professional standards for teaching and leadership at induction level.

There is a vast amount of literature available for teachers, mentors and leaders at all levels across Wales. While there are many areas that cross over and are similar with the ECF there are also elements that are unique to the Welsh context, for example the ability to use incidental Welsh language in the classroom. This is an expectation of all teachers across Wales, regardless of background and even in English-medium schools where lessons are delivered in English. Phrases, instructions and resources within the school are expected to be bilingual, and this is a focus of Estyn, the Welsh inspectorate.

Our advice to support NQTs in Wales:

- Although an important requirement in Wales, do not panic about the use of incidental Welsh language in lessons. Kate previously held a leadership position that focused on supporting staff and students with Welsh and promoting bilingualism across the school. Simply aim to master some basic phrases such as, 'Bore da' and 'Prynhawn da' (good morning and good afternoon) to begin. Tutorial videos online and Duolingo (plus other language learning apps) can be very helpful. It's important to show respect, awareness and appreciation of the Welsh language and culture even if your ability to speak Welsh is limited.
- Carefully consider how the time provided for professional learning is to be spent. This is not an opportunity to be wasted and should be taken full advantage of. Mentors should also support NQTs with this, to ensure the time is used wisely and is beneficial.

- Although the focus remains in Wales on the NQT year we both believe that the two-year shift to ECT in England is a very good thing and should be more widely adopted. While the financial support and time does not currently extend to the second year in Wales, it is vital that the mindset and focus of support remains in place as teachers enter their second year. See the QR code at the end of this chapter to find out more about the specific documentation and support available in Wales.

PROBATION YEAR IN SCOTLAND

The General Teaching Council for Scotland (GTCS) is the gatekeeping body for the teaching profession. Upon completing university, trainees (called probationers, but also known as NQTs) will have achieved the Standard for Provisional Registration (SPR) with the GTCS. The NQT year needs to be completed successfully to achieve the Standard for Full Registration (SFR). This is most commonly done through the Teacher Induction Scheme (TIS). If this paragraph has demonstrated anything at all, it's that Scottish education is the global leader in acronyms (just wait until you meet SHANARRI, GIRFEC, DYW and their coterie of friends).

Once provisional registration has been achieved, there is an interesting lottery process to go through. The TIS involves applying for a one-year post at a local authority (state, or maintained) school. Scotland has 32 local authorities and probationers have to choose their top five, in order of preference. There is then a very anxious wait to find out which council, and which school, you will be teaching at for the next year. You can also opt to be put anywhere, which pays a bit more (and will probably suit those who don't mind life on a remote island). You can also take what's called the flexible route. This covers a lot of the different situations that trainee teachers may find themselves in, and the key difference is that it takes 270 days of teaching experience (which is a year and half) rather than the 190 days that the TIS requires.

Once in post, probationers have a 0.8 Full Time Equivalent (FTE) timetable. Scottish full-time teachers have 22.5 hours of contact time, so probationers should be teaching for 18 hours per week. The other 4.5 hours should be spent in professional learning, which can be in or out of school. The mentor is called the 'supporter' and weekly meetings should take place. The year is divided into two phases, with the period from August to December involving a minimum of five observed lessons. There is also careful logging of professional learning in line with a development plan – agreed with the supporter – that is based on areas identified in an ITE profile from university. If this phase is successfully completed, onward progress sees a second phase from January to June, with more meetings, professional development and observations leading to completion of the TIS and full registration with the GTCS. However, if the interim recommendation at the end of the first phase is 'unsatisfactory' or 'cause for concern' there is a second bite of the cherry, with a satisfactory award needed by the end of the spring term. Assuming all goes well and probationers achieve full registration, they are then tasked with finding a new post, and join the mainstream profession. All teachers in Scotland have to go through a five-yearly 'health check' called a Professional Update, so continually logging professional learning with the MyGTCS website (not known for its user friendly interface, historically) is a must.

One of the most interesting features of the newly revised (as of August 2021) professional standards in Scotland is the section on 'Being a Teacher'. This section from the GTCS website gives you an indication of the cultural and professional expectations of Scottish teachers:

> *The Professional Standards 2021 includes a new section called 'Being a teacher in Scotland', which highlights the professional values of social justice, trust and respect and integrity as central to what it means to be a teacher in Scotland. This roots the Professional Standards as a framework that supports what it means to become, to be and to grow as a teacher in Scotland.*

> *The strong focus on professional values helps teachers develop their professional identity and underpins a deep commitment to all learners' cognitive, social and emotional growth and wellbeing. The Professional Standards are integral to, and demonstrated through, teachers' professional relationships, thinking and actions in their professional practice. Commitment to reflecting on the connections between values and actions and career-long professional learning is a critical part of developing teacher professionalism.*

Our advice for probationary teachers in Scotland:

- The wait to find out where you will be placed in the country is tough and can add pressure. There is a reasonable chance that you won't get your first choice of local authority, so establishing a good support network early on is really important. You won't be surprised to hear us recommending Twitter as the easiest way to connect with other Scottish teachers.

- If you are the adventurous type, the option of taking more pay to live anywhere in Scotland might be worth considering. After all, it's only for one year.
- Logging professional learning can be onerous, so develop a 'little and often' approach to it. Getting it done straight after your weekly supporter meetings is a good idea.
- 4.5 hours of professional learning each week is quite a lot, so make sure that what you are doing is effective and not just time filling activities to meet the standards. Your supporter, and indeed the leadership team at your school, really should be helping you a lot with this. If you find you are on your own, reach out for support. Keeping in touch with people from university can be an essential survival skill.

EARLY CAREER TEACHERS IN NORTHERN IRELAND

The General Teaching Council for Northern Ireland (GTCNI) has a model to support teachers from Initial Teacher Education (ITE), Induction and Early Professional Development (EPD). Once teachers in Northern Ireland qualify, they proceed to Career Long Professional Development (CLPD). This model is also linked to the progression of the upper pay scale in Northern Ireland.

The first year involves an induction where teachers are required to engage in professional development, and record and present this evidence in a portfolio and action plan which is statutory for all teaching in grant-aided schools in Northern Ireland. The action plans should also tie into the aims and school development plan. The Induction Action Plan should be revisited and reviewed on an ongoing basis throughout the induction period with the teacher-tutor and colleagues.

The Teacher Education Partnership Handbook, Section 4.1 states that:

> The overall aim of the induction is to continue to address the GTCNI Competences and Core Values and encourage the Beginning Teacher to develop their critical reflective practice in order to improve their teaching and the quality of pupil learning which will not be fully developed in Initial Teacher Education.

The role of the teacher-tutor in the induction year is explained clearly by Teaching Union NASWUT Northern Ireland in their published Induction Planner, noting that:

Your teacher-tutor should be your line manager, a senior member of staff or a suitably experienced teacher who has considerable contact with you. It could be the principal, but is unlikely to be so. Schools identify the staff they consider the most appropriate. Your teacher-tutor should be fully aware of the requirements of the induction period and should have the skills, expertise and knowledge to work effectively in the role. Your teacher-tutor has day-to-day responsibility for monitoring, supporting and evaluating you during your induction. Your teacher-tutor will coordinate observations. S/he should ensure that your induction programme fulfils the requirements of the teacher competencies, make sure that you know about and understand your role and responsibilities and inform you about the nature and purpose of any assessments.[24]

EPD takes two years after the initial induction year as part of the ongoing professional pathway. Therefore, there are three years of guided support in place in Northern Ireland, which is unique in the UK, and shows the emphasis on developing and improving during the early years of a teaching career, as well as ongoing support and focus. Again, all teachers are required to participate.

There is more information and support available from the Education Authority website, a QR code can be found at the end of this chapter.

Advice for the induction year in Northern Ireland:

- Utilise the induction planner, this can vary as they are provided by schools and unions, but it should be kept safely and referred to regularly. Keep a record of upcoming deadlines, key dates and information all in one accessible place: your planner.
- The Career Entry Profile (CEP) is a useful professional development tool for recording professional development needs and progression through all stages from ITE, induction and EPD. This can be viewed as a tick box activity and paper task but instead try to view it as an important reflective record and a key component of professional development, progression and learning.
- To complete the induction year the Summative Report will need to be signed by the principal and board of governors. This is based on evidence from lesson observations, observations by colleagues and leaders including the line manager(s), and the portfolio of professional development. Remember, the principal and governors do not expect any teacher to be

---

24. NASUWT (ND) *Induction Planner.* Available at: https://www.nasuwt.org.uk/advice/ northern-ireland.html

the finished product, but they should be able to see from the evidence a level of commitment and a desire to learn and develop. This should also be regularly emphasised by those supporting the beginning teacher to avoid pressure and mounting stress occurring while trying to collect and gather this evidence.

Naturally, there is overlap with the various policies which is reassuring, but there are also differences that we believe are worth shining a light on so we can promote further discussion, collaboration, connections and reflections. The main similarity is the focus on professional learning, encouraging teachers to become reflective practitioners and putting support in place. There is also a wealth of literature and materials available for each country we have reviewed.

The key difference is the amount of time spent supporting teachers, which varies from the initial year, to two or three years. There is also a difference in terms of funding and the support available. There are various models, approaches and lots of different terminology and acronyms, for example Wales and Scotland both refer to NQT, England has moved to ECT as has Northern Ireland after previously referring to teachers in the induction year as Beginning Teachers.

HOW TO SUCCEED DURING THE EARLY YEARS OF YOUR TEACHING CAREER

There are numerous books and blogs dedicated solely to providing advice for teachers at the start of their careers, and understandably so because there is a lot to take into consideration. We have deliberately avoided providing advice relating to a specific context, such as a phase or subject because we aren't in the best position to do so as we both have very similar teaching and leadership experiences as teacher of history and head of history, although Robin has progressed to headship.

Instead, we urge early career teachers to find others teaching the same subject(s) or phase as they will be able to offer relevant, specific and very valuable advice. It would be useful to look for these colleagues in the wider education world, as well as in your own school community. We have thought about this carefully and provided some generalised guidance which we hope will be helpful and relevant to all.

Become familiar with unions and professional bodies. Most trainee teachers and NQT/ECTs can join teaching unions for free or at a very low price. We strongly recommend you do so and also take full advantage of what the unions can offer. Teachers are often instructed to join a union 'just in case' anything happens. Sadly, there are many teachers who have had to deal with serious and unsubstantiated allegations against them, and having legal fees covered by a union in these situations is vital. However, there is often a lot more on offer so do take the time to explore this and find out what support and professional learning opportunities are available.

As mentioned previously, the CCT provides a wealth of high-quality professional learning materials and can be accessed cheaply (free membership for those training to be a teacher and more information about membership can be accessed here: https://chartered.college/join/). The CCT is not a teaching union, it is a recognised professional body for teachers and school leaders.

Embrace professional learning opportunities but also be selective. As discussed, there is so much choice available that it's difficult to know where to begin, what to go for and what to avoid; rather like an all-you-can-eat buffet! It can become easy to create a 'to be read' pile that keeps growing and eventually becomes overwhelming. This is why it's important to be selective. It can be tempting to focus on one element that you particularly enjoy when it comes to professional learning but it's important to have an awareness of weaknesses and areas for development.

Be prepared to say no. Teachers early in their career are often very enthusiastic; keen to impress and make a contribution to school life. However, this does not mean you have to attend every single performance, sporting match, and weekend activity, or volunteer at every opportunity. It is important to show commitment but do so at a time that suits you and with something you feel comfortable doing. If there is a time when you are struggling with workload don't volunteer to give up evenings or weekends. Think carefully about what for and when you offer your time. It is ok to say no; other members of staff do, so why can't you? Learn how to prioritise.

Join Twitter. We both wish we had Twitter available to us earlier in our teaching careers! It can be a wonderful platform for professional learning, inspiration, support, networking and more. If you don't have the time or confidence to contribute online, then that is fine as there are no expectations. Some teachers share, some take, and some do both. Sign up to Twitter today, if you haven't already (and see Chapter 3 for how to make the most of it).

Don't put too much pressure on lesson observations. Graded lesson observations are becoming a thing of the past (supported by the fact that inspectorates in the UK do not grade lesson observations during inspections) although sadly some schools still do this. Teachers (including us) have been known to spend much more time on lesson plans for observed lessons than they would for others, so they don't really reflect an authentic lesson experience.

The lesson observation process itself however, is important, especially during your NQT/ECT year(s). It can offer great insight and is a wonderful opportunity to gain purposeful feedback to support and improve your practice. Engage in discussions with the staff members observing you and find out if they have a particular focus. You could explain the lesson in the context of the scheme of work and topic prior to the observation, as lessons are taught as part of a sequence and unit rather than in isolation. If things don't go exactly as planned, just remember that one stand-alone lesson is not a true reflection of you as a teacher and that learning happens over time. Have clear routines firmly in place and aim to do what you always do.

Don't be afraid to ask for help. There could be a class that simply won't behave for you, or there could be gaps in your subject knowledge, or perhaps you are unsure about effective questioning techniques in the classroom. We can all improve, especially in the early years of our career when we lack experience and confidence. There is no shame in seeking support and asking for help, this is a sign of a reflective teacher who is humble, keen to learn and wants to develop.

Build positive relationships. The emphasis on building good relationships can focus on the students in your classes, but our advice applies to everyone in your school, from students and staff to the wider school community. When we refer to staff we include all staff, from teachers to support staff and administrative staff. Good relationships with colleagues can be very helpful and make your experience in school much more enjoyable, as well as enabling you to build a good support network.

In terms of students, of course building positive relationships with the students in your classes is vital but also use opportunities such as non-teaching duties to get to know other students in the school. Ultimately, be kind to everyone you work with and hope that kindness is returned (although it might not be).

A cautionary note to sound is that teacher-student relationships have to be professional, at all times. You will get questions about your personal life, and it is tempting to think that being liked personally will equate to success, but that isn't the case. Teaching never has been, nor will it ever be, a popularity contest. Observe how experienced teachers build relationships, and how they ensure that clear boundaries are in place.

Go to the staffroom. In order to build positive relationships with those in the school environment, time and effort has to be invested and the staffroom is a great starting place for this. Each staffroom is different, and it can feel a bit political at times, maybe with the same teachers sitting in the same place every day, either in their friendship groups or departments. This can be intimidating, but more often than not the staffroom is a friendly place to be. It can be tempting to work through lunch by photocopying, replying to emails or marking but often a cup of tea and a conversation at lunch is a nice way to break up the day and further develop those positive relationships with colleagues.

Create lists. Making a list is a simple and easy way to stay organised. However, often we can add too much to our lists, being over ambitious and unrealistic which will then make us feel we haven't achieved as much as we initially hoped. Post-it notes aren't great for lists as they can get easily lost or damaged. Either use a classroom planner or diary to keep a written record of lists or record lists digitally, with a notes app on a phone or an online document; somewhere that is accessible if you need to add something to the list. Also, when it comes to lists, think short-, medium- and long-term.

The short-term list should contain things that need to be done in the near future, such as photocopying or replying to an email. Another way of thinking about this is prioritising those things that are time sensitive.

The medium-term list will include tasks and goals that are not urgent but are important and achievable within a specific time frame. This could include an element of lesson planning, professional learning or something you hope to achieve by the end of term. It is worth adding upcoming deadlines such as report writing. If it is on the medium-term list it is on your radar, but not on the short-term list, meaning you shouldn't have a deadline to meet in 24 hours!

For the long-term we don't suggest looking too far ahead with a five-year plan list (although it can be helpful to have a five-year plan) but instead create a list of aims to be achieved by the end of the academic year. This could be to plan a scheme of work, research and learn about a specific area of development or to have achieved a qualification by that point.

Enjoy the holidays! Do not feel guilty for relaxing, putting work aside and enjoying the holidays. Enjoying the holidays means doing whatever it is that brings you joy and happiness; that might include reading educational books or escaping from the classroom with non-fiction or binge watching a box set.

There may be a pile of books to mark or an incomplete to do list, but they can and should wait. Ross Morrison McGill writes:

> *Teaching is a lifetime's craft. You will never perfect it, nor complete your to do list. Accept this early on and you will already begin to master the art of resilience: know when to stop, when to switch off and when it is time to look after you!*[25]

Making time to rest, recover and relax is a vital aspect of being the best teachers we can be.

Finally, this piece of advice is taken from Kate's favourite educational book: *The Confident Teacher: Developing Successful Habits of Mind, Body and Pedagogy* by Alex Quigley (@HuntingEnglish) which is highly recommended. Quigley writes: 'The day you realise you will never do the job perfectly is the day you can start enjoying and flourishing in your teaching life.' This is absolutely true, and Kate found it incredibly helpful and liberating, as it enabled her to stop striving for perfection and focus on learning, development and happiness.

How to support teachers during the early years of their teaching career

Positive language. Avoid using language such as 'surviving' or anything that normalises teacher burnout. There is a lot of literature published with a focus on 'surviving' in teaching, especially the early years. This sort of terminology and language can create and reinforce a negative narrative that this is a profession suited for the survival of the fittest, which we desperately need to move away from.

English teacher James Theobald (@JamesTheo) made this point in a tweet:

> *One of the biggest errors we make in teaching is using rhetoric around 'survival'. It starts with advice on 'how to survive your NQT year' and never stops. I think it's a language that sets so many up to fail through normative messaging.*

---

25. McGill, R. M. (2015) *Teacher Toolkit: Helping you survive your first five years*. London: Bloomsbury.

Instead, aim to use more reassuring and positive language such as 'progressing', 'developing' and 'learning' in relation to the early years to emphasise growth in contrast to survival mode.

Lead by example. Whether you are a leader or not, we can all lead by example in many elements of our professional life. It's important to be positive role models and set good examples, not just for the students we teach but also for our colleagues. We should be modelling kind behaviour and interactions, and we should be demonstrating that we are engaging with professional learning, which can easily be achieved by discussing or sharing an educational blog post or book.

Another key area where we should lead by example is through managing workload and well-being. This, again, is often easier said than done but we need to demonstrate to teachers early in their career that it is certainly very possible to be a dedicated teacher while also being healthy and happy, and recognising the importance of home life as well as work life for a balanced lifestyle.

Know the framework, policies and standards. It is an exciting time in teaching, as government, policy makers and schools are making a significant effort to support teachers as they join the profession. Time and money are being invested to recruit and retain high-quality teachers. We have already highlighted the various policies and frameworks in place across the UK and at the end of this chapter we have signposted the support and guidance available in your region of the UK. Reference to international teaching can be found in Chapter 11.

As stated at the start of the chapter we want to stress once more that regardless of roles and responsibilities we all have an obligation to support other teachers, and having an understanding of the professional standards and frameworks in place can help us do so.

Provide feedback that is kind, specific and helpful. This advice is associated with the work of Ron Berger and his 2003 book *An Ethic of Excellence: Building a Culture of Craftsmanship with Students,* and while it is something he encourages us to share with our students, we also believe it applies when providing feedback to colleagues. So often feedback is provided for the sake of it, can lack a focus on specific teaching and learning elements, and can even at times be demoralising and devastating, especially for an inexperienced teacher lacking confidence. Feedback by its very nature is personal, so kindness is key. The more specific the feedback is, the more helpful it will be to genuinely promote teacher reflection, development and improvement.

CHALLENGE QUESTIONS

■ If you are a NQT or ECT are you aware of where to find out more about the support available?

■ Do you know who can support you within your school?

■ Do you have a PLN (professional learning network) that you can turn to for support, guidance, encouragement and inspiration?

■ Mentors and middle leaders; are you familiar with the policy within your country and school about how to support teachers early in their careers?

QR CODES FOR FURTHER READING AND INFORMATION

The Early Career Framework (ECF)
https://www.gov.uk/government/publications/
early-career-framework

Ofsted Education Framework (2019)
https://www.gov.uk/government/publications/
education-inspection-framework

Wales Induction – Professional Development (GWE)
https://hwb.gov.wales/professional-
development/induction

Northern Ireland – Early Career Teachers Induction and Early Professional Development
https://www.eani.org.uk/services/early-career-
teachers-induction-and-early-professional-
development

61

**General Teaching Council
for Scotland (GTCS)**
https://www.gtcs.org.uk

CHAPTER 3

LOW COST, HIGH IMPACT METHODS OF PROFESSIONAL LEARNING

Purpose of this chapter: To share different methods of professional learning which are low cost (or free to access) but can have a high impact on teacher development and professional learning.

We have touched upon some of the changes in professional learning, and this chapter covers new, innovative and low cost methods such as social media and podcasts. We also feel it is important to discuss how teachers and school leaders can make the most of more traditional methods of low cost professional learning such as lesson observations and school visits.

All professional learning and development should have a high impact on student learning and outcomes, but this is not always the case. Time and money are sparse so we need to consider carefully how we spend them to best effect in our quest to develop professionally. In terms of 'low cost' this varies from free to relatively cheap for the individual or school. Low cost forms of professional learning are not to be sneered at or judged as ineffective. Many teachers we know claim that the best professional learning they have experienced has been through joining social media for daily doses of information, research, networking, support and more. Observing a colleague or visiting another school can also be incredibly insightful and transformative too.

READING FOR PROFESSIONAL LEARNING

Unashamedly (and unsurprisingly) we are both strong advocates for professional reading as a form of professional learning. There has been a surge of educational reading matter in recent years, and here we must refer back to our point in the introduction to this section about choice. Choice and selection are key. Books are not the only option as there are high-quality blogs and various educational magazines (both in print and online). In the following chapter we address reading with a specific focus on learning about leadership.

Blogs

For the last decade or so, teachers, school leaders and people involved with education have been blogging about education. Anyone can set up a blog page and write a blog post, and there is no rigorous process for blogging, unlike authoring a book (which is discussed more fully in Chapter 8). The benefit of this is that it is possible to read blog posts from a wide and diverse range of voices in education whether they are reflecting on their classroom practice, sharing educational research, or discussing the latest educational policies or updates. There is a lot of content available. Blogs can also be very topical and hot off the press too, relating to and covering the issues of the day from examination changes to government announcements and news stories. Social media is a great place for finding blog posts as bloggers will share their posts and others will retweet and recommend them. If you find a blog post interesting, the easiest way to read future posts is by subscribing so that all posts will be sent directly to your email.

Blogs cover a huge range of subjects and styles, from practitioners sharing their expertise, to individuals offering reflections or advice, but all are useful for two key reasons: time and cost. Blog posts tend to be (and we believe should be) relatively short to read, often taking five to ten minutes to do so. This is great news for the busy teacher who wants to read about education but is struggling to find the time. Blogs are also free to read, with no cost involved for the reader, although some bloggers provide the option for readers and subscribers to 'buy them a coffee' which is an optional donation that can be made as a way of saying thanks for their work and what they share freely.

Educational magazines

There are many high-quality educational magazines published in print and online. Schools can subscribe and place copies in their staffrooms for staff to read, but teachers sometimes prefer to have their own subscriptions so as to have their own personal copies to read at their leisure.

Research summaries

We advocate research summaries in Chapter 1 as they are an excellent resource for making educational research and evidence findings more accessible for teachers. They are a short summary, focusing on the key elements, easier to digest and understand and most of the time can be downloaded freely. At the end of this chapter we have provided QR codes to direct you to various research summaries linked to education.

Books

Blogs are great but books provide more depth and detail, and the authors have spent considerably longer writing a book compared to writing a blog post (we are both well aware of this, as we publish blogs and author books). Although there is a cost for books it is often a very low cost, and many publishers provide discounts for schools that place bulk orders.

A key question we return to is the economics of professional learning; who should spend money on books for teachers to read? Teachers or schools? We believe that every school should have a CPD library which all staff can access. This should be the norm, and it is worth asking this question at an interview, as the answer will inform you as to whether the school invests in professional reading for staff. The books in the CPD library should cover a wide range of areas linked to professional learning from pastoral, behaviour, teaching and learning, leadership and more. It is a good idea to involve all staff in the purchasing of books, for example ask staff which educational books they would like to read or have read and would recommend to colleagues. Every school should be as proud of their CPD library as they should be of their student library. A sparse or empty CPD library is a good thing, as it means the books purchased are being read by staff not gathering dust on a shelf!

Many teachers do prefer having their own copies of books, to annotate or keep so they can be referred to again (we certainly have our own collections). The frustration with a CPD library is that a specific book a teacher wants to read might not be in the library or might already be loaned out to someone else. Purchasing and reading books about education can be viewed as an investment to help us improve, develop and reflect on our practice, as well as helping us get to where we want to be in terms of career progression. If you are studying for a formal qualification in education (see Chapter 5) then reading will play an essential role in this. If you are working towards an MA there will be access to the university library, but this might not always be practical, so it is likely you will have to purchase books to support your study.

It is one thing for a school to purchase books for staff to read, but is time provided for professional reading? We both believe this can be an excellent use of Inset and meeting time. Trust is required; leaders need to trust staff to make use of the time to read and not waste it, and teachers need to make sure they take full advantage of the professional learning time provided.

CASE STUDIES: CREATING A CULTURE OF READING FOR PROFESSIONAL LEARNING IN SCHOOLS

Sharing a weekly read for all staff. Nigel Davis, Secondary Deputy Headteacher at The British School Al Khubairat (BSAK) in Abu Dhabi, sends a blog post or article to all staff each week. We asked Nigel about the weekly read concept he introduced at his school.

There was a time in education, not so long ago, where teachers were very much inward looking. Schools worked in isolation, trying to improve themselves as much as they could. There was a time where staff only improved by helping each other, by learning from each other in their own departments – but this led to the potential teaching development plateau after the first few years in the profession. Fortunately, this climate has changed!

I first came across this different (outwards looking and sharing) outlook when I came across researchEd in 2015. Since then, this has become an avalanche of online developmental opportunities for educators. Twitter and blogs, and an explosion of theory-savvy publications now means that any school that wants to see improvements in teaching for learning owes it to their staff to signpost as much of the good stuff as possible! However, therein lies the issue – the wood for the trees – how to support staff to engage with the amazing stuff out there when their professional lives are so full; teaching timetable, planning, assessing and preparing feedback? This is where I felt a Thursday Read would really help.

Pushing a weekly read that we refer to as a 'Thursday Read' – usually a blog (or sometimes an article, a Twitter stream, podcast or Vlog) to our staff has happened weekly for the last four years. I try to take the time-consuming searching out of our staffs' hands. I aim to push information that can be immediately either used in the classroom, or at least discussed in departmental teams, and also look for reads which align to my school's own developmental needs and professional learning plan. I also ask for feedback – what do you think of this Thursday Read? I have had some wonderful discussions and debates off the back of different reads, although even now, staff are not quite brave enough to 'reply all'!

Although I am sure that there are some staff, especially at pressurised times, who do not read them; but the engagement in the readings, and change of culture it has brought, has been tangible among our staff.

Setting up a school book club for professional learning. Joe Morrin is a Lead Practitioner for Teaching and Learning at the Dukeries Academy in Nottinghamshire. Prior to this Joe was a Research Lead Practitioner and implemented the Edubook club at the Evolve Trust.

Why did you decide to launch a teaching and learning book club?

I wanted our staff to challenge fads and gimmicks in education by becoming critically reflective practitioners and more evidence- and research-informed. Using pedagogical books was an extremely powerful tool in helping to break down barriers, by providing discussions on the latest research and providing practical suggestions to help inform practice in a more practitioner-friendly approach, bridging the gap between research and practice, while also providing opportunities for further research or enquiry.

How did you encourage others to get involved? How often did you meet?

There were some initial anxieties from staff prior to the book club launch. Some staff had not undertaken significant pedagogical reading since their teacher training and others considered the thought of an Edubook club to be an onerous activity and negatively impact on their workload. The book club required a high level of marketing to increase awareness and celebrate the exciting nature of engaging with pedagogical books. A staff newsletter went out to inform the staff of the books we would be looking at during the course of the year and an incentive of a free loaned copy of the text and hot drinks and cake was offered. I wanted this book club to stand-out and created a big launch day to add to the excitement of this event. This really got staff talking about the book club, which led to a high uptake from staff across our Trust schools.

I wanted this book club to be manageable and sustainable, so my approach was little and often, reading only a few chapters at a time and meeting on a regular basis to discuss the text and its implications for practice in the classroom. We met with our reflection logs in a classroom for one hour after school every four weeks. This gave a chance for staff to implement new strategies in their classrooms and to critically discuss their ideas with staff from different subject areas and phases.

How did you decide which books to focus on?

I initially wanted to choose a text that was readily accessible and applicable to all teaching staff, irrespective of leadership role, experience level and phase. I had to be careful not to specialise too early, for example on an aspect of leadership or behaviour as this would have narrowed the scope of ideas and may have led to reduced uptake from staff from across the Trust. Kate Jones' Love to Teach *was a brilliant text that provided a plethora of teaching strategies to support retrieval practice, literacy and use of technology in the class alongside ideas for their practical application in the classroom. This was a great introduction to an Edubook club and staff spoke highly of the text.*

After the initial success of the book club, I wanted to align the school priorities with the choice of text to enable book club participants to become experts in this area and support their respective schools and faculty areas. Michael Chiles' Craft of Assessment *was perfect in supporting our approach to assessment. The book club was developing the expertise of our practitioners to help support our school development priorities.*

How did you promote discussion and reflection with the book group?

I developed reading logs specific to each chapter which posed a variety of questions to summarise key aspects of the reading and to encourage greater critical analysis of the ideas presented, as well as opportunities for staff to write down their experiences with the particular chapter.

Promoting psychological safety is paramount for a book club to be sustainable. Staff may not feel comfortable sharing their experiences with the text or being critical of their classroom practice. It is important to develop trust with the participants and to ensure a degree of confidentiality within the book club. Provide opportunities for all staff to share their ideas and validate these ideas. Every meeting would start with initial thoughts of the chapter and its relevance to practice. The reading logs provided a useful structure to help shape the conversation. Importantly, the meetings were not used to read through the logs, but to pick out the significant aspects of the reading and to develop an open discussion.

What were the benefits or positive aspects of having an edu-book club?

I'm very pleased to say that the Edubook has had a profound positive impact on staff development, which has filtered through at all levels.

On an individual level, one of the book club participants decided to use the ideas from the book club to develop their Master's project title and to inform their research. The participant focused on the efficacy of recall starters with pupil premium boys in Year 11. Several staff also wrote about the positive impact on teaching and learning in the Trust's Teaching and Learning newsletter. Notably, not only did the book club have a positive impact on teaching and learning, it also provided a way to develop staff expertise by becoming research and evidence-informed and allowed the Trust to provide more meaningful, cost effective in-house professional development using the book club participants.

Do you have any advice for someone wishing to do the same?

When setting up a book club, you really need to market and promote your book club, the more participants the more fruitful the conversations will be. This is a fantastic opportunity to involve other schools within your Trust or within your local area and beyond. Make your book club inclusive, involve all school personnel; teaching assistants, supply teachers, governors, even your Headteacher. They all have a part to play in supporting teaching and learning. I would also involve the author as much as possible, either through Twitter or email. Let them know what you are covering and the outcomes of the meetings. They may even get involved with your book club which will really get people talking.

Think carefully about the frequency and timings of your book club meetings. Leave it too long between meetings and staff may have forgotten what they've read. Too short, and it won't provide sufficient time to analyse, implement and reflect on the ideas from the text. Consider when the meetings will take place and try not to host them on weeks when there are pressure points, such as assessment and data entry points, parents' evenings and moderation meetings. Plan for the whole year and get the dates out to participants so they can factor this into their schedules. You may wish to do the meetings online but face-to-face is best and provides an environment of togetherness.

Think carefully about the choice and variety of text. You may wish to discuss how you can make your book club align with school priorities by discussing with your Headteacher, or you may have greater autonomy over the choice of text. If the choice of text is too specialised this may result in fewer book club participants. After a day of teaching, offering soft or hot drinks and nibbles can be a nice reward and keep participants' energy levels up and provide a comfortable environment.

Thank you to Nigel and Joe for sharing their experiences and reflections with us. You can follow and connect with Nigel on Twitter @BSAKT&L and Joe @joe_morrin

SOCIAL MEDIA FOR PROFESSIONAL LEARNING AND NETWORKING

Professional versus personal media

The term 'social media' is nebulous. There are so many purposes and platforms that it helps, as a teacher, to make a distinction between professional and personal media, and there are settings to restrict what people can and cannot view. There have been occasions when we have posted personal announcements on our professional accounts, for example Robin announced the birth of his daughter and Kate has shared travel photos publicly. Each person has to know where to draw the line, and this will vary for each individual as some are more open than others.

If you want to use media professionally, then use open platforms and settings, in the full awareness that the whole world can see what you post. This includes your students, their parents, your colleagues and your line manager. This is about cultivating an online persona that showcases your professionalism, so you create a positive digital footprint. Remember, a negative digital footprint may cost you a job or your reputation. A non-existent footprint will neither help nor hinder, but a positive one can be transformative. This involves a little bit of courage, as some teachers are terrified of digital media and sharing their opinions, but once you cross the Rubicon it can really enhance your professional life.

The key health warning we need to issue is that sadly some online behaviour is extremely poor and can adversely impact your mental health. Trolling occurs frequently and can be caustic, and sexual harassment is not uncommon. The major platforms all have block and report functions, although these can be frustratingly limited in their impact. However, you can take gentle steps into the real world (see the advice on 'lurking' in the next chapter), and you can also develop a sense of which debates to step away from. It's the same approach as risk assessment; you can never eliminate the chance of being targeted on social media, but you can limit the chances of it happening. For example, one of our golden rules is to never engage publicly with an account that has no personal markers: nameless, faceless trolls should always be avoided.

Ultimately, we are keen advocates of using social media for professional purposes, but make sure you are safe online and supportive of others.

Platforms for professional learning

The most popular online platform globally in 2021 is Facebook, followed by YouTube, then WhatsApp, and then Instagram, with Twitter further down the scale.[26] However, these figures and statistics are ranked by the numbers of users. Social media is mainly used for exactly that: staying socially connected, for example WhatsApp is purely a messaging service. These figures are not focused on social media as a tool for professional learning and different platforms have different appeals to different audiences, with age being a clear example of this, with many younger people choosing to use Snapchat, TikTok and Instagram.

In this section dedicated to social media we are purely focusing on using social media for professional learning, but it also has other pertinent uses. It can be used for researching schools you are thinking of applying to, there can be school accounts and pages set up to promote and share what is happening day to day with the wider school community and some teachers create social media pages for students to access revision materials and content. We will share a range of social media platforms with a brief explanation of their unique features (brief because they are regularly updated and sometimes features removed) and tips on how to use them for professional learning and development.

While we advocate using social media as a low cost (mostly free) form of professional learning, we aren't encouraging teachers to use all the platforms discussed below (we don't use them all). Teachers will have their preferences on which to use, and while some teachers completely avoid social media, others reluctantly dip their toe in, and others wholeheartedly embrace it.

There is a lot of research now focusing on how teachers are using social media for professional development and the impact this is having. *Like, comment, and share – professional development through social media in higher education: A systematic review* published in June 2020 by Tian Luo, Candice Freeman and Jill Stefaniak highlighted in the abstract that:

> *In recent years, professional learning networks (PLNs) and online learning communities of practices (CoPs) enabled by social media have emerged as a conduit and communal space for faculty members to engage in professional learning.*

---

26. Statista (2021) *Global social networks ranked by number of users 2021.*https://www.statista.com/statistics/272014/global-social-networks-ranked-by-number-of-users/

This systematic review provides an overview (synthesis) of research linked to social media and professional development in higher education. This includes:

Articles published in peer-reviewed journals between 2009 and 2019 were reviewed and 23 articles that met our selection criteria were included for further analysis and synthesis in this review. Their main findings suggest 'that research and practice on social media-supported professional learning is still in its infancy stage. Despite that social media-supported PLNs and CoPs show potential for contributing to faculty professional learning, challenges exist in sustaining faculty participation and engagement, as well as effectively navigating the social media space, especially for novice social media users.

The authors also offer recommendations for future research in this field.

Who to follow

We won't create a list with individuals to follow. It would be very difficult to do so due to the vast number of educators online sharing high-quality content and offering support, guidance and inspiration across different social media platforms. It could also be a very biased list including people we relate to, know or like. Instead, we offer this advice when considering who to follow, connect and engage with online:

- Aim to strike a balance between those working in the classroom and outside of the classroom, so a combination of classroom teachers, leaders and consultants.
- Aim to follow a diverse range of people in terms of teaching methods and approaches in addition to various BAME (Black, Asian and Minority Ethnic), gender and LGBT+ voices.
- Do connect and follow educators who share a common interest or specialism as yourself. This could be subject specific, EYFS, literacy, research and so on.
- As well as connecting with experts in your field follow teachers, leaders and consultants who specialise in areas you don't know as much about.
- Keep up to date by following educational news accounts such as Teacher Tapp.

Twitter for professional learning

'Nobody ever expected teachers to adopt Twitter as the backbone of the professional learning network but it happened,' noted blogger Thomas Whitby. We think this quotation sums up well the surprising popularity of Twitter within the teaching profession. Author, blogger and educator Mark Anderson (@ICTEvangelist) often describes Twitter as 'The best staffroom in the world'. This is a lovely way to view Twitter, bringing teachers around the world together to connect, network, share, learn (and sometimes argue!) plus more. Blogger and teacher Elizabeth Peterson has written about Twitter as a form of professional learning, noting that:

> *Ask any educator on Twitter and they will tell you that the best professional development they receive is on Twitter with their PLN. Why? I argue (and many would agree) that this is because the sharing, the ideas, and the support come from other teachers who are as invested in their passion to teach as you are! My PLN has served me far beyond my expectations.*[27]

We write more about professional learning networks (PLNs) in Chapter 6, another benefit of using social media for professional learning.

Features of Twitter

We will not go into too much detail as we realise Twitter is regularly updating, adding and removing features. There is an option to write and post a thread, which is a series of consecutive tweets which some choose to use as an alternative to blogging, and there is the facility to create a poll for other users to vote on.

Twitter Spaces enables users to have a verbal conversation, although without video. Anyone can host a Twitter Space and followers can join and listen or contribute to the conversation (a very similar format to the app 'Clubhouse'). A 'Pinned Tweet' allows users to take one specific tweet they have previously posted and pin it to the top of their profile, which ensures all visitors to the profile will see it. This is useful if you are sharing content such as a blog post or promoting an article, book or product.

Hashtags have slightly lost the appeal they initially had as it seems fewer people in education are using or searching them, but they can still be useful. # is a symbol that goes before a word, term or acronym which allows related tweets to be grouped together and when there are lots of tweets using a specific hashtag

---

27. Peterson, E. (2010) PLCs and PLNs – Go Us! *The Inspired Classroom.*
   https://theinspiredclassroom.com/2010/05/plcs-and-plns-go-us/

this can result in the hashtag 'trending', meaning it is widely viewed. Hashtags are useful when attending educational events as they are a quick and easy way to view other attendees' posts.

Instagram

If you use Instagram in addition to Twitter and other social media platforms, you will likely have a crossover with some connections but you will also engage and connect with new people who don't use those sites. On Instagram users are not limited to 280 characters per post, but try to avoid writing long posts as people often won't read them!

Instagram doesn't allow users to share links on posts, the only way to do so is by providing a link in the bio, so people will write 'see link in my bio'. People are now adding 'she/her' or 'he/him' or 'they' to their profile to show which pronouns they want people to use, with the aim being to help non-binary, transgender and intersex people feel more welcomed, included and accepted.

Posting Instagram 'stories' is very popular; they last 24 hours and you can see who has viewed your story, unlike your posts, where you only know if someone has seen it if they like or comment, although they may have briefly seen it and just kept scrolling. You can categorise your stories as 'highlights' for people to view after 24 hours, and this is also where you will see if someone is posting a live video. Instagram Live stories can be scheduled and promoted in advance, or they simply happen randomly for followers to join live and view. People can comment and interact, people can also be invited to join the Instagram Live chat. Twitter doesn't have this function, but Facebook does.

LinkedIn

As described by LinkedIn.com:

> LinkedIn is the world's largest professional network on the internet. You can use LinkedIn to find the right job or internship, connect and strengthen professional relationships, and learn the skills you need to succeed in your career.

It is a professional form of social media; only work-related posts should be shared (although this does not always happen) and only professionals that work together should be connected (again, this doesn't always happen).

Similar to the other platforms discussed, users can share, network, organise, host and promote events or publications. Unlike other platforms, LinkedIn allows users to write and publish articles through the platform. The structure lends itself to using an online CV where users include their education and employment history. If you use LinkedIn it is useful to regularly update your online CV, this is good for reflection and also helps when applying for a position (see Chapter 10 for more about the application process). There is an option on LinkedIn for colleagues, or former colleagues, to write testimonials which is essentially a very short reference that can be read publicly, and people can endorse users for various skills they list, such as leadership, data management, or assessment.

It is possible to state that you are seeking a new role or position, or wish to work in a specific location. Kate did this successfully and LinkedIn played a significant role in her appointment and transition to a new school when she made the decision to relocate to the United Arab Emirates. Below Kate shares her experience of using LinkedIn to secure a teaching position.

In the half term of February 2016, I went on a holiday alone to Dubai. I went for two reasons; to visit a new country on a relaxing holiday, and to see if this was a place I could live and work. Of course, a week's holiday is very different to living somewhere, but a week was enough to confirm that the United Arab Emirates (UAE) was the country I wanted to relocate to. I knew lots of other teachers who had made the same transition and were very happy teaching and living in this beautiful country earning a higher (and tax free) wage with a comfortable package that included accommodation, medical insurance, annual flights and more.

On the Monday morning after my visit to the UAE I informed my headteacher I would be looking for a job in Dubai or Abu Dhabi. I did this because I planned to announce on LinkedIn that I was looking for a job but as a professional courtesy I felt it would be the right and respectful thing to tell my headteacher first. Prior to this I had been making connections with educators and school leaders in the UAE, which was easy to do through a simple search. Connections with individuals then led to other connections in their school or area, and before long I had developed a wide network of educators across the UAE.

I announced on LinkedIn that I was seeking a teacher of history position in the UAE. The following day I received a private message from a Head of Secondary School I was connected with who told me they were about to advertise for a history teacher at their school and asked me to email him my CV and letter of application. I already had my CV prepared and ready. I spent some time researching the school and within the week I sent my application. 24 hours later I was invited to an interview with the Head of Humanities that would be held over Skype. The interview took place the following week and shortly afterwards I found out I was successful. Within two weeks of announcing I was seeking a position in the UAE I secured a job at a school where I remained for three years. On reflection this was a quick and surprising process, but I was very grateful for the role LinkedIn played in my appointment.

Facebook

Facebook is quite different from the other social media platforms discussed, in the sense that people don't set up professional accounts but instead use their personal accounts to follow education related Facebook pages and groups. This is where the lines can become blurred with the professional and personal. It is up to you to decide what your purpose and aims are for each social media platform you use. Facebook has a range of education groups for individuals to like and/ or join. These can have a specific focus such as different age ranges, topics, or subjects, and can be another source of professional support and learning. Many people check Facebook daily, so it can be helpful to follow the Facebook TES news page to stay updated with the latest developments in education. There are also live webinars and online events that can be streamed through Facebook.

TikTok

TikTok is a video sharing social networking service that is growing rapidly in terms of its popularity and users. TikTok.com states that their mission is 'To inspire creativity and bring joy'. Admittedly, TikTok does appear to be a social media platform that is more popular with teenagers but there are also teachers using and sharing on it too. 'Teacher comedy' has emerged with students and TikTok influencers posting teacher sketches based on stereotypical and exaggerated phrases and behaviours teachers demonstrate in the classroom. But what about TikTok for professional learning?

We both don't use TikTok (as we stated, not all social media platforms are for everyone) but we have met teachers who are TikTok enthusiasts. Although limited to video content (currently links cannot be shared via TikTok other than links to Instagram and YouTube channels) there are short videos posted by teachers offering advice and tips to other teachers. It is easy to find these by searching the hashtags #edutok, #teacherpd and #thetiktokteacher. There is also a 'Question of the day' (QOTD) where a question is posted by a teacher about an element of practice or professional development for other teachers to respond. Again, these can be found via the hashtags #teacherqotd or #teachertalk .

YouTube

We don't need to explain how popular YouTube is, it is a phenomenon. For many, YouTube is the first stop when they want to find out more about something, and education is no exception. Previously, any event or presentation had to be attended live and in person but now that has all changed. There is a vast amount of content available on YouTube for teachers to view as part of professional development. researchEd events have gained momentum in recent years and when the pandemic broke out and lockdown occurred researchEd, like many others, adapted to continue to provide high-quality professional learning for teachers and school leaders. On the website https://researched.org.uk/ it states:

The goal of researchED is to bridge the gap between research and practice in education. Researchers, teachers, and policy makers come together for a day of information-sharing and myth-busting. We aim to bring together as many parties affected by educational research – e.g. teachers, academics, researchers, policy makers, teacher-trainers – in order to establish healthy relationships where field-specific expertise is pooled usefully.

While many researchEd events globally had to be postponed or cancelled in 2020, researchEd Home was created. researchEd Home consists of a wide range of presentations delivered by leading experts in their fields, including teachers and leaders. They are available to access freely on the YouTube channel, and again a QR code at the end of this chapter will direct you to the channel and online presentations. It was not just researchEd that expanded their online offering, many organisations and events made similar adjustments, such as Seneca Learn, BrewEd events (more explained about this below with TeachMeets), and more.

All the social media platforms described above are user-friendly and available to access freely, although you can pay to upgrade features on some sites, for example LinkedIn has the option to upgrade to premium membership which has additional features. All the platforms provide access to a worldwide network of educators that you can connect with, interact with, share with and learn from. Regular updates, blogs, and news surrounding education are posted daily, and there is great potential if you are searching for a teaching position. It is becoming more common to see teaching and leadership positions advertised on social media to widen the recruitment field. Social media platforms can also be a fantastic platform to showcase your skills, experience and passion for education, and for sharing your work widely.

Platforms vary significantly in terms of how formal or informal they are, from a TikTok tutorial video to a published article on LinkedIn. Teachers spend a lot of time educating students about the potential dangers and risks of social media, and it is just as important that we are also informed as to how to protect ourselves online. All social media platforms have options to remove or block another user that is bothering or harassing someone, and e-safety is something we should always consider and keep in mind when using any online site for professional learning. Additionally, social media and apps can be just as addictive for adults as they can be for children, so we need to self-regulate and monitor our own screen time as these things have the potential to become all consuming.

PODCASTS FOR PROFESSIONAL LEARNING

Podcasts continue to grow in popularity, and the education sector is no exception as there are various podcasts and radio channels dedicated to teaching and learning. Podcasts are great because they are simple to subscribe to and listen to, and they are flexible in the sense that people can listen to them while driving, exercising or relaxing. Everyone with a smartphone can access a podcast via Apple Podcasts, Anchor, SoundCloud and other platforms, and they are free to access.

Most educational podcasts involve leading voices in education being interviewed about their work but there is a wide range available, including those with subject-specific content, and podcasts shared by examination boards offering advice to teachers and students. We both have a history background and we listen to podcasts that focus on different periods and aspects of history. We do this because it is an area of interest and as a way to develop and deepen our subject knowledge. We recommend you find podcasts that are either linked to general education or are more specific to your interests and professional development needs. In Chapter 8 we offer advice on how to launch your own educational podcast.

TEACHMEET EVENTS AND CONFERENCES

A 'TeachMeet' refers to a grassroots event for teachers, often hosted and organised by teachers. Originally TeachMeet events consisted of short presentations delivered by teachers and leaders on a subject of their choice linked to education. They are intended to be an informal method of professional learning and networking, and the model has developed and evolved over recent years with many TeachMeet style events happening online. Whether in person or online, these events tend to be free or relatively cheap.

TMIcons (TeachMeet Icons) was set up in 2015 by Tom Rogers, with the first event, TMHistoryIcons, held in 2016. Kate was part of the original founding team and the aim was to host a free event for history teachers across the UK which had a subject-specific focus. This grew in popularity and developed into TMIcons which now hosts events, in person and online, for a wide range of subjects and continues to grow. You can follow @Teachmeeticons on Twitter to find out about free events taking place for teachers.

'BrewEd' is another grassroots movement for teachers. The founders Edward Finch and Daryn Simon launched BrewEd for teachers interested in pints and pedagogy (although 'brew' can refer to tea, depending on your preference). Simon and Finch write:

> *BrewEd is a grassroots movement for people from all phases, sectors, and areas of education. BrewEd events provide a space for educators to come together, enjoy each other's company and have some robust, open and challenging debate around thought-provoking ideas and issues. They should also provide a platform for local educators to have their voices heard within their community. Events are organised by volunteers and are completely free from corporate sponsorship. They are inclusive events and, as such, ticket prices should be kept as low as possible.*[28]

To find out more about BrewEd events in person or online follow @BrewEd2017 on Twitter.

Although researchEd has a YouTube channel where presentations can be viewed, there are various events held around the world. Previous researchEd events have been held in London, Amsterdam, Philadelphia, Cape Town, Chile, Dubai, Geneva, Melbourne, Toronto and Glasgow, with more planned for the future. At a researchED event, there is a keynote speaker, and also six or seven rounds of sessions led by various voices in education who are passionate about research and what it looks like in the classroom. Each session is about 40 minutes long, and attendees can build their own day using the timetable and programme released a couple of weeks before the event. We have both attended and presented at researchEd events, and Robin has organised and hosted researchEd events in Scotland. We highly recommend learning more about the researchEd movement, either by attending an event or viewing presentations online.

---

28. BrewEd (ND) Available at: http://brewed.pbworks.com/w/page/120273042/FrontPage

LESSON OBSERVATIONS

Firstly, we don't think the term 'lesson observation' is the most fitting description as it only focuses on observing and viewing the lesson; not considering the feedback, reflection and learning elements that come with watching teachers teach and having conversations about it. However, that is the terminology we will use, although it's important to acknowledge that it is all encompassing, going beyond the observation aspect.

The work done by Professor Robert Coe on lesson observations is now fairly well known, but if you haven't come across it, then it's worth reading.[29] Coe points out that even when observers are trained, they can differ widely in their view of the quality of a lesson. If two observers watch the same lesson, and the first observer rates it as 'outstanding', there is a three in four chance that the second observer will disagree. It's even stronger when the lesson is deemed to be inadequate; 90% of the time the second observer will disagree. Coe develops this by talking about 'poor proxies for learning', which are the things we believed to be indicators of learning, but are possibly red herrings. Are the children well behaved? Have they covered the curriculum? Have they answered questions? All these things might be true, but it doesn't necessarily mean students are learning; they might just be doing simple tasks they have already mastered. So if lesson observation is so hard to agree on, and we might not even be seeing learning taking place, why bother using it as a source of professional learning?

Well, a key point is that while observing for grading purposes may be highly unreliable, observing for the sake of learning new things is not. An interesting question here is whether or not your school has a lesson observation form. If so, what is on it and why? The reason we ask these questions is because observing and subjectively evaluating the teacher is a flawed concept, so instead any form should be about the observer and what they've learned from the lesson. How did the lesson help them to reflect on their practice, and inspire new and improved ways of doing things? Ultimately, do you even need a form for this? The problem with a form is that it is a template; it lends itself to generic reflections and recording, and is probably just there to support a system that is really about accountability. Do you need to have observed others to pass an annual review? If so, is it being done for the right purposes?

29. Coe, R. (2014, January 9) *Classroom observation: it's harder than you think.* Centre for Evaluation and Monitoring. https://www.cem.org/blog/414

And if we know what the poor proxies for learning are, what are the good ones? The best advice we can give you is to read Graham Nuthall's excellent book, *The Hidden Lives of Learners*. It makes a real difference sitting in a lesson and thinking about the three worlds that Nuthall outlines: the public world of the teacher; the complex world of peer relationships; and the hidden, private world of the learner. Try observing a lesson and thinking about those three dimensions, and you'll see things in a very different light.

We both believe that lesson observation, when done for the right reasons and in the right way, can be a powerful tool. The key to getting it right is firstly to decide what particular aspect you want to focus on; what do you want to see in the lesson? Then approach someone who is experienced, knowledgeable and willing to have you join a lesson. A key thing here is professional respect; you are entering someone else's classroom as a guest, and it's amazing how often people (usually senior leaders) can get this wrong. Once an observation has been agreed, have a conversation about the particular group of students and the prior learning that has taken place. If you don't know the context of the lesson, you will struggle to decode what is going on. Then, afterwards, have another good discussion with the teacher and see if you picked up on the many subtle and nuanced things that have taken place. A classroom is a complex environment, so don't just assume that you can learn from observing alone. Without wrap-around professional dialogue, you run the risk of wasting both your time, and that of your colleague.

SCHOOL VISITS

This is perhaps the most under-rated form of professional learning. Being able to visit another school is an eye-opening, and often very self-affirming experience. The two most common outcomes are either a significant degree of inspiration (you see things being done really well that can be transferred to your own context) or a realisation that the grass is not necessarily greener on the other side after all. Both are highly desirable outcomes.

The reason that school visits are less frequent than, say, attending courses is perhaps due to difficulties around time and organisation. After all, it isn't just a case of one teacher needing cover to be out of school, a visit demands a lot of time from the host. If you're going to have someone visit you, you need to accept that any pockets of time you have in the day will be totally taken up. You need to be well prepared in advance, and will probably have to make a few additional arrangements for the visitor, which might not always be straightforward. This is why it often works really well to arrange a reciprocal visit, so that you both get the benefit of the experience.

If you do manage to pull this off, what should you aim to get out of it? Well that depends entirely on what you are looking to learn. You should have a focus for the visit, whether that's to see a school-wide approach to behaviour management, or to be embedded within a department to learn about curriculum design. You need practical takeaways, and things you can discuss with colleagues when you return to your school.

What school visits and lesson observations have in common is that they are specific forms of ethnographic research. They involve watching people (in this case, teachers and students) in their environment and trying to understand their behaviour. This is very complex, and one of the recurring dangers highlighted by ethnographic researchers is that you often see what you want to see – even more so when it isn't there – so there is a danger that you can delude yourself based on your preconceptions. Secondly, you need to be keenly aware of your influence on your environment. Are people behaving differently because there is a different (or strange) person in the room? They almost certainly are. If you are interested in this particular area of research, we can recommend the work on participant observation by Dr Sara Delamont at Cardiff University, it may well change your approach to how you visit someone else's school or classroom.

CHALLENGE QUESTIONS

- How often do you read for professional learning?
- Do you vary the types of blogs/books that you read for professional learning?
- What do you want to achieve from your presence on social media?
- What are your aims?
- Have you gained anything professionally already as a result of social media?
- What are your concerns about using social media?
- Have you taken advantage of the free professional learning that is available online?

QR CODES FOR FURTHER READING AND INFORMATION

Teachers Talk Radio
https://www.ttradio.org

HWRK Magazine
https://hwrkmagazine.co.uk

researchEd
https://researched.org.uk

One of the difficulties of preparing yourself for leadership is that other people will notice. You may have come across this already but ambition is often a dirty word in education. Who wants the reputation of being ambitious, career-

CHAPTER 4

LEARNING ABOUT LEADERSHIP

Purpose of this chapter: To help you plan and make decisions about professional learning to support your development as a leader.

A few years ago, Robin was interested in what the route to senior leadership involved, and how to go about it. The first step? Ask someone who knows. Their answer? Just watch people who are currently doing it. Really? That's it? Yes.

That was a short-lived experiment in effective professional learning. Observation can be useful, but it needs more than just being a body in the room when a deputy head leads a briefing. What you really need is an insight into the reservoir of experience that really great school leaders have, and ideally from a range of leadership levels and roles. In fact, the leadership pathway probably has such a bewildering array of options when it comes to professional development that it will leave you feeling paralysed by choice. Which books to read? Which courses to go on? What things to volunteer for?

This chapter is not about the theory of leadership. It is, instead, about preparing yourself for leadership by doing the right kind of professional learning, which opens your eyes to the reality of the day job. How to go about making transitions from one role to the next is the focus of Chapter 9, and it may help to read these chapters back to back in order to sharpen your focus. As you'll see throughout the book, we believe in making informed choices, so learning about leadership really needs to come before the actual practice of leadership. Don't try to backward map it, unless you really want to induce stress in yourself and others.

One of the difficulties of preparing yourself for leadership is that other people will notice. You may have come across this already, but ambition is often a dirty word in education. Who wants the reputation of being ambitious, career-minded, and angling for promotion? Actually, there is nothing wrong with any of these things, otherwise we wouldn't have written this book. Healthy ambition is a good thing, and having a clear strategy for making progress is a very sensible way of going about that (see Chapter 12). It is certainly better than drifting unconsciously into leadership, or being thrust into it because a role is vacant and no one in their right mind wants it. In short, if you are interested in leadership, it is an inherently good thing to spend time studying it before you embark upon it. You definitely won't get time to do that after your first appointment.

READING ABOUT LEADERSHIP

The literature on leadership (both specific to education and generic) is not so much a mountain, as a mountain range. It's not just that you can't read it all, but you can't even read all the literature reviews either. So, where do you even begin?

Broader reading on leadership can be useful, although you may wonder whether learning about the psychology of Wall Street CEOs, command structures in the US Marine Corps, or management of air traffic control, has any practical relevance for making sure uniform rules are adhered to by Year 9 (they are strangely resistant to motivational quotes from Simon Sinek). That said, it might be an idea to start with this body of literature, because what you get is perspective, and a sense of the unique context in which you work.

When you are reading about leadership, do so selectively. What practical utility does this have for you, your colleagues and your students? A pleasing by-product of this kind of reading is that it can provide great material for assemblies, or memorable anecdotes for use in the classroom. Essentially, if it gets you interested in reading more, it has already served a purpose, and if it shakes up your reading away from a narrow focus on education literature, that's also beneficial. Keeping a broad perspective is increasingly difficult to do as you take on more responsibility, so these kinds of books are worth dipping into if you want to change your lens on the world.

Even if you are a bit unsure about the broader books on leadership, you do need to be less sceptical about the literature on educational leadership. This might seem like an edict, but we say it for two reasons. Firstly, there are some fantastic books out there which are context-specific, and they are absolutely worth reading. Secondly, if you are serious about leadership, it's hard to get to where you want to be without some form of academic study (see Chapter 5 as to why), and don't forget that a pretty standard interview question will be about which leadership books have influenced you and why.

We are still faced with the problem of where to begin on the reading list, but that depends on what you want to learn. We can break the categories down into theory, bespoke areas of leadership such as curriculum or professional learning, or the operational side that deals with things like finance or HR. The best way to do this is to consider your strengths and weaknesses, and where you have gaps in your professional knowledge. This requires some self-assessment and reflection, but should give you laser-guided precision when it comes to choosing what to read. Asking for recommendations is useful, and reading lists on university courses are freely available. Many journal articles will be pay-walled, but there is such a wealth of reading available that you should never find you are stuck.

There are many blogs that are worth reading; it's not really useful to list any here, because by the time we go to print they may have changed, but doing a bit of web-savvy research is always a good idea. Many of the best blogs are written by people who are currently in leadership positions, so are up to date, informed and practical. The best advice we can give is to check out the provenance of the blogger. What leadership experience do they have? Is it current? Or did they do a couple of years as a deputy head and have since spent the past decade as a consultant? If the source looks good, it's worth exploring further.

How about challenging yourself to read one blog a day? Most take three to five minutes, so whether you're waiting for a bus to arrive or a meeting to start, use the time wisely. It's a simple, but very effective, investment of your time.

SOCIAL MEDIA FOR LEADERSHIP LEARNING

This links with blogging, but social media has been transformative for professional learning because it has allowed teachers and leaders to share ideas and experiences and debate the issues of the day. We've already covered the basics of this in Chapter 3, but what follows is specific to leadership learning.

If you are using social media for professional purposes, keep in mind that whatever you say is visible to your students and their parents and families, and your colleagues and line-managers. The more you progress as a leader, the more likely it is that people will actively look for your account. Many aspiring leaders choose not to post things, but just follow (or 'lurk', as it's known, a tad unfortunately). You can then observe what good leadership practice looks like online. Also, if you use Twitter to cultivate your own education news timeline by following constructive, informative accounts, it's a great way to build up your resources and focus your professional learning. This can keep you up to speed with new policies and developments which are essential for school leaders to know about.

It's fine for this to be a one-way street where you just take on board good quality information. Hashtags like #SLTchat and #honk (the hashtag associated with the work of author and leadership expert Andy Buck, who we both love) are great, and will give you ideas for further accounts to follow. Online chats are really good, as they allow you to get a range of perspectives on a current key issue. You'll also find that these forums are usually more considerate and supportive than the conversations which follow after a provocative post from a virtual gunslinger. There is further discussion of social media throughout this book, which illustrates how it has shaped and influenced both our professional learning and career progression.

COURSES ON LEADERSHIP

We are both fairly sceptical about the value of these courses, because leadership is one of the busiest market-places, and therefore a money spinner for a range of firms and consultants. The 2015 TEDx talk by David Weston (@informed_edu) entitled *Unleashing Greatness in Teachers* shows that most such professional learning opportunities for educators fall short of the mark; only 1% can be described as 'transformative', where impact is assessed as being at the top of four levels. The vast majority have marginal returns for the simple reason that they tend not to make a difference to what participants do in their day-to-day practice. It doesn't really matter how brilliant or entertaining the course leader is, if what they cover doesn't translate back to your school and change your practice for the better, it simply isn't worth it.

We've already argued that professional learning about leadership is the horse that goes before the career progression cart, so you should be wary of attending a course just for the sake of adding it to your CV. If it doesn't help make you a stronger, more effective leader, don't do it. That sounds logical and easy, but the tricky part is knowing that before you sign up. How then, do you sort the wheat from the chaff?

A common theme we're developing here is around provenance. Do your research. If the course being advertised lists the presenters, research all of them and see if you really want to spend a lot of time hearing what they have to say. Also, check to see if anyone else has done the course, and don't just rely on website testimonials; we don't trust what 'Brian from Surrey' says because we don't know if he really exists. Good courses should also provide ongoing tasks, and especially reading, so you keep on learning. If you have to attend more than one day, with tasks to get on with between the sessions, there's more chance that you will apply what you learn.

To give an example, one of the things that leaders struggle with is public speaking. For whatever reasons, many teachers find addressing an audience larger than their class to be daunting. If you want to be a senior leader, fear of speaking in public or on camera can be a major obstacle. Robin took a media training course that focused on the craft of speech writing and presenting, which was stretched over three sessions. In between each session, participants had to find an opportunity to speak publicly such as an assembly or parents' evening presentation. The workshops then allowed the pitch to be developed, rehearsed, refined, and peer-critiqued (a process that is pretty similar to the training given to TED speakers). This led to all participants making a lot of progress in an area that is often overlooked in professional learning. After all, just about every leadership job specification cites being a 'good communicator' as a prerequisite, but it's rare to find anyone who has actually trained in communication skills. It's usually just left to natural talent, and explains why extroverts are over-represented at leadership level, which isn't a healthy thing. Did this course make a difference to everyday practice? Absolutely. Will the course you are currently looking at have as much impact? Hopefully, you now know how to benchmark a course being advertised so you can make an informed decision.

CASE STUDY: RESIDENTIAL LEADERSHIP LEARNING WITH COLUMBA 1400

Columba 1400 is a residential leadership centre on the Isle of Skye, and also Loch Lomond, founded in 1997 by Norman Drummond CBE. It offers something a bit different, and is best described as an experience, rather than a course. In essence it is a leadership academy, social enterprise and a charity, so not your normal training provider. While it is only available to teachers in Scotland, it is worth thinking about finding something similar wherever you are working, because this is what transformative professional learning looks like in practice.

As Robin discovered, it's for people who want to feel part of a community and focus on their own values in education. What you get out of it is a support network that lasts for many years afterwards. You are part of an alumni network, and there are reunion events later on. Cohorts typically stay in touch and support one another whenever it is needed. If one of the key metrics of good professional learning is that it should build up a wider support network, then this does the trick, hence why Robin was keen to shine a spotlight on this as a form of leadership learning.

Christine Couser (@ChristineCouser) is a Secondary Deputy Headteacher in Perth and Kinross, and is one of the WomenEd Scotland leads. Christine is interested in leadership, having been a Major in the Territorial Army. She's a Columba 1400 alumnus and says that 'If anyone asked what's the best CPD I've ever done, I would say Columba 1400.' She describes it as 'A movement within Scottish education that is not part of the establishment, but is accepted by it. You leave your job at the doorstep, and it is a fully immersive experience. The purpose is really about realising the greatness within you.' Their work is based on a quotation by the novelist John Buchan, that reads 'Our task is not to put the greatness back into humanity, but to elicit it, for the greatness is there already.' She adds that 'Everyone I know who has done it has loved it, and felt the full benefit.'

Before you think that this is a liberal retreat with little practical application, it should be noted that many of the tutors are former teachers and headteachers, and the 'course' is accredited by the General Teaching Council for Scotland (GTCS); on completion of the essay aspect of the course, GTCS recognition in Values Based Leadership is awarded. It also has a focus on school improvement, but the main thrust is about the Columba 1400 values: awareness, focus, creativity, integrity, perseverance, and service, and developing your own values-based approach to leadership. They also run leadership academies for young people, parents and carers and families.

So even if residentials are not for you, or you don't work in Scottish education, do consider whether the leadership course that you are doing has the same depth and impact that this seems to have.

LEARNING BY DOING

A pretty solid maxim is that you have to do the job before you get the job. What does that mean? It means that any entry-level opportunities to take on a degree of leadership should be grasped. It might not carry a title, a remittance or a pay rise, and is likely to be pretty thankless, but it is a starting point. It isn't just about showing willingness to the leadership team, but it's about yourself; finding out if you really enjoy the added pressure and workload first before you take it on at a higher level. There is an ethical dilemma here; surely you should expect a tangible reward for taking on such a post? If you agree that there should be an upgrade in terms and conditions, that's fine. You are making it a bit tougher to progress though, as just about any middle or senior leader will be able to point to a project or role they had which opened up their leadership pathway and carried no additional reward. That is the nature of schools as a workplace, and if the opportunity that comes up has no perks attached it should be low risk. In other words, walking away from it shouldn't be an issue if you find it isn't for you.

Often the best way to 'learn by doing' involves being part of a team which is led by someone you can observe at close quarters, as you are looking to build your own experience, and learn from the experience of others. If, for example, you get yourself onto a working group like a curriculum committee, then try to have a discussion with the person leading the group outside of the meetings. What experience or knowledge did they build up in order to be able to lead the group? How can you help them with the work being done? Good leaders know that you delegate the good stuff, not the drudgery, otherwise you never really mobilise your team. If you volunteer to take something on, the chances are that it will be something good. If it isn't, you can always (politely) retract the offer.

Good leadership learning involves a balance of theory and practice. If you are actively studying the craft of leadership, and taking on some additional responsibilities, then you are definitely progressing. If you are only doing one of those things, it won't have the impact you need it to.

CASE STUDIES: AN INTERVIEW WITH SCHOOL LEADERS ALLANA GAY AND BRUCE ROBERTSON

We thought the best way to tackle this section on leadership learning was by speaking to two experienced school leaders we have huge respect for. After all, if standing on the shoulders of giants was good enough for Sir Isaac Newton, then why not teachers?

First up, Allana Gay is a teacher, education advisor and speaker. She started teaching and leading at inner city London secondary schools and is currently the Headteacher of Vita et Pax Preparatory School. Allana co-founded the BAMEed Network in 2017 (you can read more about this in Chapter 6) with the aim of bringing attention and action to the issue of normalising ethnic diversity throughout the education sector.

Secondly, Bruce Robertson is the Rector of Berwickshire High School and author of *The Teaching Delusion* trilogy. As a chemistry teacher and senior leader, he has been working in education for almost 20 years. Bruce is also active as a consultant and conference presenter.

What, in your view, is the best professional learning you can do for leadership?

Allana: There are two parts: try small whole-school projects, and speak to and shadow as many leaders as you can. The first allows you to think through the main areas of leadership: structuring ideas; communication; getting others to follow; budgeting; impact measurement etc. The second widens perspectives on leadership. It helps you to think about the whole school and learn from the successes and failures of others.

Bruce: Professional reading is top of the list. To be a great leader, you have to be clear about what it is you are leading. In schools, I think this should be the continuous improvement of teaching and learning, by which I really mean curriculum and pedagogy. It's impossible to learn too much about these areas, which means it's impossible to read too much about them. The best leaders keep upskilling themselves by learning more and more through reading. That said, professional reading doesn't tend to be enough in itself. You need 'to do something' with what you've been reading, to help clarify and consolidate your learning. Professional discussion, practising something, or articulating your thinking in writing are all very useful professional learning activities, too.

There is a huge amount of literature out there on leadership. What three books or resources would you recommend to teachers who are just getting started on this?

Allana: Leadership Matters *by Andy Buck gives a great summary of the leadership ideas and thinking in education.* An Ethic of Excellence *by Ron Berger shows the significance of student learning and the influence that leaders and teachers have over this. And thirdly,* Quiet: The power of introverts *by Susan Cain.*

Bruce: There certainly is! And the pile of books to choose from keeps getting bigger. That's a great thing, but it can also make it difficult to know where to start. In addition to the The Teaching Delusion *trilogy (obviously!), my three recommendations would be:*

1. Aligning Professional Learning, Performance Management and Effective Teaching *by Peter Cole. This is a relatively short seminar paper that is available online. It's about the development of professional learning cultures in schools. It has had a huge influence on my thinking about school leadership.*

2. Creating The Schools Our Children Need *by Dylan Wiliam. If you're going to be an effective leader, you need to have clarity about what you should be focusing your leadership on. This book nails it.*

3. Leadership, Capacity Building and School Improvement *by Clive Dimmock. There is a huge amount of breadth and depth to this book. It's a more challenging read than my first two recommendations, but no less important.*

Did you get any help in the form of mentoring or coaching in your leadership training (either formal or informal)?

Allana: Yes. *There was formal mentoring provision through Future Leaders. That was extremely useful. I have had a coach through the NPQH. Less useful in a professional sense but it did allow a space for thoughtfulness.*

Bruce: When I first took on a formal leadership role as Principal Teacher of Professional Learning, I had a weekly meeting with a Deputy Headteacher, who acted as a coach. This was invaluable. The meetings gave us a regular opportunity to touch base and discuss how things were going. The time was protected. Rather than tell me what it was I should be doing – or how I was doing – he would ask me questions designed to help me reach my own conclusions. He guided and nudged, rather than pushed or pulled. I learned a lot.

When I became a Deputy Headteacher, I made sure I protected time each week to have meetings like this with the staff I line-managed. As Headteacher, I continue to do this, and ask other leaders in my school to do the same.

Did you take any leadership courses or qualifications, and if so, were they helpful?

Allana: I undertook the now defunct Future Leaders training in 2013. At that time it was a five year path to Headship. The reading, mentorship, projects and discussion partners through those years were excellent. It allowed long-lasting acquaintance with leaders across the country. I was able to understand various circumstances schools were in throughout the country through the networking and sharing opportunities. I have also completed an NPQH. It wasn't as useful in practice or theory as there was focus on leadership ideas rather than the gaps in practice that move a Senior Leader to Headship. Finally, I am on an apprenticeship Master's in Leadership via the NCE. The content is great as it undertakes all ideas of business leadership rather than school only.

Bruce: As of 2020, to become a headteacher in Scotland, you need to have achieved the GTCS Standard for Headship. I achieved this via an 18-month Master's in Leadership course with The University of Edinburgh. This is the only leadership course I have ever been on. Was it helpful? Absolutely. Believe it or not, before I embarked on this programme, I did very little professional reading. I credit the programme with lighting a fuse which led to something of a professional reading explosion! Now, I read a lot. I don't think I would be doing that if this programme hadn't got me started.

The assessment structure of the programme involved essay writing. At first, that was a real shock to the system! I hadn't written anything close to an essay since I was an undergraduate. To be honest, I wasn't best pleased about having to do anything like that again. But what I discovered was that the process of writing helped sharpen my thinking. Having to articulate something in writing forced me to become clearer about what I thought. If it weren't for writing these essays, I'm pretty sure I'd never have written a book – far less three!

In your experience, did the theoretical learning you did about leadership match the reality of practice?

Allana: Not always. The theoretical learning was more useful as a source of ideas to trial within school or as a reflective tool to review the impact of actions. The challenge of theoretical learning is that it tends to hold bias on the things that are examined, ignore wider viewpoints on some education ideas and does not transfer well from one environment to the next. The political nature of education means that some aspects are deliberately presented in favour to others even if not impactful.

Bruce: I used to think that you couldn't learn anything about leadership from a book, and that experience was what mattered most. I've completely changed my mind on that. While I think it is possible to be an effective leader in schools without doing much professional reading, every leader would be better at what they do if they read more.

Leadership theory taught me the importance of focusing on teaching and learning, of developing culture, and about the attributes staff tend to value most in their leaders. Some of what I read confirmed what I already thought; some challenged it. Ultimately, leadership theory has helped me develop my own set of 'leadership principles', which I keep returning to as I reflect on how things are going in my school. The most important of these are:

1. *Leadership is about getting the best out of people.*
2. *Great leaders make time to talk to people and listen to them.*
3. *Keep the focus on teaching and learning as much as you can.*

Which leader (or leaders), in education or beyond, do you admire and why?

Allana: *I do not have a hero of education. I admire people in public life like James Baldwin who speak of what they believe and work towards it. I have more of a general admiration for leaders who are open minded, authentic in their belief and seek to build the sector rather than being engrossed in their school.*

Bruce: *In education, it's Sir John Jones and Dylan Wiliam. There are others, but these two stand out for me. Why do I admire them so much? Well, Sir John Jones has written one of the most inspiring books on education that you're ever likely to read,* The Magic-Weaving Business. *He's also a wonderful, authentic, motivational speaker. If leadership is about getting the best out of people, there's no one better than Sir John to help inspire you to do that.*

Dylan Wiliam is also a superb writer and speaker. He talks so much sense about education and what we need to be focusing on in schools. As I have said, effective leaders need to have clarity in their own mind about what they are leading. Dylan Wiliam will help you get that.

What advice would you give to anyone looking to learn about leadership?

Allana: *Be clear on your own beliefs and identity. Leadership can be done in many ways but it has to be through means that you believe in.*

Bruce: *Remember what leadership is about: getting the best out of people in the pursuit of a clear goal. Leadership is about influencing people. To do that, you need to take time to get to know people well. What motivates and inspires one person will not necessarily do the same for another. Make time to sit down and listen to people. Don't let 'being busy' get in the way of that. One of the worst leaders I have ever worked with talked a lot about the importance of doing that, but never did it herself. She referred to 'cup of coffee conversations', but she never made time to even put the kettle on.*

Also, remember that the power of a team will always trump that of an individual. Create the conditions for ideas to emerge. Empower the people you are leading to lead initiatives themselves. Do that, and the impact of your leadership will grow exponentially.

What's the best thing about school leadership?

Allana: Knowing that through your actions, you can influence the futures of a large number of students. Having control over the vision and direction of your school.

Bruce: Watching people and teams transform. The satisfaction that you get from watching people get better at what they do as a result of your leadership – or leadership you have helped develop in others – is hard to beat.

The better people get at what they do, the more they tend to enjoy what they are doing, and the better the results they will achieve. Leadership that supports and challenges people to keep getting better is the sort of leadership we should be aiming for in schools. If you can develop a culture of professional learning and a mindset of continuous improvement in the team you lead, transformation is all but guaranteed.

Thanks to Allana and Bruce for sharing their answers and advice.

This chapter should, we hope, have given you some ideas for the kind of professional learning that you need (as opposed to what anyone else thinks you need) for developing your leadership. It is a blend of getting the right experience, and supporting it with effective professional learning, so you can evolve into the leader you want to be.

CHALLENGE QUESTIONS

- What professional learning have you done so far to prepare yourself for leadership roles?
- How effective was that professional learning?
- What are your strengths and weaknesses currently?
- What professional learning do you need to do to address weaknesses or lack of experience?
- Which leaders in your school can you speak to for advice or insight?
- Are you making the most of professional media?
- What opportunities are there for you to take on entry-level leadership or whole-school roles?

QR CODES FOR FURTHER READING AND INFORMATION

Honk – Andy Buck
Leadership website
https://www.andybuck.org.uk/honk

Columba 1400
http://www.columba1400.com

Bruce Robertson
Teaching, learning and
leadership blog
https://theteachingdelusion.com

CHAPTER 5

ADVANCED PROFESSIONAL QUALIFICATIONS

Purpose of this chapter: To learn about different professional qualifications available in education and how they can support professional learning, leadership and development.

Welcome to the big time. This is where professional learning hits the Champions League. Chapter 3 focused on how to do things with a tight budget but this chapter is about choosing to make a significant investment of both time and financial resources. The advanced professional qualifications we cover here are typically university level qualifications (leading to credits or an entire degree), take at least a year, and usually come with a fee or funding requirement. They are a major undertaking and involve engaging with academic literature, research, assignments and project management. They are not for the faint hearted.

We will look at four specific forms of advanced professional qualifications: National Professional Qualifications (NPQs); Master's degrees in education; PhDs; and the Master's of Business Administration (MBA) degree. This doesn't cover all qualifications that can be considered 'professional', but it does give a flavour of the top end of professional learning as we try to balance breadth and depth.

So why go down this route when there is so much out there for free, and how much of a commitment will it be? Well, the two core reasons for making this choice would be the sheer intellectual challenge, and ultimately career progression. Either reason is entirely valid, and actually making it through such a demanding process might well need the motivation that comes from a combination of both. There is a good chance that you will work with someone who has already undertaken one of these qualifications, so speaking to them about their experience is invaluable. You really need to be aware of the workload involved, and the fees required. At the top end, one of these qualifications can set you back a five-figure sum, and can take anything from one to six years to complete.

Part of the challenge, especially for those who qualified as teachers quite a few years back, is the sense of being a student all over again. It is incredible how often people who have done this kind of professional learning discover a new found sympathy for their students. Assignment deadlines and receiving feedback on written work become nerve-wracking experiences once more. That is another reason these programmes can be so rewarding; you are left in no doubt whatsoever that you are a learner, and old habits die hard, a revelation we've both had during a late night essay crisis, usually a few hours after we've told our students that the secret to success is to plan ahead and get lots of sleep.

One of the key decisions to get right is the focus of any research or project that you do. There will be some degree of choice involved in each of these courses, whether they are taught, modular, or research-based. Getting the choice of focus right is essential as you don't want to end up being demotivated by working on something you aren't truly passionate about. That may well be the best way to start thinking about this; what, if anything, would you really like to spend time on to enhance your expertise in?

Once you've got the qualification, there is also the question of what you're going to do with it. Does it have practical application? It may not be the content *per se*, but the skills you gain such as academic writing and research methodology. How will the qualification enhance your practice and make you better at what you do? If you are considering going down this route, read on. The following case studies shed some light on what each qualification involves and should help you to decide the best pathway for yourself.

NATIONAL PROFESSIONAL QUALIFICATIONS (NPQS)

The NPQ framework had, at the time of writing, recently undergone a restructuring, and NPQs are now offered for senior leaders (NPQSL), headship (NPQH) and executive leadership (NPQEL). The framework also has three qualifications that provide an alternative pathway to hierarchical leadership roles. These cover Leading Behaviour and Culture, Leading Teacher Development, and Leading Teaching. This is a very welcome development and recognises that senior leadership isn't the only game in town. It is fair to say that the previous iteration of NPQs had their share of critics. A common refrain was that they focused on 'hoop-jumping' and concentrated on approaches to leadership. The new framework makes a distinction between domain-specific knowledge, and the practicalities of applying that knowledge in practice.

Another significant change has been the impact of the Apprenticeship Levy, which has injected a significant funding stream into professional learning for leaders. NPQs are a good example, and this funding is well worth considering when looking at how much a particular qualification will cost you.

NPQs and leadership learning

To get a clearer picture of the new framework, we spoke to former Deputy Headteacher Kathryn Morgan (@KathrynMorgan_2), who is now the Head of Leadership Content at the Teacher Development Trust (TDT).

The new framework looks like quite a departure from the previous NPQs. What do you think the main differences are?

In the last ten years, we've made huge strides with teacher-led research and evidence-informed practice relating to the classroom. We are making a concerted effort to engage with evidence and research to help us make more informed decisions about how students learn, curriculum and assessment, and professional development. Broadly speaking, we have more confidence in where to 'place our bets'. However, the same can't necessarily be said for school leadership.

Historically, national school leadership development has been heavily influenced by generic knowledge and skills taken from the world of business with a focus more upon the how to lead and, perhaps, less upon the what to lead in terms of domain specific knowledge. For example, when I did my NPQML in 2012, I learnt a lot about generic leadership theory, styles and concepts but very little about the core knowledge that would help me to lead across the range of domains that underpinned the work I was doing as a middle leader. This was also true of the NPQSL and NPQH which I went on to facilitate in other leadership roles that I've had.

Therefore, the brand-new suite of NPQ frameworks have been designed to intentionally refocus our attention on the domain-specific knowledge school leaders need to be confident and successful in their role, making more informed decisions relating to the common and persistent challenges they face. By adopting a similar format to the Early Career Framework (ECF), the NPQ frameworks will provide much needed clarity on the fundamental things school leaders need to be able to know and need to be able to do, which will better support them to develop their leadership expertise.

Another significant change is the inclusion of the specialist suite of NPQs, which replaces the traditional middle leadership qualification (NPQML) and provides a deep and purposeful exploration of a specific school leadership domain, building expertise in a targeted area and improving school capacity. The specialist areas are in: Leading Teaching (NPQLT); Leading Teacher Development (NPQLTD); and Leading Behaviour and Culture (NPQLBC).

If these changes aren't enough, another important aspect to the reformed NPQ suite to note is the changes to assessment. It would be fair to say that with the old assessment model it was difficult to see the purpose or value in what we were being asked to do. To mitigate against this in the new suite, participants will complete an open-book assessment requiring a structured 1500-word response to a real multi-resource scenario or case-study. This will provide participants with the opportunity to apply the core knowledge from the programme to an unknown scenario, demonstrating breadth of understanding, the thought-process for their decision-making and the scope for adaptive expertise.

Who do you think would be interested in this new suite of professional qualifications?

The specialist qualifications (NPQLT, NPQLTD, NPQLBC) are ideal for those who want to develop expertise in one of the core areas, rather than having to engage with school leadership knowledge more broadly. For example, being a pastoral leader requires different knowledge from someone responsible for teacher development. By providing the opportunity for specialist expertise to be valued and developed in this way, classroom teachers will hopefully feel there are more options to grow their practice closer to the classroom rather than having to choose leadership roles out of the classroom as the only option for career progression.

The NPQLT is ideal for anyone whose work is focused on supporting effective teaching across the school. This might include phase leaders, key stage leaders, heads of department (or similar titles) and they might be considered to be part of the middle leadership team.

The NPQLTD is ideal for anyone whose work is focused on supporting initial teacher training, early career teachers as well as the wider development of all colleagues across the school. Many of those leading teacher development who will take this qualification might be considered to be part of the middle leadership team and they might indirectly manage a team of mentors or coaches.

The NPQLBC is ideal for anyone whose work is focused on ensuring good behaviour and a culture of high expectations and learning are maintained across the school. Many of those leading teacher development who will take this qualification might be considered to be part of the middle leadership team and they may indirectly manage a team of class teachers or form tutors.

In addition to the three specialist qualifications, there are the three leadership qualifications that were common in the previous NPQ suite. The NPQSL would be most suitable for anyone who contributes to all aspects of the school through the leadership team in addition to having a core area of responsibility. Their role might primarily be an operational one although they will also be involved in some strategy. The NPQH is most suitable for those who have responsibility for the whole school and is primarily a strategic and operational one. The Executive Leadership qualification is for anyone with responsibility across a group of schools and is overwhelmingly strategic.

Why might someone opt for an NPQ over another form of advanced professional learning, such as a master's degree?

The NPQs will support leaders to better mitigate against the complexity of schools and leading teachers, students and their wider community. A master's would be a helpful next step on from the NPQs and further develop critical analysis, working with people from different disciplines and cultures, time management and working independently. In addition to this, a master's provides the opportunity to engage with theory and concepts which are no longer drawn upon in the new suite of NPQs.

What benefit do you think they bring in terms of career progression?

Historically, once teachers have established themselves in the classroom, the only viable option for career progression has involved them taking on more responsibility for a subject area or whole department, often resulting in them moving further away from the classroom. To mitigate against this and enable more teachers to deepen their classroom practice in tandem with developing their school leadership expertise, the specialist qualifications will allow middle leaders and senior teachers the opportunity to develop further specialist expertise without stepping away from the classroom.

The three leadership qualifications (NPQSL, NPQH, and NPQEL) will better equip school leaders to solve the common and persistent challenges that are inherent to complex environments such as schools. By providing participants with a codified body of knowledge, underpinned by a rigorous evidence base, school leaders will be better informed when it comes to the decision-making process and dealing with the challenges they face. Rather than seeing the NPQs as a means of accelerating promotion opportunities, the new suite is designed to add breadth and depth to participants' domain-specific knowledge so that they feel more confident and capable of doing the complex role of school leadership.

What advice would you give to anyone considering taking an NPQ?

Take time to really think about the aspects of your practice that most interest you and, without sounding twee, bring you joy. If you are someone who really enjoys engaging with research and is driven by better understanding where to place our best bets in the classroom then consider the NPQLT. If you are driven by understanding how we can better maximise the impact of professional development so that it leads to sustainable improvements in practice and student outcomes, then consider the NPQLTD. If you are interested in how to create the styles of classroom cultures and school environments where students and teachers thrive then consider the NPQLBC.

If it is less of a specialist area that you are interested in and you would like to focus on deeply learning the domain-specific knowledge that will better help you to solve the common and persistent challenges that are prevalent in school then consider one of the three leadership qualifications. The key thing here is that there are now far more options, with career progression feeling less like climbing a ladder and more like on-going, interconnected, professional growth.

CASE STUDY: NPQ EXPERIENCE

John McCance has been coaching, teaching and leading in primary schools since 2010. Before this, he worked with children and young people, in various roles and settings, in his native Scotland and the USA. You can connect with him on Twitter via @AlbaMcCance

You've done a lot of work on NPQs, which ones have you done, and over what timescale?

From 2016 to 2017, I completed my NPQML with UCL (London) and Infinite Learning (Dubai). I have just submitted my NPQH documentation with the same providers. I started my NPQH in 2019, but it took me longer than most to complete it due to Covid hitting and having a baby son. I am awaiting the results of my NPQH. I have mentored a colleague through their NPQSL as well.

What do you think the main benefit has been?

I gained a lot from the in-person sessions in Dubai. I met a range of other teachers and leaders from various countries, curricula and age ranges. The facilitators were all fantastic as well. There were acting headteachers, principals and academics.

How hard has it been to manage the day job, family life and your professional qualifications?

The beauty of NPQs is that they are vocational and tie closely to your day job for the central part. With NPQMLs and SLs, they directly link to something that is a developmental need of your school. Hopefully, it is something you already lead on or can easily lead on as part of your current role (or additional responsibilities) in addition there were three assessed tasks too.

What career benefit do you think they bring?

It helps you develop as a person leading a project in a school. There are no hiding places when you lead, get mentored and submit evidence of meeting certain competencies. It shows that you are resilient and can see something substantial through.

What advice would you give to anyone considering taking an NPQ?

Look at where you want to go in your professional life. Some people like to complete a Master's first (if they have not already done so), and others like to go down the NPQ route due to the vocational nature. The new syllabus and specialisms at the NPQML level sound interesting and great practice.

1. *Plan your time (work backwards in timescales and keeps notes).*
2. *Follow the evidence (to choose a project task, analyse and measure change).*
3. *Network with experts in the field you are working on and beyond.*

Thank you to Kathryn and John for sharing their insight and experiences.

MASTER'S DEGREES (MA)

These need little introduction in terms of what they are, and are perhaps the most common form of advanced professional learning. The key question is whether you want to tackle a taught programme, or a primarily research-led one? The former is typically more popular but has the potential disadvantage of needing to attend university seminars at a specific time. That may mean a request for the dreaded lesson cover, and we all know how popular that will make you. You are therefore well advised to check with your line manager to see if they will support you in this respect; the last thing you need is more stress as you go about the Master's, and friction with work commitments will do just that.

The other consideration is the timeframe. There are different options here, but most courses seem to involve part-time study over two years. Some stretch to three years, and modular approaches can offer a longer time frame for completion (the longest we found in researching this was an incredible 96 months). The alternative to part-time study is to go full-time for one year, though not all courses offer that. It is a huge commitment and might require a sabbatical (if such a thing is offered by your school), career break, or part-time teaching.

How much will it set you back financially? There is a pretty wide range. At the most affordable end of the market, the University of Glasgow offers a Master's in Educational Leadership for £2,889 full-time, and has an impressive range of funding opportunities which are all easily accessible on the webpage. If you're on a budget but don't live near Glasgow, then the University of Buckingham has an online Master's programme that costs £3,150 (plus a £275 registration fee). A mid-range option is the National College of Education which offers an 18-month research Master's at £5,995. Moving up a price bracket, the IoE courses at UCL cost £10,500, and at the top end Oxford University weighs in at £13,600. Note, these costs are all for UK students, for studying from autumn 2021; if you are international then prices are much higher.

Young teachers are often advised to invest in bricks and mortar, but should you put your hard-earned cash into a mortar board instead? What emerges from this is the importance of looking at entry requirements and sources of funding. You should definitely ask your school if they can help, as they may have a policy on this. Even if it is £100, it all counts when you're looking at these kinds of sums. At the risk of sounding mercenary, you should also consider whether this is money (and time) well invested. Will it lead to an enhanced salary later on, and end up paying for itself? Or will it lead to you being – as one of our colleagues once sardonically said – 'hideously overqualified and heavily in debt'? Some calculations are needed here, and not the sort that fit onto the back of an envelope.

CASE STUDY – MA IN EDUCATION WITH SARAH MENZIES

Sarah Menzies is a primary teacher in Scotland. Throughout her career she has gained experience teaching in the independent, state and special education sectors and has completed a Master's in Education.

Why did you choose to do a Master's in Education, and was it a taught course or by research?

While studying for my Postgraduate Diploma in Education, I was provided the opportunity to submit the main pieces of coursework for consideration at Master's level. As a lover of learning and self-progression, I decided to do so. Moving forwards, I continued with this path of study (distance learning) while teaching full time. Ultimately, I felt that completing my Master's in Education would provide me with a broader understanding of the education system, as well as set me apart from some other applicants when looking at career progression in the future.

The initial part of my course was taught face to face (while completing my PGDE) and latterly it was predominantly completed through action research and critical engagement with professional reading. While I was allocated a tutor to support me throughout (and with my dissertation this was an invaluable resource), the majority of the work was self-led.

What was the focus of your Master's?

My Master's degree was awarded in Education: Leading Learning and Teaching. The coursework included evaluating my own professional ethos, looking at pedagogical theories, innovation in the curriculum and the purpose of action research in education. Additionally, I was required to complete a module of research methods and ultimately engage in an empirical study for my dissertation. My dissertation focus was Mindfulness vs. Physical Activity: Developing Children's Resilience in Problem Solving. This was a small scale, mixed methods study that focused on a small group of students.

Did you receive any financial support for the fees?

I received a student loan during my PGDE year and during my probation year I completed a module that was discounted by University of Dundee as an incentive for completion. The last module and my dissertation were self-funded.

What were the main challenges you faced?

The biggest challenge for me was time management. While completing my Master's I was working full-time at a big, busy all-through school. As such, my holidays became a 'MEd protected zone'. I would spend full days in the university library, doing as much reading and research as possible as I knew my availability during the term was limited.

In what ways has it enhanced your skills as a teacher?

Alongside improved time management and an ability to prioritise tasks, I feel that I am now able to engage with documents, articles and policies in a more professionally critical way. More importantly, within the classroom I am less afraid to 'just have a go'. If we expect our students to develop resilience, give of their best and not be afraid of failure then we too need to model this. I have found my attitude towards perceived failure and mistakes has changed greatly, to the extent that my students now get excited at the prospect of using my giant 'Oops' rubber.

Has it helped you with your career progression?

As yet, I have not applied for a promoted post. However, I fully believe that my Master's has helped win me interviews for some incredible jobs that have allowed me to develop my experience. While it is certainly not the sole reason that I was offered these positions, it is likely that it helped me to 'get in the room'. Most interviewers with whom I have engaged have wanted to hear more about my project, which then opened the door to showcase professional commitment, an understanding of the education system, enthusiasm for a subject and critical reflection; all of which are essential skills in teaching.

What did you learn overall from the process?

Mainly, I learned that we are never the finished product. Even once I had completed and submitted my dissertation, I was considering how the project could have been improved and what I could do to enhance the results in the future. I think many teachers (my previous self included) view research as a scary enigma that we don't fully understand, or feel is not necessary unless we intend on writing a book or completing further education. When, in actual fact, we are all completing action research all the time: we have an idea, we action it, we reflect on how it is going, we amend it. This can be with something big like implementing a new literacy scheme or something small, such as switching to flexible seating. The worst thing we can do as educators is utter the phrase 'but that's how it's always been done'. This is the perspective my dissertation in particular has given me.

What advice would you give to anyone considering undertaking a Master's degree?

I would suggest to anyone that, if you are a keen lifelong learner wishing to enhance your pedagogy and professional understanding, this is an excellent way to do so. While it is not for the faint of heart, the rewards and feeling of accomplishment certainly outweigh the long hours in the library.

If you do decide to embark on this journey:

- *use your time wisely*
- *cite your sources as you go*
- *discuss the process along the way with your support system*
- *and (most importantly) make sure you have a never ending supply of highlighters and good coffee.*

I adore learning and am always looking for the next way to enhance my practice and add to my skill-set (even if this means giving up some of my very precious holidays). Undertaking a Master's in Education was a big consideration for me, as I was just beginning my career, but it was the best decision I could have made.

Thank you to Sarah Menzies for answering our questions about her MA experience.

PHD

This is the marathon, but is the only one where you get to add a title before your name, rather than just letters after it. That makes all the difference, right? Well, maybe. A PhD does open up career opportunities because the world of academia might beckon, and there are many teachers who have gone from schools into further education (FE). A PhD might lead to different pastures and academic clout, but will it make you professionally and financially better off? The answer is not clear cut, and if any of these qualifications are really about intrinsic motivation, it's this one. You're going to need buckets of the stuff.

It is of course a great intellectual challenge, and you are very much in control of what you research. The relationship with your supervisor is integral to success, and there is no doubt that this will open up a whole new world for you. It is probably reasonable to suggest that collaboration and dialogue between schools and universities still needs to improve, so doing a PhD will help break down those barriers for you. It is also a chance to specialise in a very well-defined area of education, and this confers a high level of expertise and authority that might be the career definition you want. If you have that one thing that you are truly passionate about, more so than anything else, the PhD might just be the best path for you.

The investment in time and money is substantial. If you are doing this part-time, then you are looking at (optimistically) six years. That means if you have a child who is starting secondary school when you start your PhD, you need to finish on time or run the risk of bumping into them on campus when you trudge in for your viva (a powerful incentive to meet deadlines, if ever there was one). Annual fees can weigh in at between £3,000 and £6,000 for full-time study, and half that for part-time. The Open University is nicely in between, at £4,500 a year (full-time), but if money is no object then a Cambridge education PhD costs £8,844 per annum. Multiply that by three and you've got your ball-park figures.

It is a long haul and the fees are high, so this is the biggest commitment of them all. Do you have the deep-seated intellectual curiosity needed to keep your motivation going for this length of time? Will it be worth it in terms of career progression? Most people who have gone down this route only really care about the first question, so it is interesting to think about what your reaction was to being asked them both. It might be an indication of whether or not this is for you.

To find out more, we spoke to Dr Maria O'Neill, Deputy Head of Wellbeing at St Christopher's School in Hampstead, and author of the excellent book *Proactive Pastoral Care*. She spent five years doing her PhD, and her motivation for sticking at it for that long clearly came from a combination of the intellectual challenge and professional skill set she acquired.

Maria explains, 'I love studying, I am a forever student. I also feel that I need to have a deeper understanding of the topics which turn into buzz concepts in education. I prefer making my own decisions based on the knowledge I acquire and my practice.' Interestingly she didn't approach her school for financial support as she didn't want to feel that she owed them any kind of debt, so had to finance her studies to the tune of £2,400 a year. It wasn't easy to keep on track, between her pastoral workload and her home and family life, so she took what she calls a 'temporary withdrawal'. The main benefit of doing the PhD was that 'It enhanced my critical thinking and reflective skills. I believe that reflection and critical thinking are essential skills for teachers. I don't think that my aim was to learn from the process, I am already quite self-aware. I thoroughly enjoyed it, and it enhanced my knowledge of my topic of interest which is wellbeing.' So overall it is something that Maria recommends, though she does add, sagely, that you really shouldn't attempt to write a book and complete a PhD thesis at the same time. Thanks to Maria for sharing her experience.

MBA

You might be surprised that we've included an MBA, because most people think that it's for executives in the business world. It is, but then there are educational variants because – wait for it – being an executive head is increasingly commonplace. In fact, senior leadership in schools is becoming more complex (see Chapter 9 and the discussion on New Public Management as to why). In fact, in the US, High School Principals are classified by the Bureau of Labour Statistics (BLS) as being managers rather than education professionals. Above principal level is superintendent, a position that involves line managing all the schools in a given district. With the development of executive headship in the UK, and the rise of Multi-Academy Trusts (MATs) it seems there is another tier of leadership that will only grow in size and influence. So it is logical to assume that the number of MBA programmes will increase in line with growing demand from education leaders.

MBAs of the strictly business variety are usually very expensive, so by comparison the MBAs that are tailored for education are, at UK universities, much more cost effective. For example, UCL's Global MBA weighs in at £42,500, but their Education Leadership (International) MBA is £9,500; a full £1,000 less than their education Master's degree costs. Anglia Ruskin's MBA is a mere £50 more, and Liverpool Hope's education MBA is £9,400, but drops to £7,600 if you've completed the NPQEL.

The National College comes in at a much higher £25,000 but some of the fees can be offset by accessing the Apprenticeship Levy. When you consider what CEOs of Multi Academy Trusts earn, this is starting to look like the smartest investment of all the advanced qualifications. Any idea what the top salary was for a Trust CEO in 2021? The prize goes to the Harris Federation's boss, who takes home a cool £455,000, earning almost three times as much as the Prime Minister. In fact, there are 98 CEOs of trusts who earn more than the PM does.

What distinguishes the MBA is that it has a more operational focus than other qualifications, and is really about system level leadership. It is for those who are more interested in how to run complex organisations at a high level, as opposed to dealing with the technical aspects of curriculum design or assessment, for example.

MBA CASE STUDY WITH ANNE WATSON

Anne Watson is a Deputy Head and languages teacher at Robert Gordon's College in Aberdeen, and has the (dubious) privilege of working with Robin. She worked for fifteen years in manufacturing industries before coming into education, and has completed both an MBA and headship qualifications (Into Headship, at Aberdeen University). She is therefore very well placed to compare the two levels of study.

You worked in industry before coming into teaching, so what benefits does that bring?

The development of general skills which have been critical in quickly getting to grips with teaching: presentation skills, communication skills, organisation and planning, managing customer (parent) relationships, general admin and minute taking, people management, direct reports and managing through others; the business I joined from university gave formal training in all of these areas which was directly transferable to teaching.

You also get an understanding of the broader picture. In industry I was moved into different roles in different parts of the business over a short space of time to enable me to gain an understanding of how the organisation functioned as a whole and as a result an understanding of the impact of any decision on different parts of the organisation.

Finally, an experience of working with and developing strong relationships with a broad range of people in different roles and from different backgrounds, and of the value everyone brings. I found it less hierarchical than education.

What were the main things you learned from doing an MBA?

The theory behind the experiences I had gained day to day and the opportunity to apply these different theories on a practical basis over a long period. I did the MBA over four years through distance learning and had three jobs within the organisation in different areas during that time, which allowed me to view different practical situations within the context of the theory I was learning. I gained enhanced organisation skills through fitting in study on a regular basis over a long period of time.

I also acquired an appreciation of new areas which I wasn't exposed to in detail through my job, such as finance and accounting, HR, project planning, and strategic planning. This gave me a very rounded understanding of business but also enough detail to use these skills and the knowledge as I progressed into management roles. Areas such as strategic planning also helped me to look more broadly, consider all options and think longer term when putting proposals together or problem solving.

You've also done headship qualifications, so what overlap is there between the two qualifications?

There was some overlap in terms of functions through the work set by Education Scotland but the Into Headship work was at a much higher level but it didn't give the detail of understanding I had from my MBA. I felt that between the MBA and the education-specific experience I have from my current role I had covered most areas prior to doing the course.

The university modules had quite a lot of crossover in terms of strategic planning approaches although it was good to update and to think about these in an educational context. I found the learning and teaching elements useful but mainly gained from seeing other perspectives. This was particularly true of policy areas which feature less in my day to day work than in local authority schools and I found it really interesting and helpful to understand more of how policy is applied on a day to day basis.

MBAs are becoming more popular in education now, especially for executive headship. Would you recommend doing one?

I would recommend an MBA over the Into Headship programme. I think the learning is deeper and broader and a longer course provides more opportunity for useful practical application of your learning. The MBA also covers areas which may not have been experienced in roles prior to headship, depending on the school context and deputy remits. I found the project element of Into Headship too short to achieve any significant change; while this was impacted by lockdown, I'm not sure it would have been significantly different under normal circumstances.

How hard is it to balance work and university level study, and how did you manage it?

Although my family circumstances were different for each course, I took the same approach of working continually and gradually through the course and planning study over the whole year, setting interim deadlines to break things down into manageable chunks. When I did the Guidance and Pastoral Care course, my daughter was young and it only worked by having set times each week to study and by setting myself weekly deadlines. I applied the same approach to Into Headship and used holidays to complete bigger pieces of work for submission. I think it's important to commit fully, recognise the amount of time needed from the outset and that weekends and holidays are critical to get through everything. I think it's also important to have people you can chat to; I didn't have colleagues doing any of these courses at the same time as me but did discuss with family and friends, line managers and mentors. I think it is inevitable that you will tire of the course at some point and it's important to have support to get you through those times!

What advice would you give to anyone taking on either an MBA or Into Headship now?

- *Be very organised with a weekly plan which you put together for the year.*
- *Don't wait to be told what to do; order texts early and read as much as you can as early as possible.*
- *Ask if you are unsure – especially if the course is online or if something is unclear – don't leave any queries as the time passes very quickly and this may cause you a problem.*
- *Try to build in other activities and socialising alongside work and study so that you keep a balance.*

- *Be focused during your study time so that it doesn't encroach into the time you have for family and other commitments.*
- *Work at the time you are most effective; for me this was predominantly early mornings at weekends rather than late at night.*

Thank you to Anne for sharing her unique insight and experiences.

This gives you an interesting menu to choose from if you do want to invest in substantial professional learning. As we explore in later chapters, the difficulty with recruitment to senior leadership posts is showing not just that you are capable of doing the job, but are more capable than all the other candidates in what will likely be a crowded field. Which route is best for you, and whether it will ultimately be worth it, are things that need to be assessed in many ways and from both personal and professional perspectives. No one can give you an absolute guarantee, but the simple advice is just to ask those who have already done it. As we will keep saying, without apology for repeating ourselves, do your research. This book has done a bit of it for you already, so just keep going.

CHALLENGE QUESTIONS

- Would an advanced professional qualification be something that you would enjoy enough to see it through to the end?

- Do you have the time, and the financial resources, to undertake advanced professional qualifications?

- What would your motivation be for doing such a qualification?

- What would be the benefit, based on what you want your career path to be?

- What changes might take place in your life in the full timeframe of the qualification? (Remember what happened to the best laid plans o' mice an' men ...)

QR CODES FOR FURTHER READING AND INFORMATION

 **Teacher
Development
Trust (TDT)**
https://tdtrust.org/

 **National
Professional Qualifications
(NPQs) reforms**
https://www.gov.uk/government/
publications/national-professional-
qualifications-npqs-reforms/national-
professional-qualifications-npqs-reforms

CHAPTER 6

PROFESSIONAL LEARNING COMMUNITIES AND NETWORKS

Purpose of this chapter: To promote a wide range of professional learning networks (PLNs) and professional learning communities (PLCs) with a focus on both support and representation in education.

The term professional learning network (PLN) has various meanings but ultimately it is about creating a support network to learn from and collaborate with in a professional capacity, and tends to refer to connections online. A professional learning community (PLC) is very similar although it can have a more specific focus – specialised communities within the education community – and tend to meet more in person, if possible. Those are our own definitions, but the terms are so widely used that there are various interpretations of both PLN and PLC.

PLN co-ordinators Chris Brown and Cindy Poortman write:

For us, the term Professional Learning Networks (PLNs) represents any group who engages in collaborative learning with others outside of their everyday community of practice; with the ultimate aim of improving outcomes for children.

We agree this is an excellent definition. They also add:

Networks of educators, (from different schools) such as teacher design teams, research learning networks, data teams and lesson study teams appear to provide such promising forms of teacher development. What's more, as well as teachers and school leaders, policymakers and researchers may also be involved as facilitators and/or participants, enabling all parties to benefit from a wide pool of knowledge and expertise.

This emphasises the inclusive and diverse nature of PLNs.

The *Glossary of Education Reform* describes PLCs thusly:

A professional learning community, or PLC, is a group of educators that meets regularly, shares expertise, and works collaboratively to improve teaching skills and the academic performance of students. The term is also applied to schools or teaching faculties that use small-group collaboration as a form of professional development. Shirley Hord, an expert on school leadership, came up with perhaps the most efficient description of the strategy: 'The three words explain the concept: Professionals coming together in a group – a community – to learn.

There are different types of PLNs and PLCs in education and while we can't write about them all we have tried to shine a spotlight on examples that will be relevant and interesting, as well signposting readers to where they can find more information. There are some PLNs and PLCs that are free, for example an online forum or community, whereas others cost a membership fee that can be paid for by individuals or a school budget. We explore free, low cost and more expensive options.

Teaching in the classroom as the only adult in the room or being based in an office in a school can at times be lonely. There are many benefits to having a PLN (discussed in more detail below), and a question Robin frequently asks candidates at interview is:

Can you tell me about your professional learning network(s) and connections and how they have enhanced your professional learning?

Can you answer this question? In an interview it can be great if a candidate is able to discuss various PLNs and explain how a PLN has supported their ongoing development and professional learning.

BENEFITS OF PLNS AND PLCS

The main benefits include having connections with people who are knowledgeable, experienced, and from whom we can continue to learn. A PLN or PLC is another example of a low cost and high impact method of professional development (as discussed in Chapter 3).

We are an example of a professional collaboration that has developed from a PLN, as well as building a strong personal friendship. We connected on Twitter and realised we had a lot in common from our history backgrounds, experience teaching in the UAE and our shared interest in evidence-informed practice. We later met in a pub in Glasgow, alongside some other mutual friends and connections who are also teachers and continued to stay in touch. We are both very grateful for Twitter which has connected us not just to each other, but to many others around the world. Some we have met in person, and others we only know online, which is something we are sure many other Twitter users can relate to.

Another very significant benefit of a PLN is having access to people who can offer advice, guidance and support when needed. There are various challenges within our profession and we all need support at some point, which might involve helping us manage workloads, deal with work related stress or work through personal issues that are having a negative impact on our day to day teaching and leadership.

Connections outside of our school walls are important for numerous reasons. It can be useful to have someone in your PLN that is experienced and trustworthy if there is a sensitive question or situation you would rather talk about with someone outside of the school environment, such as clashing with a line manager and how to deal with this. Even if the main motivating factor for finding, joining and connecting with a PLN is for support, we think it is worth it. It is an investment in well-being and that investment is priceless. Good mental and physical health are vital to being a good teacher and leader and are at the heart of the teaching life.

Finding a PLN online is very easy, but how you do this depends on who and what specifically you wish to connect with. If you simply want to connect with other teachers and leaders outside of your school environment, then sign up to Twitter and/or LinkedIn. Connect and follow with other educators and there is a PLN at your fingertips that you can curate. You decide who to connect with and follow, and this selection could be niche or broad. Elizabeth Peterson has rightly pointed out that, 'Social media has hit education by storm and many teachers are embracing it as a professional tool'[30] and developing a PLN is one aspect of this.

Our colleagues can inspire us but those we don't work with often have ideas, resources, suggestions and more that are worth tapping into. We can and should

---

30. Peterson, E. (2010) PLCs and PLNs – Go Us! *The Inspired Classroom.*
https://theinspiredclassroom.com/2010/05/plcs-and-plns-go-us/

contribute to a PLN – both give and take – as there is often a relevant audience with whom to share blogs, resources, ideas and created content. As well as seeking support we can also support those that need it whether that be teachers early in their career, those new to a specific role or colleagues who simply require any help we can offer. It's important everyone feels valued within a PLN so members can confidently share reflections, ideas and insight. Critique and feedback should be welcomed but it should always be – as Ron Berger advocates – kind, specific and helpful.

PLNs and PLCs can promote and support inclusivity. On Twitter you can find @ LGBTed which is an account that aims to empower LGBT+ educators to be visible and authentic in schools for the benefit of LGBT+ young people. The LGBTed team have published a book, *Big Gay Adventures in Education: Supporting LGBT+ Visibility and Inclusion in Schools*, edited by Daniel Tomlinson-Gray, which has an excellent range of contributors. The LGBTed website https://www.lgbted.uk/ is, at time of writing, under construction but once launched will aim to further support educators and help schools learn more about LGBT+ inclusion.

In 2021, Kate was diagnosed with hearing loss and now wears a hearing aid in her left ear. This has been a difficult adjustment in many ways, but Kate decided to be open about this on social media, sharing her experiences with hearing impairment. This has led to others connecting with Kate to share similar experiences and offer support. There are a range of networks available that can support with mental and physical disabilities and difficulties.

BESPOKE PLCS

Are there PLCs within your school community? Examples can include working parties with a particular focus, or a professional learning book club as discussed in Chapter 3. People with shared interests often find each other within a school environment and organically form a PLC without initially realising or planning to do so. Below are examples of bespoke PLCs that each have their own focus and aims.

WOMENED

Teaching is a female dominated profession yet the data and statistics from England highlight the lack of female leaders in education. WomenEd continue to raise awareness of this, sharing that in 2015 although 62% of teachers in secondary schools were women, they accounted for only 36% of secondary headteachers.[31] They also shared that only 7% of women in education will attempt to negotiate their salary offer, compared to 57% of their male counterparts. Another alarming statistic revealed that one in four teachers who quit the classroom in recent years were women aged 30-39.[32] More recently a list of the twenty highest paid Academy leaders was published, with only one woman on it, again illustrating the need to support and encourage more female leaders in education.[33]

WomenEd also aim to support female educators with other issues they may experience in the workplace, such as discrimination, harassment, maternity related issues and fleible working hours. Their website explains:

WomenEd is a global grassroots movement that connects aspiring and existing women leaders in education and gives women leaders a voice in education. Even though women dominate the workforce across all sectors of education, there are still gender and racial inequalities in terms of the numbers of women in senior leadership, the large gender pay gap and the number of women who want to stay in education yet whose requests for flexible working are not met. Our mission is for more women in education to have the choice to progress on their leadership journey. To achieve this, WomenEd works to remove systemic and organisational barriers to such progress and to empower and enable women to achieve their next leadership step, if they choose to progress in leadership roles. Any income received by WomenEd, including royalties from our books, is used solely to run this website and other communication channels. No individuals or organisations directly profit from WomenEd.[34]

So, how can you get involved with the WomenEd movement and community? WomenEd are very active across different social media platforms, @WomenEd is the main Twitter account although there are many other WomenEd accounts for different regions in the UK and globally. There are two main hashtags used when sharing posts or searching for content: #WomenEd and #10percentbraver. The Twitter page also includes the handles of leaders within the community who you can connect with and follow.

31. Future Leaders Trust (2015) *1700 Female headteachers 'missing' from England's schools.* https://s3.eu-west-2.amazonaws.com/ambition-institute/documents/1700_FEMALE_HEADS_MISSING_FROM_ENGLISH_SCHOOLS.pdf

32. Porritt, V. and Featherstone, K. (Eds) (2019) *10% Braver.* London: Sage.

33. Antiacademies.org (2021) *The highest paid academy bosses.* https://antiacademies.org.uk/2021/08/the-highest-paid-academy-bosses/

34. WomenEd (ND) About us homepage. https://womened.org/about-us

There is an official Facebook page https://www.facebook.com/womened where people can 'like' and sign up to the page to stay connected and informed, and the hashtag #WomenEd is regularly used on Instagram. #WomenEd Being 10%braver is the name of their YouTube channel where you can subscribe and view a wide range of presentations and online events hosted by the WomenEd community.

WomenEd have created and developed their own website: https://womened.org/ with more information. There is a specific section to find out about WomenEd events taking place (in person and online) and you can also search for these on Eventbrite. To stay up to date with their published blog posts there is an option to subscribe to their mailing list. Regular posts cover a wide range of important issues and topics, written by a diverse range of contributors and authors. The website also contains information about regional WomenEd networks as well as content about their campaigns and the resources they offer. It really is worth taking some time to explore this website and learn more.

WomenEd have also published two books thus far. The first is *10% Braver: Inspiring Women to Lead Education* (2019) and the second is *Being 10% Braver* (2021). Both were edited by Vivienne Porritt and Keziah Featherstone, Global Strategic Leaders at WomenEd. If you wish to contact the team directly you can do so by emailing womenedleaders@gmail.com

THE BAMEED NETWORK

The acronym BAME refers to Black, Asian and Minority Ethnic. The BAMEed Network is a movement initiated in response to the continual call for intersectionality and diversity in the education sector. They aim to connect, enable and showcase the talent of diverse educators so they may inspire future generations and open up possibilities within education careers. We asked co-founder, senior leader and teacher Amjad Ali to answer our questions about this network for educators.

What is The BAMEed Network and how did it begin?

BAMEed is a grassroots charity run by educators that seeks to make the education sector more representative of society. It began over four years ago with a desire to have more representation in leadership but has since grown into leading education through ethnic diversity recognition. The BAMEed Network has regional hubs all across the United Kingdom and has engaged in both virtual and face to face events, with hundreds of people attending and learning from across the education sector and a variety of individuals.

Why is it important for teachers and school leaders to be aware of BAMEed?

To educate you have to consider who you are educating. To change you have to join with those in practice who can share their journey; understanding and connecting. It is vital for all educators to know about anti-racism practices along with being confident in addressing diversity, equality and inclusion (DEI) issues in their classrooms. By joining in with The BAMEed Network educators are able to benefit from the vast amount of resources we have signposted on our website along with being able to access a qualified mentor to support with career progression.

What is the benefit of being involved with your community and how can it help teachers with professional learning?

Teachers are likely to avoid creating an inclusive environment through simply not knowing where to start. So it is vital for all to not just be diverse in name, but through their actions and by being a member of this network and through engaging with this professional development of social understanding and DEI, it will help broaden our minds and our students' outcomes. Every journey like this is better with a community to learn, support and connect yourself with.

Thank you to Amjad Ali (@TeachLeadAAli) for answering our questions. You can find out more about BAMEed by following @BAMEedNetwork or visiting the website https://www.bameednetwork.com/

SUBJECT ASSOCIATIONS

The main purpose and benefit of subject associations is that they offer specific resources, training and support for subject specialists. Generic pedagogy, assessment, curriculum and leadership professional development can all be beneficial, but depth of subject knowledge and understanding is an essential component of teaching and learning. Associations can support teachers and leaders to stay up to date with the latest news ranging from published reports to exam guidance (they are often independent from the government). A subject association aims to create a community where all members are bonded by their passion for the subject they teach and are keen to learn more and share this passion with others, either in person or online.

A Model for Great Teaching is an evidence review published by Evidence Based Education in partnership with Cambridge Assessment and the toolkit has four key recommendations for teachers:

1. Understanding the content.
2. Creating a supportive environment.
3. Maximising opportunity to learn.
4. Activating hard thinking.

The first point links well to subject specialist professional learning. The report states that as teachers you should have a 'deep and fluent knowledge and flexible understanding of the content you are teaching' adding the importance of the curriculum being taught, assessment, activities and content. Subject associations can assist with these elements. You can read the full evidence review at: https://www.greatteaching.com/

There is usually a fee to be paid for subject associations, including individual or group membership, which vary in terms of cost and packages. Heads of Departments really should join relevant subject associations so they can share useful content with their team as well as leading by example and engaging with subject-specific professional learning. Subscriptions often include access to online materials, regular publications, events and webinars, courses, conferences and teaching resources. We both agree that joining a subject association is a good investment offering bespoke professional learning opportunities and materials. However, it can be easy to pay the subscription and then struggle to stay informed with the latest offerings. Our advice would be to regularly check what new content is on offer and accessible, and take full advantage of all you can. Subject associations usually share primary teaching materials too, but of course the challenge at primary level is teaching a wide range of subjects. We advise subject leads at primary level to sign up to the relevant subject associations to help them in their role leading and supporting colleagues.

To find out more about subject associations we recommend visiting The Council for Subject Associations (CfSA) directory online: https://www.subjectassociations.org.uk/our-members/

REGIONAL NETWORKS

This is once again difficult to write as there are lots of differences among the regions, from localities, cities and counties in the UK and beyond. There can be local grassroots events taking place as well as more formal networks within the regional community. An example of regional support across Wales is that of the regional school improvement services working alongside local education authorities. Within each of these regional services are networks that bring together teachers who teach the same phases, subjects or hold similar leadership positions.

GwE is the service provided for schools across North Wales and on their website they describe their vision and focus:

Our work is driven by genuine ambition to see that schools and organisations we work with achieve their aspirations and to see all learners succeed. Proudly Welsh and internationally informed, we will support our schools to become successful and confident learning organisations. We will collaborate to provide learners with the climate and education they deserve so that they become capable and resilient individuals to realise their full potential.

Schools across Wales should take advantage of the school improvement services provided and teachers can also find out more (see the QR codes at the end of this chapter).

It is worth asking colleagues or your line manager about regional networks and searching online for any local events and meetings to attend.

If teaching internationally then a PLN or PLC can be very helpful; both professionally and personally. People within a PLN or PLC in the same country can often give very useful advice based on their lived experiences as well as being able to answer specific questions and queries. It is worth connecting with as many teachers as possible before relocating. This can be done easily online; simply ask, send a tweet or share a post asking for connections in a specific country or region, and join online pages and forums (Facebook is great for this). There is more discussion about teaching internationally in Chapter 11 and you can visit our website www.theinternationalteachinglife.com to find out more.

CASE STUDY: EDUCATION ROUNDTABLES – AN EDUCATION NETWORK FOR SCHOOL LEADERS WITH BEN BROWN

Ben Brown is a former primary school teacher and Deputy Headteacher with 17 years of classroom experience. He left teaching following a stress-related breakdown to work in sales and marketing before setting up Education Roundtables.

Education Roundtables (EDRT) started as an idea in 2018. As a teaching deputy, I had struggled finding someone to talk with, to share some of the challenges that I was facing and to find solutions. I ended up regularly working 90-hour weeks, often reinventing the wheel, or doing lots of research and reading to get a better understanding of how I could achieve something, without always fully understanding it. Things caught up with me and I had a breakdown and ended up leaving teaching. What I had needed was a network, that wasn't within my local authority or cluster of schools, where I could ask questions and share challenges without being judged, and without having to deal with local politics.

Teachers are a judgy lot, as even a short amount of time on Twitter during the summer break quickly shows. What I realised was, that if this was true for me, then it was also true for headteachers. After all, they face even more intense scrutiny, and the buck stops with them. The aim of the idea was to create a network for individual headteachers to meet in a space where trust is a given. The 'Vegas' of education: what is said in EDRT stays in EDRT.

Professional growth and development thrive in high trust environments, which is why the basis of membership to the group must be an understanding that we trust each other. The Vegas comment may be a light-hearted phrase, but confidentially is something that everyone takes seriously. Without trust, many of the conversations that we have would not be as open and honest as they are. Without that underlying trust we can't help each other effectively and challenge each other with empathy and understanding where appropriate.

Physically getting heads together to talk is challenging. Time is precious and arranging a day when everyone can take time out of school to talk, is nigh on impossible and limited by geography. It is the main reason that schools have stayed in local authorities, cluster groups and geographical Multi-Academy Trusts for their conversations and training. I tried to introduce heads to the concept of Zoom in 2019, something I was very familiar with from my work in US sales. No one had heard of it. That soon changed when the pandemic hit.

The first Roundtables session was in March 2020, shortly before the first lockdown when schools were closed to everyone apart from the children of key workers and vulnerable children. The topic of conversation was 'How do we realistically support the most vulnerable if schools close?' Throughout the next five months primary heads from around the UK sat around the virtual table and talked. They supported each other, shared hopes and fears and found a way through the pandemic. We released summaries of the discussion, on topics ranging from supporting the vulnerable to remote learning and transition. The latter document was downloaded over 3000 times and distributed through other education communities too.

Thank you to Ben for sharing more about EDRT. You can follow Ben on Twitter @EdRoundtables and visit the website to learn more at https:// educationroundtables.co.uk/

ARE THERE ANY NEGATIVE ASPECTS OF PLNS AND PLCS?

While we are both advocates of promoting both PLNs and PLCs we do think it's important to discuss the potential pitfalls. No strategy or method of professional learning is perfect, but it is important to note that the points below are only potential issues:

- There can be PLNs/PLCs that can seem quite exclusive, lack inclusivity and make others feel alienated or left out because of cliques and close groups.
- Divisions exist, which is especially notable online with social media and Twitter as an example. This can lead to tension and arguments that go beyond debate.
- PLNs and PLCs might have high expectations and demands, for example expecting regular attendance at meetings and requiring commitment which could potentially add to workload.
- Lines can become blurred, again social media is an example of this, where teachers can be reading, discussing and tweeting about education late into the evenings and weekends. If this is what people wish to do, that is fine, we are not judgmental as we have done so, but social media can become consuming and even addictive.
- There could be financial implications (this is rare) but there are some PLCs that require payment for membership and subscriptions that schools would be unwilling to pay.
- It can be difficult to measure the impact of being part of a PLN or PLC. There can be barriers, for example a teacher might learn about a new innovative strategy via others in a PLN but is unable to trial or implement it in their classroom due to school policy. It is worth reflecting and evaluating if there is a significant and notably positive impact of being part of a PLN or PLC. That impact might be visible in your classroom or it could be the enjoyment of feeling part of a team and having a support network.

If there does not seem to be a PLN or PLC for something you are searching for then simply create your own! This can easily be done either within your school community, local area or online to gain a wider reach. Also, if you are part of a PLN or PLC which is not having a positive impact on your life then it is worth reflecting on that and considering how you invest your time in the future. Ultimately, we believe that any PLN or PLC has to enrich our lives professionally – and perhaps personally – in many positive ways.

CHALLENGE QUESTIONS

■ Do you have a PLN or PLC, and if so how do they support your professional development?

■ Are there PLNs/PLCs in your local area/region?

■ Have you considered setting up a PLN/PLC?

■ How can you support other PLNs/PLCs to promote and encourage representation in your school community?

■ Are you a member of a subject association(s) and if so, are you are aware of all they can offer? Do you take advantage of your subscription benefits?

QR CODES FOR FURTHER READING AND INFORMATION

WomenEd
https://womened.org

BameEd
https://www.bameednetwork.com

Education Roundtables
https://educationroundtables.co.uk

The Council for Subject Associations for Schools
https://www.subjectassociations.org.uk

Here are two simple questions to get the conversation started:

1. ...how long do you want to be a teacher?
2. What do you want to achieve in that time?

SECTION 2

CAREER PROGRESSION

This section of the book is about your career as a teacher. In this sense, *The Teaching Life* is about the period of time between your first and your last day as a teacher. This teaching life will have various twists and turns, and while this book is not explicitly about teacher wellbeing, we do think this is an area which can be improved significantly by taking control of career progression. Making the right decisions, at the right time, for the right reasons, will add up to a happier professional existence, which in turn makes for a happier personal existence.

Career planning is something that is usually discussed in the context of the next step you intend to take, and this very often revolves around moving school or taking on a leadership position. This is a very short-term approach, but thinking about career planning for the full duration of your time in teaching is talked about less often. That duration is one of the major challenges facing the overall education system.

In 2018, the Department for Education admitted that one third of newly qualified teachers in the UK leave the profession within the first five years. Highly effective professional development and support are critical to retaining good teachers, and you will notice that much of this section of the book has significant overlap and synthesis with the first. To borrow a phrase from President Harry Truman, professional learning and career progression are two halves of the same walnut.

Here are two simple questions to get the conversation started:

1. **For how long do you want to be a teacher?**
2. **What do you want to achieve in that time?**

How long you have left as a teacher depends on several variables, and only you can know what they are. Will you consider changing profession? Will you take a career break? Will you retire early? If these considerations aren't currently clear to you, it's worth thinking about them as you progress through the following chapters.

For those in their early twenties, there could be well over four decades in education, and an awful lot will happen in that time. For those who are in the final stretch, you may think there is less in this part of the book that's of interest to you, but a significant consideration is how to end your career well. What we all want, ideally, is the perfect dismount. The final day in your classroom, having packed up and left marking and emails behind forever, should be one in which you have no regrets and feel that you have never been more valued than at that point. Pulling this off isn't easy, so there will be plenty of discussion on how to finish on your own terms.

A significant preconception we wish to challenge is the idea that career planning is about promotion, when in fact it is about *progression*. Not everyone wants to be in a leadership position, or have additional responsibilities, but career progression is just as important to this group of teachers. Progression means you are evolving and developing so you can continue to be the best teacher you can be for your students. It means that you feel professionally fulfilled and valued. It means that you never stagnate, falling into the trap of 'going through the motions'. It means that you mature in your practice and continue to grow in your understanding of the craft of teaching.

There is no such thing as perfection in teaching. If you are constantly evolving and progressing as a teacher, you will find yourself getting even better, and probably realising the full complexity and subtlety of what you do. If that is the paramount driver of a teaching career, it is perhaps the most noble one of all. For those of you interested in promotion, we also recommend that you frame this in terms of progression. Not every 'promotion' is a forward step, and making sure you get the right role, in the right setting, is critical to your professional fulfillment. If promotion is thrust upon you by circumstance, and you are not truly ready for it, then it can lead to unhappiness and impact significantly on your sense of wellbeing. You have to make sure that you are taking on additional responsibility because you intrinsically want it, not because someone else wants you to.

Taking on an advanced post because other considerations come first is not the right way to go about it. There is a crucial distinction to be made here; taking on a leadership role because of career progression is inherently a good thing; doing it primarily for the status and salary that come with promotion is not, although these are important to many. The challenge question to ask yourself is this: Why do I want to go into leadership? Hopefully you will be able to articulate the answer to this clearly and rationally to yourself when you have finished reading this book.

A key message we develop is that you should be in control of your career, even if your career path plans and goals change along the way, so that you don't find yourself in a position where you are professionally unhappy. Sadly, this is easier said than done, and if it never happened there would be little point in writing this book. Any career planning has to dovetail with your personal life, and as we all know there can be difficult tensions at play here. Major life events, and the changing nature of life with family and friends, will have a significant impact on your career. Compromises will be made in both your professional and personal life, but if you are making decisions from a position of strength, you are likely to get what you want in both dimensions. Effective career planning, by thinking ahead and being clear about what you want to achieve, makes this much more likely to happen.

With this in mind, a (polite) recommendation is to have a notebook to hand as you read on. It's not to take down notes on what we write, but to collect your own thoughts and reflections, and where there is a gap in your thinking get some questions down. After all, this is not a manual, but a stimulus for your own decision-making. Reading back through your notes should be the most significant reading about education that you ever do. We aim to promote opportunities for self-reflection and enable you to offer support, guidance and advice to those around you with their career progression.

#THETEACHINGLIFE

CHAPTER 7

THE ART OF REFLECTIVE PRACTICE

Purpose of this chapter: To explore the methods and benefits of reflective practice to support professional learning, development and progression.

'The unexamined life is not worth living.' – Socrates

We have titled this chapter 'The art of reflective practice' because we believe it is more of an art form, rather than an exact science. This is despite the OECD stating in the Anticipation-Action-Reflection Cycle in its *Conceptual Learning Framework* that 'Reflection is a systematic, rigorous, disciplined way of thinking, with its roots in scientific inquiry.' As Jennifer Moon has pointed out, the bulk of the literature on reflection is conceptual rather than scientific in nature, and we should be very wary about trying to be too narrow in how we define and apply it. We believe it comes from having an open and critical mindset that develops with experience, that it has great value when done well, and that it is a difficult skill to master. In this regard, no one should presume that all teachers can do it well, or easily.

To be a 'reflective practitioner' is a commonly used phrase that is now a core expectation of all teachers and school leaders, and is a common theme throughout this book. The term needs some unpacking if we are to fully understand what it means, and what we're meant to do with it. When done well, reflective practice can be a powerful driver of teacher professionalism and career development. When done badly, it can entrench habits that inhibit personal development and student outcomes.

The Department of Education's 2016 *Standard for Teachers' Professional Development* states that:

> *In particular, the standard should be used to support regular reflection on*

existing practice and discussion between teachers, headteachers and leadership teams, and those providing and supporting professional development.[35]

Furthermore, teachers are to 'reflect systematically on the effectiveness of lessons and approaches to teaching.' This is very much a 'broad-brush' statement that presumes there is common agreement about what it means to 'reflect systematically' on anything, when in fact there is a lot of critical debate about what such processes involve.

In Scotland, the latest iteration of the *Standard for Full Registration*, published in 2021, sets this out more fully:[36]

3.3.2 Engage in reflective practice to develop and advance career-long professional learning and expertise	
Professional Actions	As a registered teacher to demonstrate your professional skills and abilities you are required to: • commit to lifelong learning, through an ongoing process of professional review and development that impacts on the learning of children and young people; • reflect and engage critically in self-evaluation using the relevant professional standard; • adopt an enquiring, reflective and critical approach to professional practice; • enhance learning and teaching by taking account of feedback from others including children and young people and actively engage in professional learning to support school improvement; • work collaboratively to contribute to the professional learning and development of colleagues, including student teachers; • maintain a reflective record of evidence of impact of professional learning on self, colleagues and learners; and • engage with the Professional Update process.

Here, reflection is paired with engagement; there is an exhortation to some form of action as a consequence of that reflection. In the third bullet-point, 'enquiring' and 'critical approach' stand on either side of reflection, like sentries making sure the prisoner can't escape into the ether. Reflection in and of itself is insufficient, and needs to be anchored in something more direct.

WHAT IS REFLECTIVE PRACTICE?

You will not be at all surprised to find that defining reflective practice is problematic and depends on which body of literature you look at. The four

35. Department for Education (2016) *Standard for teachers' professional development*. London: DfE. https://assets.publishing.service.gov.uk/government/uploads/system/uploads/attachment_data/file/537031/160712_-_PD_Expert_Group_Guidance.pdf

36. General Teaching Council for Scotland (2021) *The Standard for Full Registration*. Edinburgh: GTC Scotland. https://www.gtcs.org.uk/web/FILES/Professional-Standards/2021-Standard-for-Full-Registration.pdf

principal writers on reflection are John Dewey, Jurgen Habermas, Daniel Kolb and Donald Schönn, but none of their work was in any way empirical. The concept defies thorough research, because you can't really measure what 'reflection' is taking place in someone's mind, and how it influences their actions. A further problem is that the concept isn't really a recognised construct by psychologists, and writers who have explored it further have tended to narrow their definition in order to avoid the term seeming simply nebulous. That narrowing hasn't really been productive, because it usually means looking at reflection in a very specific context.

Jennifer Moon has looked for common denominators in the literature and has produced the closest thing to a catch-all definition:

Reflection seems to be a form of mental processing with a purpose and/or an anticipated outcome that is applied to relatively complicated or unstructured ideas for which there is not an obvious solution.[37]

Moon therefore feels it is 'a useful concept … [which] helps those in learning and professional situations to make sense of an area of human functioning.' If we agree with this, then it does have practical usage in education because we are all, on a daily basis, trying to make sense of what is happening around us. The academic literature does have some common threads about the nature of reflection, and it is interesting that it is consistently associated with the performance of a task; in this sense, it is not generic navel-gazing, but linked to something tangible.

As a thinking process, reflection is also assumed to be metacognitive, and is often linked to critical thinking. Dewey, who was the first to write about reflective practice back in the 1930s, argued that reflection occurs when a person experiences 'cognitive discomfort' because of a problem that needs to be solved. That might also help us to frame reflective practice in education, because there is an element of struggle in the thought process about something that is complex. It is not a quick look back at what we did, and a light-touch comment on that, but a more rigorous process of self-analysis. Another theme that emerges from the literature is that reflection happens when the subject matter is not straightforward, and the outcome is not clear.

---

37. Moon, J. (2000) *Reflection in Learning and Professional Development: Theory and Practice.* Abingdon: Routledge.

This leads to another area of controversy; when does reflection take place, and for how long? Kolb developed two themes; reflection-in-practice and reflection-on-practice. The former is something that happens in the moment, in the middle of a task and is part of the problem-solving process. The latter is something that takes place later. Kolb's experiential learning cycle (see diagram below) might provide a useful framework for many teachers, and appears attractive because it is self-sustaining. However, the length of time involved in the process varies, and the distinction between phases is fluid. This has implications for things like coaching and annual review processes, as discussed below. Moon makes an excellent point when she says that 'While no one can force another to reflect, it is possible to create conditions in which another is induced to reflect.' Creating those conditions should be a priority for school leaders.

Ultimately, the key determinant of the success of reflection depends on the depth of thought that goes into it, the level of self-criticality, and the tangible outcomes the process produces. That takes time, conscious cognitive effort, and the right conditions for inducing such thought.

The Experiential Learning Cycle

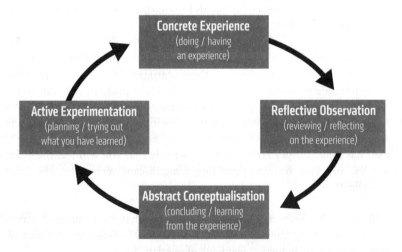

BEING A REFLECTIVE PRACTITIONER – FREQUENCY AND METHODS

One of the most practical and useful ways to reflect on your practice is to annually update your CV. This doesn't need to be preparation for an application, it's just for your own benefit. Doing this over the summer is helpful, because it allows you to look back on the past year and think about new experiences, skills and achievements you can be proud of. If you look at your CV and the only change you can make is the date, then you have to ask whether you have really progressed in the past year. There should always be something you can add or tweak, because no two school years are the same.

It might just be adding some new professional learning you've done, but even that is a valid form of reflection. After all, if your professional review process isn't all it's meant to be (see below) this might be your best chance to self-evaluate and set yourself some challenges for the coming year. It also has the added benefit of you being prepared in advance if a golden opportunity comes your way suddenly and unexpectedly, slap bang in the middle of the busiest week of the busiest term (as these things invariably have a habit of doing).

Professional support for career progression: mentoring, coaching and sponsoring

There are typically three distinct forms of support for progression, two of which are widely understood and practised, and the third less so. The most commonly known are mentoring and coaching, and the third is sponsoring. In reading this section, a critical consideration for you is whether you are in need of this kind of support, or whether you would like to become a provider of such support to your colleagues.

As mentioned previously, the duration of teaching careers is, on average, becoming much shorter which means there is a significant 'brain-drain' effect. One way to counter this is by having better levels of professional and pastoral support, and offering this support, and pathways to practising that support, should be part of a long-term strategy at national level to improve teacher retention and job satisfaction. Seen this way, becoming a mentor, coach or sponsor has a pleasing symbiotic effect: it's likely that you will feel the benefit personally, and you are also providing a significant service to your fellow professionals.

The difference between mentoring and coaching has been much discussed, with some suggesting they are distinct, and others feeling they are part of a continuum that has important elements of overlap.

Mentoring is perhaps the easiest of the three to define and articulate. It usually involves an experienced teacher providing instruction and counsel to a trainee, in order for them to become qualified and established. This involves a variety of techniques, such as questioning, suggesting, advising and instructing. When done effectively, it is critical in bringing new teachers up to the required level of competence and has significant influence on whether the trainee does indeed remain in the classroom after the critical five-year mark.

The relationship aspect is vital, and whenever the authors have worked with trainees and asked what makes for a good mentor, the two most common answers are time and approachability. However, when done badly, the mentee can become demotivated and feel lacking in ability, and this of course enhances the likelihood of them changing career path sooner rather than later. The most common cause of this type of negative mentoring is when the mentee feels they are being appraised rather than supported. It's what Hobson and Malderez call 'judgementoring', and if you want to be a mentor then it's worth reading the research around effective mentoring so you avoid this kind of pitfall.

A significant problem with mentoring is that it usually stops after the mentee has become established and is deemed ready to 'fly solo'. It may be more down to capacity and resource than anything else, but mentoring still has an important role to play in career progression. When taking on a new role, especially in middle or senior leadership, you would definitely benefit from the guidance of an experienced mentor. This does happen, but it is far less systematic than it is for initial teacher education. Many leadership courses offer a coach and/or mentor, but not everyone embarking on a middle leadership role will be taking formal courses in doing so. If you are making a step into more senior leadership, then do ask either if you will be provided with a mentor, or if there is support in the form of a course that has mentoring built into the framework. Robin has benefited immensely from having an experienced headteacher as a mentor as part of the HMC induction process.

Coaching has grown in stature in recent years, but it isn't at all new. The value of coaching in education goes back to the work begun by Summers and Joyce in 1980, and their conception of peer coaching has real consistency with what is now being practised much more widely. However, there are many misconceptions about coaching, which has much to do with its different applications depending on the sector. It looks, and feels, very different in education compared to other contexts, such as business. What is needed to help teachers develop is very different to business, life or sport coaching (although the latter does have some similarity with instructional coaching, more of which below). Crucially, coaching is not about performance management. If you ever feel that a coaching session is becoming a critique of your practice, linked to a judgement, you are perfectly entitled to leave the room.

Coaching is distinct from mentoring in that the relationship should be different, as the coach and coachee do not need to have different levels of experience. In essence, the coach's job is to ask questions in the belief that the coachee is capable of answering them, based on their own professional knowledge and skills. The person being coached needs help, in the form of questions and feedback, to reach the answers desired. It is inherently self-reflective, and like mentoring it is much more likely to be successful if there is a relationship based on mutual respect. It involves a level of openness and trust that can be unsettling at times, and it can definitely have a pastoral dimension depending on where the conversation goes. However, it is a very effective form of teacher development that has a growing body of research to support its efficacy.

To become a coach is no simple thing, and if you are ever offered a paid course that promises to make you an effective coach in one day, don't waste your time (or money). It takes a long time to become skilled at it, and the benefits are that you will be much sharper in your questioning technique (which has obvious classroom applications) and – perhaps even more importantly – much better at listening. One of the core tenets of coaching is that there are three kinds of listening: micro, what the person is saying; macro, what the person's body language is saying; and me, which is your own internal monologue. Turning the 'me voice' off is tough, and you soon realise how often it takes over when you're in the middle of a conversation. If you have the chance to become a coach, it is fascinating work and provides a real element of challenge for your development. Like mentoring, it has the dual benefit of personal progression as well as providing service to your colleagues.

Coaching between peers can have two key professional benefits. The first is around career progression, because understanding what you want isn't always obvious. Sometimes the coaching session will lead you to realisations that lurk beneath the surface, and you intuitively know to be true once you have articulated them openly, but probably didn't recognise before. The challenge questions in this book are essentially coaching questions, but it is a good idea to get a trusted colleague to pose them to you so they can become a coaching conversation.

The second benefit is around classroom practice, and this is where instructional coaching comes in. This has more in common with mentoring because it does involve being coached by someone who has expertise in a given area and is looking to pass it on. Crucial to this process is the idea of deliberate practice. This is an idea you will probably have come across before, but if not then reading

Anders Ericsson's book *Peak* is advised. The basic idea is that true improvement comes from specific, focused practice on a particular skill, which is observed by a coach who gives feedback. The practice is then refined according to that feedback, and continued until expertise is reached. This is what happens in sports coaching, and the same is being offered in classroom practice. A lesson could be observed, or filmed, and feedback given on a specific aspect such as questioning or behaviour management. Refinements are made through specific interventions, and then reviewed again after a period of further practice. As you can probably imagine, this kind of professional development is quite intensive and is made all the more effective if it is combined with other training to complement it.

The concept of sponsorship differs significantly from both mentoring and coaching in that it is informal. It is one of those brilliant things that tends to happen over a cup of coffee in a staffroom, or anywhere informal when two people at different stages of their career just hit it off. A sponsor is someone who advocates on your behalf, and essentially takes you under their wing. They don't do it in a recognised capacity, and they combine the best aspects of both mentoring and coaching. They give the benefit of their experience, provide valuable insights, and ask all the right questions. Interestingly, Catalyst, a business organisation that aims to increase opportunities at leadership level for women, stated in their research report *Sponsorship and Mentoring* that sponsorship had a greater level of influence than formal mentoring programmes. A key finding was that sponsorship could make promotion opportunities more equitable:

> *Sponsors use their influence or leadership status to advocate for the advancement of an individual. They are often senior leaders or other people of power appropriately placed within an organization who help protégés obtain high-visibility projects or jobs. When women have sponsors, it can narrow the advancement gap between women and men.*[38]

A useful distinction made in this report is that:

> A role model talks *by example*, a coach talks *to* you, a mentor talks *with* you, and a sponsor talks *about* you.

It is very often sponsors who help you make progress by speaking up on your behalf when you're not in the room, which helps to break down barriers and allow others to recognise your talents. It also provides a crucial level of support

---

38. Catalyst (2020) *Sponsorship and mentoring: ask Catalyst Express.*
   https://www.catalyst.org/research/sponsorship-mentoring-resources/

that may not be there when early career mentoring has gone, and coaching isn't an option. It should also be noted that sponsorship should not be confused with nepotism; it is not about advancing the career prospects of 'mates'. Sponsors recognise talent and act as critical friends, and this is underpinned by professional integrity. They encourage others because it helps the organisation (in this case, the school) to progress.

So what does this all mean for reflective practice? It is safe to say that if you are being mentored, coached, or sponsored, then you are in a state where you are actively engaged in reflective practice. The challenge questions keep coming, and you think deeply about what you are doing. If you don't have such a person in your professional life, you have to ask yourself if you are being reflective enough. Are you treading water? Are you able to recognise your strengths and weaknesses, and act accordingly? If you are concerned about your answers to these questions, what are you going to do about it?

Furthermore, what does this mean for career progression? There are two pathways open to you. One is to enlist the help of a mentor, coach or sponsor, and the second is to become one. The beauty of this is that virtually everyone can become one of these once they have become qualified. An NQT can give great advice to a trainee, and we have both seen RQTs who have soon gone on to become excellent PGCE mentors because they have recent experience of the process themselves. The more experience you build, the more you are able to become a mentor, coach or sponsor; and remember, you don't need anyone's permission to become a sponsor. You just have to recognise the integrity and potential of a less experienced colleague and ask them if they want to have a coffee. Providing professional support to your colleagues is one of the most rewarding, and least advertised, pathways for career development. It is well worth spending some time factoring it into your overall career plan.

CASE STUDY – COLLECTIVED WITH PROFESSOR RACHEL LOFTHOUSE

Rachel Lofthouse (@DrRLofthouse) is Professor of Teacher Education at Leeds Beckett University. She is the founder and director of CollectivED, The Centre for Coaching, Mentoring and Professional Learning in the Carnegie School of Education. Rachel was a secondary teacher and middle leader throughout the 1990s prior to becoming a full-time teacher educator and researcher.

How did CollectivED come about, and how does it support teachers in their professional learning?

CollectivED was founded following a strategic planning conversation among five professors in Carnegie School of Education at Leeds Beckett University. Three of us were newly appointed and the Dean of the school, Professor Damien Page, was keen that we could each successfully bring our research credentials and current interests into the public domain. We agreed to each establish new research and practice centres to achieve that. The aim of CollectivED is to support education practitioners and researchers (who are often the same people) in a shared endeavour of enabling professional practice and learning that has integrity and the potential to be transformative.

As a centre we make a conscious choice to recognise the value of all colleagues working in education, regardless of their role, their career stage, the sector or phase that they work in or their geographical location. We invite them to participate and contribute, knowing that their experiences and voices are relevant. We publish working papers related to coaching, mentoring and professional learning and wellbeing which are written with a broad audience in mind. Teachers and school leaders are among the authors of each type of working paper; research working papers, including summaries of empirical research, case studies, action research, practice insight working papers, book and conference reviews. Together the papers provide significant insights into educational contexts as workplaces and the decision making that shapes them, and opportunities for a wide range of people to share opinions, reflections or critiques of education practice, research and/or policy.

CollectivED hosts a range of opportunities for professional development and learning, with our session formats giving priority to dialogue and the sharing of expertise. These include one-off sessions, short courses and PGCert in Coaching and Mentoring for Education Practitioners. We also facilitate an international network of CollectivED Fellows who meet regularly online to share their research and practices.

We know that mentors are a key part of helping teachers to develop, but what qualities do you need to be an effective mentor?

The teaching profession is diverse, and teachers will occupy a range of roles during their careers. Mentors need to be drawn from across the workforce but share a common interest in creating great professional development opportunities for others. They need to be motivated beyond the natural inclination of assuming that to be successful the person that they are mentoring should think and act in a way that they recognise in themselves and thus find reassuringly familiar, easy to model and to explain.

A mentor needs to be able to build a secure working relationship with their mentee, based on deliberately being curious about them, offering practical, but not constraining, advice and helping them to make good connections between the new challenges that they are facing and their past and current learning. A mentor sometimes needs to act as a broker, recognising when their own skills or understanding are being tested and knowing who else in the wider school community can offer the necessary support and guidance that the mentee needs. Mentoring requires good and fair judgement, used sensitively to sustain formative assessment of the mentee's progress as well as summatively if they share responsibility for final judgements of professional competency. Mentors who are only interested in the role for instrumental reasons to support their own CV are unlikely to sustain their role as mentor for long enough and with sufficient frequency to develop the depth and breadth of skills that great mentors need.

Coaching is something that teachers and leaders are increasingly encouraged to do, but there are many different approaches. How should coaching be used in education?

Coaching in education is an interpersonal and sustained dialogue-based practice in which the coach works with a coachee to facilitate self-reflection and effective decision making in the context of their own personal and professional challenges. Coaching should be a confidential, reflective and collaborative process allowing current practices to be expanded and refined. A range of types of coaching are adopted in education settings, but their common goal is to provide the coachee with an opportunity to build their capacity to do their most impactful work in the sector. Coaching in education always holds a positive stance and as such it is not focused on deficits or limited to external benchmarks or criteria. That might be as a result of focusing on pedagogic or leadership practices, wellbeing or career choices. Skills of coaching are nuanced and strike a fine balance between supporting individuals to thrive in their contexts and enabling them to become agentic to create positive changes in that context.

How does instructional coaching differ, and what situations would it work well in?

Instructional coaching is not defined as a trademark or copyrighted practice, and it exists in a variety of forms. Instructional coaching originated in teacher development practices in the US, where the word 'instructional' is a synonym for teaching and learning or pedagogy. An instructional coach should have expertise in pedagogic practices relevant to the coaching context and purpose. Traditionally instructional coaches work in specialist fields, such as literacy coaching. This gives them the relevant insight and knowledge to be able to provide teachers with credible feedback and advice. They should have effective coaching skills, particularly the ability to provoke reflection, support enquiry into the teacher's teaching routines and its impacts, and the capacity to work in partnership to co-create new understanding and a motivation to make adaptations in teaching and learning. It works best when the coach is able to take into account the individual contexts and needs of the teacher being coached, as well as the specific needs of their learners and the curriculum. Although it sounds like a cliche there is value in working towards the coach being redundant, in that the teacher they are working with has developed habits of reflective practice and problem solving which mean that they can self-coach through many of the inevitable dilemmas that they will experience in their classroom.

Thank you to Professor Rachel Lofthouse for answering our questions. You can follow Rachel on Twitter @DrRLofthouse.

PROFESSIONAL REVIEW AND DEVELOPMENT

Professional review and development (PRD, or an equivalent acronym) is one of those thorny areas that can either be highly effective and lead to successful reflection, or a cumbersome and bureaucratic process that just leads to a tick-box conversation and another year melting into the next (if it's the latter, there's a good chance you know it as 'appraisal'). Worse still, it might not be happening at all, and you are left questioning whether anyone even cares how well you are doing your job.

Firstly, the paperwork. How long is the form, and what data is being asked for? Typically, the longer the form, the less meaningful the conversation because why would a reviewer need to delve into areas that have been so rigorously documented already? Also, the longer the form the more likely it is that the reviewer hasn't read it fully either, which also devalues the conversation. And of course, the paper trail is in place so what comeback is there for managers who can demonstrate that a meeting has taken place and that the forms have been signed off by all parties?

Forgive the cynicism here, but we are both people who detest the bureaucracy that teachers labour under, when time can be better spent doing other things. This is a case in point. Review forms that are a light touch in terms of data entry, but lead to good conversations, are what is needed. If you are a senior leader reading this, and you have responsibility for annual reviews, go back to that form now and start culling it. If it doesn't lead to healthy professional dialogue, it isn't fit for purpose.

What you get out of the process depends on the spirit in which you enter it. That, of course, depends on who is conducting the review and your relationship with them. You will know if the conversation is open, honest, and leads to effective professional reflection. If so, it is a really valuable opportunity to take stock of what you've been doing, the rationale for it, and how effective your efforts have been. If, however, the review meeting is a PR exercise, or worse, conducted with a tin hat on, then you are missing that chance to objectively assess your professional life. That is likely to be highly demoralising, and throws into sharp relief how counterproductive review processes can be if not done properly. What you need to consider here is whether you are getting the right level of support from this (typically annual) review process. You have to tread carefully if you're going to challenge any process, and it should come across as being constructive and driven by a genuine desire on your part to make positive progress.

Interestingly, many companies are now moving away from annual reviews, and that theme has been picked up by Multi-Academy Trusts (MATs). Instead, a 'little and often' approach is adopted that focuses on both performance and development, but the person leading the process has a responsibility to provide much more in the way of feedback. There is a shared responsibility here, and meetings can be as frequent as every six weeks. Paperwork is much less onerous, and for recording purposes the emphasis is on tasks rather than minutes. This approach lends itself much more to a coaching methodology, and although it increases the number of meetings, it does prioritise dialogue over paperwork. Mandy Coalter, in her book *Talent Architects: How to make your school a great place to work* argues that:

The benefits of this approach include staff having more ownership of their objectives and staff receiving more regular and timely feedback, as well as better retention and performance along with less time wasted on form filling.

It is also worth keeping in mind that review processes are a chance for middle and senior leaders to think about talent spotting, and succession planning. Coalter cites the use of the nine-box grid by senior leaders in business, which again is increasingly being used in schools. It looks like this:

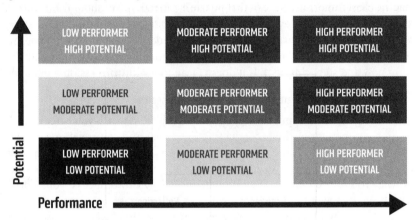

If you are reflecting on your own situation, where would you put yourself on this grid? Where should you be? And where do you think the leadership team in your school sees you? If there is a disconnect, how can you address this? A good review process should allow you to do that. Don't be afraid to ask tough questions in the meeting because it is also a chance for you to find out how healthy your career progression really is.

The purpose of professional review and development overall should be to provide a chance for genuine reflection on your part, and meaningful feedback on the reviewer's part. This should create a clear way forward, with specific tasks to be done, that help you stay engaged with what you do. It should lead to you feeling valued and challenged, and intellectually curious about what you do as a teacher. If that isn't the case, it's worth spending some time thinking about why that is, and what you can do – if anything – to address it.

The diagram below was created by Kate and focuses on how teachers can get better at getting better. The key concept is that all four elements; learn from others, research, experience and reflection are all connected, hence the jigsaw puzzle. In terms of learning from others, this is a vast area as it may include informal conversations with colleagues, lesson observations, professional learning communities, and more. We discussed in Chapter 1 the importance of engaging with research and becoming evidence-informed practitioners. Another key aspect of being evidence-informed is combining evidence from research with our own professional judgment, knowledge and experience. There is wisdom and confidence that teachers can acquire from experience in the classroom and the same applies to school leaders and their role. We believe that the most important piece of that puzzle is reflection. We should continually reflect on all elements: reflection is key when learning from others, engaging with research and of course we should regularly reflect on our experiences too.

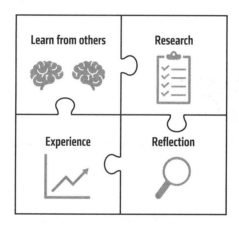

CHALLENGE QUESTIONS

- How often do you reflect on your practice?

- How do you reflect on your practice; a journal, a record or something less formal?

- Do you reflect on your practice with others? This can include your line manager, or if you are a leader having conversations with those you lead and work alongside.

- Have you got the qualities needed to be an effective mentor or a coach?

- How might coaching be of benefit to your practice?

- Do you currently have a sponsor, or could you be a sponsor to someone?

- How do you approach the professional review process, and are you making the most of it?

QR CODES FOR FURTHER READING AND INFORMATION

Leeds Beckett Research
https://www.leedsbeckett.ac.uk/research

Catalyst: Workplaces
that work for women
https://www.catalyst.org

CHAPTER 8

NON-LEADERSHIP CAREER PROGRESSION

Purpose of this chapter: To explore the benefits and pathways for career progression without adopting leadership.

There has long been a traditional and rigid career progression model for teachers based on hierarchical leadership. After a few years of teaching, you apply for middle leadership, and after a few years more you step up to senior leadership. While this model of career progression has enabled many teachers to flourish as leaders, as we have noted, it isn't for everyone, and *The Teaching Life* is about following a career path that is enjoyable and feels right for every individual. It is possible to progress without a promotion – not having a leadership title doesn't equate to failure or a lack of ambition.

It is certainly possible to be fulfilled as a teacher without leadership and this section focuses purely on that. Alternatively, there are opportunities for leadership outside of the school environment which can support professional progression and provide valuable experiences, skills and knowledge. It is about having the teaching life that you want for yourself, which is based on a level of professional challenge that helps you to feel you are progressing as a person and a teacher. Progression is therefore a key word in our concept of the teaching life; it doesn't matter if you are moving up (or down) in terms of position, but it does matter that you are always moving forward in your development as a teacher. Staying static means stagnating. Progressing means thriving.

We have both achieved progression with various leadership roles in addition to success outside of leadership. There are now a variety of ways in which teachers can branch out and progress in school without a leadership title. There are ways to achieve career progression within education without having to line manage others, have difficult conversations, and take on extra responsibility and accountability.

If leadership within your school isn't for you then it is worth reflecting on why that might be. Is there a specific reason or is it linked to the people and environment, or from viewing others in their leadership roles? Once you have reflected on this, it is easier to think about other options for non-leadership career progression that would be the best path for you.

BEING THE BEST TEACHER YOU CAN BE

Firstly, this point is not to suggest leaders are not always striving to be the best teacher they can be, but the higher up the leadership ladder a teacher progresses the less time they spend in the classroom. There is nothing wrong with wanting to progress by remaining full-time in the classroom. It is possible to move forwards without moving upwards. In addition to the professional learning previously discussed, such as pursuing a qualification like an MA in Education, there are other ways to have an impact without a leadership title, which will be explored in this chapter.

CASE STUDY – FREYA ODELL: LEADING LEADERSHIP BEHIND

English teacher Freya Odell (@FreyaMariaO) held various leadership positions but felt a change was needed in her life. She relocated to teach at a British curriculum school in Rome, Italy and also stepped down from leadership to be a full-time teacher of English. This change was transformative for Freya, both professionally and personally.

In 2018, I walked away from a strong leadership position. I was Head of English, Director of Learning, Line Manager to Humanities and Modern Foreign Languages, Literacy Co-ordinator and mentoring three new entrants to the profession. I was busy. But I was also so busy that I was shattered and unfulfilled. I felt as though I was existing rather than living. So when a job came up in Rome, I made the decision to move back to Italy (having lived there between 2008-2010) and take a step back onto the main-scale, as a Teacher of English.

Some may say that taking such a step is a sign of professional regression: that after years of hard graft, skill building and learning on the job that walking away from such a position is reductive. I would argue the opposite and suggest that it is both liberating and satisfying.

This is especially true when it comes to professional development. Having no leadership responsibility, I have found I am now more invested in my own professional development than ever before because I have both the time and the headspace to be invested. On top of this, I am also more in control of my own professional development, having the freedom and the luxury to only invest in things that I feel will be beneficial to my own practice and develop me as an individual, within my classroom.

And let's be honest, we are living in a time of great richness when it comes to professional development and the ability to self-direct our work as educators. The 'edu-book' market is thriving with books available on almost all aspects of educational practice. If time-poor, blogs are a fantastic way of accessing research and learning from other practitioners about what is working in their classrooms. If really time-poor, just being on Twitter and engaging in some of the discussions and collaborative opportunities is incredibly beneficial to stimulate our thinking and enrich our own provision.

The ability to clarify our own thinking and reflect upon our own practice can be done by having our own blog or by contributing to a range of publications. Arguably, many writers have said that the writing process has really helped them to reflect upon the research they are engaging with and offered them a space to critique their own practice as well. I have certainly found this is the case when contributing to The ResearchEd Guide to Assessment *(2020), providing a case study for* Fiorella and Mayer's Generative Learning in Action *by Mark and Zoe Enser (2020) and now also contributing to* The Teaching Life!

Similarly, with the onset of the COVID pandemic, there has been a marked increase in the popularity of online webinars, such as researchEd Home, the IB Virtual conference, the World Education Summit and TeachMeet Icons (with a subject-specific focus), to name but a few. These webinars have proved to be incredibly popular: one, because of the plethora of sessions available; two, because many can be watched in your own time at your own pace; and three, because they are extremely cost effective. Furthermore, practitioners are encouraged to get involved and present at such events and I've been fortunate enough to participate in the Seneca English conference, Teach Meet English Icons and the Team English Conference on both reading for pleasure and writing – areas in which I am particularly passionate about developing my own thinking.

There are a range of distance-learning courses available to us, most notably, the Chartered Teacher Programme from the Chartered College. This is a fantastic course that again puts you at the centre of your own professional development by allowing you to choose key areas of your practice to focus on, while receiving excellent support and guidance. But let's not forget an MA in Education, one of the new NPQs or a subject-specific post graduate study should that suit you more.

Finally, for me, the opportunity to get involved in Teachers Talk Radio. Although incredibly nerve-wracking, an experience like this has enabled me to have discussions with educators all around the world about teaching and learning and has helped to really extend my thinking on a more global level.

So, if leadership isn't for you, or if you are considering stepping away from leadership, just know that it doesn't mean the end of a fulfilling and rewarding career. In fact, it simply empowers you to seek out new opportunities for growth and enables you to take even greater control of your own professional development. In an edu-rich world, never has it been more easy to self-direct our own professional development so that we can grow in the direction we wish to grow – even if this does not involve leadership. This is not only incredibly energising and stimulating, but ultimately the most satisfying position we can find ourselves in.

Thank you to Freya for sharing her experiences and advice with us. You can follow Freya on Twitter @FreyaMariaO and visit her teaching blog engteacherabroad.com

GOVERNOR

There are numerous benefits of being part of a governing body, and various ways to go about it. There are teacher governor roles for those that teach at the school, or a parent governor or governor position at a different school. Usually, governor positions are advertised but schools can also approach an individual to apply. If this is something you wish to pursue, a good starting point would be to express an interest at your current school or make a connection with a local school (we stress local because often meetings happen in person, so a close location is much more convenient, although some schools are making the permanent transition to virtual meetings).

Kate was on the advisory board of a school in Abu Dhabi for three years, at a school she did not teach or ever work at. She was asked to join the advisory board as the Principal wanted someone outside of the school environment, but who had a knowledge and understanding of teaching, learning and education. The Principal felt it was important to hear from a range of voices and as he was not Kate's employer he trusted her to offer him honest advice, feedback, critique and support.

What does a governor do? This can vary significantly, and context is key. Governorsforschools.org explain the role of the governor as follows:

> *Governors are responsible for overseeing the management side of a school: strategy, policy, budgeting and staffing. They enable their school to run as effectively as possible, working alongside senior leaders and supporting teachers to provide excellent education to children. Being a school governor is a commitment to attending governing body meetings which consider issues such as setting the school vision, mitigating financial risk and scrutinising educational outcomes. They are also involved in the school community, acting as critical friends to the headteacher and senior leaders. Governors bring a wide range of skills and expertise from their professional lives to the governing board and schools benefit greatly from working with skilled volunteers, for example anyone with experience of finance, law, premises management or human resources. A governor with business know-how can transform the running of a school.*

There are many hard-working individuals who contribute to ensuring a school runs smoothly day in and day out. School governors are often unsung heroes working behind the scenes, involved in important decision-making and contributing to future developments and planning.

Becoming part of a governing board can also provide an opportunity to build professional relationships and connections with different people and become a valued member of a team. While this isn't a paid position and does require time, effort and dedication, being a governor can be very rewarding as it involves making whole school decisions which can have an impact on the entire school community, including teachers, students and families. It is not something to take on lightly, but it is a different approach to contributing to whole school development and improvement.

To find out more about the role and responsibilities of a school governor we have included links to websites containing information as well as the *Department for Education Governance Handbook* (2020) at the end of this chapter.

BECOMING A WRITER

There has been a surge in recent years of classroom teachers and school leaders writing about their practice and experiences and publishing on various platforms. This can act as a great form of reflection as well as helping others in the profession who chose to read the writing of others. We both thoroughly enjoy writing; from writing short informal blog posts, writing for national magazines and authoring educational books.

There are many teacher authors who have followed a similar path; beginning with sharing content on social media, then progressing to blogging to expand further on resources, ideas and opinions, then perhaps writing for educational magazines and potentially becoming an author. Not all bloggers in education wish to become published authors (and not all educational authors have a blog) but if becoming a published author is something you are considering then our initial advice would be to start a blog (if you haven't already). We've found this to be one of the most effective ways of being a reflective practitioner, because it really encourages you to think deeply about what you do in the classroom.

BLOGGING

Blogs have reinvigorated the teaching profession, providing an online voice for classroom teachers and school leaders around the world. Blogs are opportunities to share thoughts, reflections, views and opinions with others within the educational community. Whether you are a keen blogger, someone who has started a blog but doesn't feel like it has quite taken off yet, or are a complete novice in terms of blogging, we hope to provide some guidance and advice to help you.

Starting an educational blog

Setting up a blog is relatively straightforward and easy to do with hosting platforms such as wordpress.com, blogger.com and Wix. It is free to create your own blog but you can pay for upgraded features such as a specific domain name and options to upgrade your platform and website design. There are various tutorials online documenting how to begin or you could reach out to an educational blogger and ask for their advice as to how they set up and launched their blog. Don't be put off by the technical elements as it is easier than most people realise.

When creating a blog you will need to create a unique domain name that is available – the title of your blog. We advise you to keep it simple and aim to show in the blog name that you will be writing about education. If you have a specific area of focus within education you wish to write about, such as Early Years Foundation Stage, then EYFS can be included in the name as this will indicate to readers what you will be focusing on and help attract your chosen target audience.

Before even writing and posting a blog post our advice would be to read lots of existing posts published by teachers. Not only could this provide plenty of food for thought and professional reading, but it can also provide inspiration in terms of the content, tone, structure and style you choose to adopt for your blog.

Writing a blog post

There is the flexibility with a blog post to write about any topic you desire. A blog can be a topical look at a current issue, it can refer to and examine an educational development or it can focus on a theme of pedagogy or leadership. There are no deadlines or set word limits. A blogger can blog frequently or simply when they have the time to do so, although if you are aiming to build up an audience then it is advisable to be consistent in terms of how often you blog.

Blog posts shouldn't be too long but instead clear and concise; 800-1000 words would be our recommendation, but you have the choice and flexibility to write as much as or as little as you want. If you begin to get carried away and find a post to be longer than originally intended, a good idea would be to divide it up into different sections and publish a series or collection of shorter posts over time.

While there are many aspects of blogging that are informal, it is still being published in the public domain, so there are some key aspects to keep in mind. Anyone can read it; this may include your employer, future employer, colleagues, students, governors or anyone in the wider school community and beyond. While you may have a specific target audience, be prepared for people outside of that to read your post. Proofreading is another important aspect of blogging and while starting out it can be useful to send blogs to colleagues or friends for their feedback and initial reaction, as well as getting another set of eyes to check it over for literacy errors.

When writing a post focus on writing about an area, field or topic where you have experience and an interest. Imposter syndrome may occur, making you feel that perhaps you do not have anything of any real value to add or cannot contribute anything that hasn't already been said, but it is highly likely that others will find what you write interesting and helpful. Your audience can potentially be global so keep this in mind when using acronyms as they may not be as well known in other regions or countries, and may not be familiar to early career teachers.

Make sure you credit and reference where applicable. This can be easily done by including hyperlinks to original sources and also provides the reader with the further information to find out more should they wish to do so. Images and videos can also be included in blog posts. It is important to have an awareness of copyright when including images. There are many websites that provide a vast choice of high-quality images that are royalty free, thus allowing you to include them in your posts without any possible complications or copyright issues. Recommended websites for freely available images to use are:

www.pixabay.com
www.unsplash.com
www.vecteezy.com/free-photos

If you wish to personalise images by adding text and captions you can use Adobe Spark Post which is available via browser or as an app, you simply need to set up an account by email to be able to use it. Canva.com is another popular and user-friendly website for graphic design creation or alternatively there are various apps such as Typorama for creating typographics with text.

Consider the structure of your blog post. If offering advice and tips, short sentences using bullet points can be an effective way to do so. Headings and subheadings can also be used to ensure the layout is clear and focused. Although a blog can be conversational and informal in style – in contrast to an academic essay – it can still be beneficial to reach a judgment or summary at the end of the post.

If for any reason you are hesitant about posting something, simply save in your drafts. This is a better option than later deleting or retracting it as the post will have already been in the public domain and screenshots of texts can be kept. If in doubt take some time to wait, think and reflect and ask someone you trust for their honest feedback.

Sharing your blog post

Once the publish button has been pressed, effort and energy has to shift to attracting readers. This will become easier over time as people subscribe and will automatically receive blog posts as they are published. The best way to reach a wide audience is to share widely. Social media is a fantastic way to do this, and it is advisable to share on various platforms; Twitter, LinkedIn, Facebook and Instagram are all great places to share your latest blog post. We believe blogging and social media go hand in hand; blogging without using social media platforms to share your posts will make it very challenging to attract readers, views and visitors to your website.

Self-promotion can be difficult but there should be no shame or embarrassment in doing this. It is important to regularly share each post as followers and connections online may have missed it when it was originally published. Striking a balance between sharing pertinent content on a regular basis without spamming and overwhelming people's timelines is important. It is a good idea to share posts at different times to ensure connections on different time zones are signposted to your latest offering.

Should educational bloggers share their posts with colleagues? We would argue yes. Sending the blog post to a relevant audience, whether that be members of your department or the whole school staff can be more challenging than sharing online, after all, these are your peers who you work with and see every day. When emailing a blog post, make a comment about how colleagues can subscribe to keep up to date so they can choose if they wish to continue reading your content, and there is then no need to send out future emails for each blog you publish.

Once your blog post has been shared it can be useful to view the analytics. This information can show how many people have read your post or visited your site. In addition to this, information can be provided as to where in the world your readers are based, if they clicked on hyperlinks included in the post, and how they were directed to your site. A blog doesn't become successful overnight; gaining traction and engagement can be a slow process but do stick with it and don't become too fixated on statistics and figures. Blogging can be highly enjoyable, rewarding and motivating in terms of promoting continual reflection and professional learning, and can also create connections as people will respond, comment and provide feedback.

Not everyone in education shares the same views, opinions and experiences, but a difference in opinion or critical comment shouldn't stop anyone from writing, although the first time this happens it can be disappointing and even upsetting. Resilience is an important element of being a writer as anyone who writes is being very brave by opening themselves up so publicly and widely. There is an element of vulnerability when writing about our passion, experiences, interests and views on education, but respectful debate can be healthy and can help us develop as professionals.

WRITING FOR EDUCATIONAL MAGAZINES

If you are a regular blogger or perhaps a keen writer but reluctant to set up a blog, then the alternative is to write for an educational magazine. There are many advantages of this over blogging. There will likely be an editor that can proofread, edit and even improve your original piece. There are some educational magazines that provide payment for articles written. A magazine will have their own existing reader base which will promote and share your writing to a wider audience.

The disadvantages for writing for a magazine in comparison to blogging are that you may be set a deadline that has to be met, you can be restricted to a specific word limit and the editor may alter your content by adding, amending or removing key points. There may be a topic or focus you wish to write about, but which a magazine might not wish to publish, in contrast to a blog where there is freedom and flexibility.

How to write for an educational magazine? There are various ways to do this. The easiest way will be to find the contact details published in the magazine or on the website. It is important when contacting a magazine to not pitch yourself but instead have a clear idea, concept or topic that you wish to write about. You may have even already written the article and be ready to submit it. If one magazine rejects your article or idea, then try another and be persistent.

AUTHORING AN EDUCATIONAL BOOK

If blogging regularly and/or writing for educational magazines it is likely you will improve as a writer and grow in confidence. Regular bloggers can attract a readership which follows their posts closely and this can have an indirect effect on social media accounts by attracting more followers and increasing engagement. As we are both bloggers and published authors, we are well aware of the significant differences between the two, not just the noticeable income and recognition that authoring a book has over writing a blog but also the time and process itself.

Securing a publisher

Firstly, to become a published author (we are not referring to self-publishing) a publisher will need to agree on the initial pitch and then a contract will be signed. Some educational authors decide to write their book and then find a publisher whereas others will approach a publisher with their ideas and start writing once a contract has been agreed. In some instances publishers will reach out to those in education that are bloggers or have a profile within the educational community and ask or persuade them to write a book.

There are a number of educational publishers, including John Catt Educational, Crown House Publishing, Independent Thinking Press, Bloomsbury Publishing Company, David Fulton Publishers, and Routledge. You may have a preference based on the books you enjoy reading or you may not have a choice if one publishing company doesn't accept your submission. The submission process for each publisher varies but if you are considering authoring an educational book then be prepared to potentially answer the following questions:

- What is the title/sub-title of your book?
- Describe your book in 100 words.
- What is the main focus/theme of your book?
- Who is the target audience for your book?
- Are there any current books that are similar?
- List books that would be considered as competitors and how will your book compete with these books?
- How is your book different from others, how is it distinctive?
- What time frame do you plan to work towards?
- How will you promote your book?
- Why is this book needed now?
- Does it fill a gap in the market?
- What is the shelf life of your book? Will this book still be relevant next year, in two/three/five years?
- Can you send us a sample or extract of your book/writing?
- What is your vision for the front cover/design of your book?

For each publisher you can find out more on their website about the submission process. Once the submission or application form has been completed, publishers have different methods for reaching their decision, which can include a peer review, editorial assessment or further questioning.

If you are unsuccessful you can ask for feedback and guidance and can consider the option to self-publish. There are pros and cons to self-publishing. The most obvious advantage of self-publishing is higher royalties in comparison to those offered by publishing companies. However, there will be no support in terms of editing and promotion, and it certainly involves more hard work and effort to attract readers. If you are successful in securing a publishing contract, then the writing journey begins.

Writing your book

Prior to writing our books, we both spend a huge amount of time reading; this is a crucial element as we draw on and reference educational research and evidence-informed practice. When reading and researching it is important to make notes, write down quotes you may wish to include and page numbers for future referencing. It's essential to keep a record or log during the reading and research stage, as you may want to revisit books and websites multiple times, and it's far easier if you can find the articles and pages you want quickly. Keen writers are often keen readers so be prepared to invest in lots of books and dedicate time to reading them, which will help you with your book.

It is important to consider the impact writing a book can have on workload and well-being. It is incredibly rewarding and fulfilling to become a published author but it is not an easy thing to do. There are many factors to consider: when will you write? This might be evenings, weekends or during holidays. Will your book have a positive impact on your current role, or will it hinder it? Is it worth considering co-authoring a book? The benefits of co-authoring a book include sharing the workload, ongoing support, encouragement, motivation and the enjoyment of working with someone you know well and get along well with. It can be challenging co-authoring a book if your co-author doesn't share the same vision or views and of course co-authors have to share and divide the royalties!

There are many well-known and successful educational authors that are still based in a school such as Mark Enser, Michael Chiles, Jennifer Webb, Victoria Hewitt, Carl Hendrick and Jon Tait to name but a few. We both know how challenging it can be to write a book in addition to having a full-time role in a school; it requires a lot of time, dedication and organisation. Obviously, our teaching roles in school take priority; while authoring a book is important it does need to fit around a schedule that will work for you and any other commitments you may have. Every author has their own routine and approach, for example some authors can spread their writing out over a long span of time whereas others prefer to write intensely in a shorter period.

Promoting your book

As with blogging, writing is an incredibly important part of the process, but it is only one part of becoming a published author. Once the book is published and available it's important to promote it as widely as possible. It is the responsibility of the publisher to promote their books and they will have a marketing team, but they will have several books to promote at once so authors need to get involved too. Kate has published three books focusing on retrieval practice. All three have reached number one as a best-seller on Amazon in the classroom category. Kate makes full use of Twitter, Instagram, LinkedIn and Facebook to share and promote her books in addition to the work done by John Catt Publishing. She is well aware that social media has played an integral role in the success of her books, but of course it is not the sole contributing factor.

Authors may deliver webinars, be interviewed on podcasts or radio shows and speak at events as a way to discuss, share and promote their book. Another idea is to send copies to friends, colleagues and people in the wider educational community to encourage readers to leave positive reviews and recommend your book through word of mouth. Competitions are another useful way to promote books; a simple way to do this on social media is to ask followers to retweet a competition tweet which contains the book's details, and a winner can be selected randomly via retweetpicker.com

Any author who has written a book has done so in the hope that others will read their work and hopefully enjoy it, and find it interesting, helpful and thought provoking. Again, there is no shame in celebrating hard work and success; self-promotion is an important element of being a published author, especially in education where our target audience is a specific profession and perhaps even a narrower sector within that. When it comes to being an author, once a publishing agreement has been secured, the focus will be to read, write and share!

PODCASTER

Podcasts have grown in popularity over recent years, as they can be listened to when driving, exercising or relaxing. There is a wide variety and choice available, including podcasts specific to education. Everyone with a smartphone can access a podcast via platforms such as Apple Podcasts, Anchor, SoundCloud and as mentioned in Chapter 3 they are free to access.

In the same sense that setting up a blog is much easier to do than people often realise, the same applies to launching a podcast. The technical elements really aren't that complex, and a podcast can be set up simply using a smartphone, although you can purchase specialist equipment such as headphones and microphones. Once you have recorded and published a podcast episode, the same advice applies as with writing in terms of gaining traction and reach, and once again using social media is a great way to do this.

EXAMINER

Becoming an examiner might not appear exciting and lucrative but it can offer an excellent opportunity for professional learning and networking. Some teachers will strongly recommend being an examiner while others may say to avoid it! As with any type of progression there are pros and cons to be aware of and consider. Different examiners for different exam boards and subjects will have different experiences so it is worth asking around with colleagues or teachers online to get a broader view.

The criteria for becoming an examiner varies but generally it is necessary to be teaching the content being examined or to previously have taught it. If you can demonstrate strong experience in a particular field or topic, but have not yet taught it, that can also be accepted too. Naturally, this is a great opportunity for a teacher of examination classes.

The main benefits to becoming an examiner are:

- **Valuable, relevant and useful CPD.** There is often an examiners' conference or meeting, either online or in person, which is usually compulsory as it is so important. This discussion will explicitly and carefully go through the examination paper and mark scheme. To ensure consistency, it is important that all examiners are clear about the questions and criteria. This can be incredibly insightful and give teachers further understanding of the exam content and technique they teach their students. In terms of teaching examination classes this can be an excellent – arguably the best – form of professional learning, benefiting teachers and their students. This can lead to increased confidence in the classroom, and the insightful and useful knowledge and experience can also be shared with colleagues.
- **It is an opportunity to network and meet other teachers.** Examiners will be teaching the same specification, content and questions. If possible, try to remain in contact with other examiners. Although there will be confidential

information that cannot be shared it can be beneficial to stay in touch during the process to offer support and motivation to one another. In this way a new professional contact and relationship can be formed which can lead to further support and sharing good practice.

- **Timing.** Being an examiner is not a full-time and year-round responsibility. Exam marking often takes place when teachers have been released from lesson time after examination classes leave school in June and July, although there are opportunities to become an examiner at other points in the academic year. Exam papers are not allowed to be marked in school or any public place (exam boards have strict rules and regulations about this) but what it can mean is that teachers can concentrate on school-related work during the gained lesson time and focus on exam marking outside of school.

- **CV enhancement.** Becoming an examiner shows a commitment to further professional development and can enhance a CV. It illustrates time management, the ability to meet deadlines and manage multiple complicated projects.

- **Leadership opportunities.** If leadership within a school isn't the desired option but leadership itself is still appealing, there are also opportunities to progress to a leadership role as an examiner.

- **Extra money.** It is worth finding out how much money you will receive as different exam boards and different subjects pay different amounts; the payment can vary considerably. If becoming an examiner for the main exam season in May, the payment is often made during the summer holidays. There is also payment for attending the conferences and expenses, such as transport and hotels are usually paid for too.

Being an examiner is very time consuming and will add considerable pressure to your out of hours workload. There are deadlines to meet, which can be stressful. It is worth finding out about the payment to consider if it is worth the time, effort and energy invested; again, is the juice worth the squeeze? There is also a lot more to this than marking papers. Some scripts might be scanned digitally, meaning a lot of screen time. Paper scripts can also be delivered but this will mean returning them with postage and packaging as well inputting raw marks and total scores. There can be administration to complete too. Becoming an examiner need not be a lifelong commitment, it can be done for one year and then, based on your reflection on the process, you can decide whether or not you'd like to do it again.

As we stated at the start of this chapter, it is possible to move forward with career progression without moving upwards. It is a very exciting time to be involved in education as social media, podcasts, blogs and more are offering alternative and enjoyable methods of professional learning. There are roles and responsibilities linked to education that exist outside of your school environment, from being an examiner to a school governor. Whether it is speaking, writing or following a specific area of interest, there are a variety of ways to extend your skill set and make progress without holding a leadership position. The examples we provide are far from being comprehensive, but they are challenges that we've taken on which are not linked to leadership roles and they made us better teachers. It is also possible to do any of those things in addition to having a leadership role, but we need to take care not to spread ourselves too thinly. Taking a 'less is more' approach can help; doing less but doing it well can result in us making more of an impact on the areas we choose to focus on and can result in more balance in our lives too.

CHALLENGE QUESTIONS

■ Have you considered any of the options discussed as an alternative to leadership?

■ If you would like to branch out into blogging, writing for a magazine or authoring a book, what are the factors holding you back?

■ How can you support others – perhaps colleagues or those you lead – who do not want to progress to leadership?

■ What do you enjoy most about teaching and how can you develop that passion and experience further?

QR CODES FOR FURTHER READING AND INFORMATION

National Governance Association

https://www.nga.org.uk/Governance-
Recruitment/Be-a-school-governor-or-
trustee.aspx

Joint Council
for Qualifications
(JCQ – role of an examiner)

https://www.jcq.org.uk/examination-
system/the-role-of-an-examiner

Anchor (platform to create,
host and share a podcast)

https://bit.ly/3GNc3KD

The Blog Starter

https://www.theblogstarter.com/

CHAPTER 9

LEADERSHIP CAREER PROGRESSION

Purpose of this chapter: To help readers to prepare for leadership roles, at different levels within a school from middle leadership to headship.

In Chapter 4 we looked at how to learn about leadership in a professional learning sense. This part of the book is more about praxis; how you go about taking on a leadership position, and what the transition looks like. One of our contentions is that leadership pathways in education are more diverse, and less hierarchical, than are usually recognised. This is due to the legacy effect of a very traditional model of leadership progression, which looks like this:

Headteacher/Principal	
Deputy Head/Vice Principal (Often still in academic/pastoral silos, and possibly with a senior deputy role to add to the hierarchy)	
Assistant Head/Assistant Principal Academic focused – primarily teaching Pastoral focused – primarily behaviour/well-being	
Middle leader (pastoral)	Middle leader (academic)
Classroom teacher	

The idea was that once you pinned your colours to one of two middle leadership masts (academic or pastoral), that dictated which opportunities were available to you at senior leadership level; win your spurs here, and the door to headship opens up. This, of course, looks very straight-jacketed now, and also had a habit of producing heads who leaned either to the academic or pastoral side of things, because that was their core experience of leadership.

In fact, it's much harder now to draw a diagram which shows the typical progression, because there is a greater leadership diversity in the education world. For example, what about becoming a governor, or leading a co-curricular activity, or even an operational team? More emphasis is put on breadth of experience, and that's worth considering when you are looking to build expertise as your teaching life evolves.

This chapter is really about the different expectations and challenges that come at each level, and should prompt you to think about where your natural fit might be. It is also about knowing when the time is right to make a move. You can't perfect any given stage of leadership, but you can be ready and confident to progress to a new one. Very few people are destined for, or suited to, headship, so which area of leadership are you best suited to, and what would that entail? And if you need a leadership fix in your professional life, do you need to get that from school? Or would you prefer an outside organisation like a charity or a social enterprise, or by being a governor at another school? This is a case of making the weather for yourself. You are often told to think about what type of leader you want to be, and while that is important, career planning involves thinking just as much about where and when you want to lead.

THE CHANGING FACE OF SCHOOL LEADERSHIP

Schools have become more complex places in the twenty-first century, not least because of the greater range of expectations placed on teachers. For those of you who have been around for, say, at least 20 years in education, think back to how many operational staff you came into contact with when you started in teaching. How many HR staff were there back then? Or health and safety specialists? Or IT technicians? Yes, life is more complex, but with complexity comes opportunity. There are more areas in which teachers can develop leadership skills, and the career roadblocks caused by a senior colleague who will be on that next rung of the ladder for many years to come are not so problematic as they once were.

Much of this change in both the proliferation of leadership roles and the nature of those roles came from New Public Management (NPM), which began in the 1980s and was heavily influential in education from the 1990s onwards. What NPM aimed to do was make public services more efficient and consumer friendly, which meant greater accountability and collection of data to demonstrate that. School league tables are a classic example, as are inspections (the first ever Ofsted inspection took place in 1993). This has transformed the culture of education as a sector, for good and bad, and we need to consider the effect it has had on school leadership. It is, without doubt, more technocratic now than it was in the past. Paradoxically, the more school leaders are meant to be 'consumer' – in this context child and parent – facing, the less time they get to spend on things that really matter for their students.

What does this mean for your progression into leadership? Well, it is reasonable to assume that management of staff now takes up a far greater proportion of middle and senior leadership remits, and this trend will only continue. Going back a generation, being a head of department was often a case of just being a really good teacher. Admin came with the territory, but it wasn't death by spreadsheet as many middle leaders feel it now is. Equally, being a pastoral leader usually meant being very good at dealing with children, but now there is much more in the way of dealing with external agencies, following policies, and producing detailed reports. This might all sound very demotivating, but keep in mind that much of it is for good reason.

You might think that accountability, regulation and compliance have ruined education, but spend any time looking at cases of historic child abuse in schools and you'll see these things in a different light. The reason we are saying all this is because it is worth knowing that leadership entails managing staff, understanding policies and legislation, having financial nous, and being skilled at data processing and analysis. Within this bewildering array of responsibilities, the one that most school leaders find hardest of all is the HR aspect; it turns out that children are often easier to deal with than adults.

So the first thing to ask yourself, is whether or not this is the progression you want to make. We both have a range of leadership experience, and it is fair to say that having a positive impact with a colleague is just as rewarding as doing so with a student. It is a different kind of work, but it is still for the same end: the best outcomes for young people. The roles may be different, and the skillset more diverse, but the rationale is really the same. We both feel that there is little point complaining about leadership decisions without offering solutions, and that is another major reason to take this step. You get to influence things in a way that you believe is positive and will make a difference. If that's your mindset, then leadership is most likely for you.

MIDDLE LEADERSHIP

Middle leadership is a highly flexible term, and can cover a wide range of roles (you might also come across the term meso-level leadership in academic literature). At entry level, these roles may be of the 'volunteer' variety; no salary attached, no time remission, just building up a store of professional credit that will come in handy when a bigger role is advertised. These roles are good to experiment with, because you can get a sense of whether leadership is really for you or not. If more than one of these is undertaken, it can broaden your experience and give you a sense of which pathways would be best for you. Join the curriculum review committee? Sure. How about the school magazine? Why not? These are testing grounds that allow you to cut your teeth. It also gets you on the radar of the school's senior leaders, which is no bad thing. The key thing is to reflect on these experiences and start to formulate a strategy in your mind as to what you would like to do next.

What impact does it have on you when you move into middle leadership? Undoubtedly there is more work, more pressure, and a steep learning curve. There should also be a higher salary, and a lighter teaching load. You are, of course, still expected to teach very well, even though lesson planning time probably contracts to a greater degree than your teaching load does. You are also more front line with parents, and not necessarily in a good way, so the art of dealing with complaints is one of the most difficult things to come to terms with; sadly parents don't call up middle leaders to say 'We love your work' as frequently as they call to raise an issue.

A stinging email, terse phone call, or bumpy face-to-face meeting can have a nasty habit of resurfacing in your memory when you least want it to (like when you randomly wake up at three in the morning). The same applies to dealing with colleagues, and most heads of department will say that having difficult conversations is one of the aspects of the job they struggle with most. It is never a good idea to be confrontational as a leader, but people will be confrontational with you. That's hard to handle and you won't know if your skin is growing thicker until you've experienced it quite a few times. The net effect of all this is that middle leaders are highly prone to burnout, perhaps more so than any other group in the profession, because their answer to pressure and stress is often to work harder, and shoulder more of the burden. It may come from a noble place, but it is self-destructive. It is also career destructive. Failure to delegate effectively, or cope with pressure, raises questions about suitability to take on more pressure at senior leader level.

So why should you do it? Well, there is no doubt that good middle leaders perform very well under pressure, because they get better at it with experience. They play a critical role in effecting change, through intelligent leadership of their own remit, and by influencing decisions made at senior level as skilled consiglieres. They are the belt-buckle of the school, who know the fine detail of what is happening in and out of classrooms, and also get insight into what is happening at a strategic level. In the previous chapter we talked about teacher agency, but actually one of the key drivers for taking up middle leadership is a desire to have more agency within the school community. The reward for being a middle leader is relatively slender in financial terms, but in having a greater ability to shape the immediate environment, it is fairly rich.

One of the toughest skills required by middle leaders is the ability to lead both up and down equally well. Leading down is fairly self-explanatory; it means being an effective leader to your team, getting the best out of them by creating the optimal conditions for success, and providing the right balance between support and challenge. Leading up is arguably harder. It means you deal just as effectively with your senior line manager as you do with your team. You need to be able to toe the party line when necessary, but also speak truth to power diplomatically when the occasion calls for it. This is a case of providing the right level of support and challenge for senior leaders. When you are given feedback, you need to be able to listen objectively, even when it might be difficult to do so. Being honest about mistakes is essential; this means taking principal responsibility for your remit, and only calling in the cavalry when a problem grows beyond your control. All of this is hard, as it involves a constant state of tension. It is easy to curry favour with your own team by positioning yourself as their advocate and protector, but leadership is not a popularity contest. Leading up and down means seeing things from both sides, and using your professional judgement accordingly.

On a bad day it can feel like that scene from *Star Wars* where they all fall into the garbage compactor: walls closing in, everyone screaming, surrounded by rubbish, unseen creatures dragging you under and trying to drown you, and when you call up for help no one answers. However, when it goes well it feels euphoric – like blowing up the Death Star – and there is certainly something addictive about it. As with classroom teaching, there is no such thing as perfection here, only a case of refining what you do to try to make those incremental improvements that ultimately lead to better working conditions for your team, and successful learning being more likely for the students. And that's another key consideration: what you do has a greater impact on young lives as a middle leader than it does as a classroom teacher, because the effects of your decisions and your actions reach a wider constituency.

The importance of a good middle leader is shown by the contention that teachers can be happy in a school where they have a great head of department but a lousy headteacher, but not the other way around. Whatever improvement needs to happen in a school is led by senior staff, but enacted and embedded by middle leaders. That in itself can be a very fulfilling purpose, so middle leadership is undoubtedly very hard, but it is absolutely worth it.

CASE STUDY: BECOMING A MIDDLE LEADER – AN INTERVIEW WITH EMILY FOLORUNSHO

Emily (@MissFolorunsho) became Head of History in September 2020 and had her first experience of middle leadership during the COVID-19 pandemic. In addition to her middle leader role, Emily is also an SLE, governor and Teachers Talk Radio host.

What made you want to make the step up into middle leadership?

It was ultimately curriculum design. I never aspired to be a head of department (HOD), however, as time went on I saw changes that needed to be made but I knew I would have to be HOD in order to do so. Furthermore, I felt stale. I am a classroom teacher at heart, and I resented taking extra responsibility that would mean less teaching time; however, I did feel like I was plateauing as a classroom teacher for five years. So becoming HOD was a natural next step for me. I needed the extra challenge to grow.

What other responsibilities did you take on in order to prepare prior to becoming a head of department?

In year three of my career I was a Head of Key Stage 3 History and then in year four of my career I was Head of KS4. As a result, this made the transition much easier. I never applied for these roles; they were given to me. It must be noted I never did them in order to become an HOD as becoming an HOD was never what I wanted until the fifth year of my career. I did these roles because they needed filling, but I can now see that these roles were my stepping stones into middle leadership.

Which aspects of the role have been the most rewarding?

The ones that involve seeing ideas and thoughts come into fruition. It's also wonderful watching others grow. I had a Teach First trainee, and she has been amazing. It works best when you have staff buying into the vision.

Which parts of middle leadership are the toughest to get to grips with?

Being firm and assertive – killing the people pleaser inside of me – which involves saying no to staff at times, and having difficult conversations. I also had to have the confidence to allow myself to disagree with my line manager at times. You have to get used to the constant internal questioning of your decisions. Finally, delegating and trusting staff to do an equally great job on tasks is a hard balancing act.

What's the best piece of advice you've been given on how to be an effective middle leader?

I will never forget when Kate Jones told me to have a vision and share that early on with the department. As a result, my very first meeting with my department in September 2020 was about the vision and therefore changes that needed to be carried out. Communication with staff is key, especially because I am in charge of history on a dual campus, so communication ensures much-needed consistency and organisation.

Thank you to Emily for answering our questions about transition to middle leadership. You can follow Emily on Twitter @MissFolorunsho.

SENIOR LEADERSHIP

Conventional wisdom has it that the hardest career move to make is from middle to senior leadership. This is because the pool of talent who are interested in being an assistant headteacher or deputy head, and have middle leadership experience, is the largest pool of all. Think about it, middle leaders are in charge of bespoke groups; the head of maths advert isn't going to attract anyone from the French department. Now count up in your head all the middle leaders in your school (*how* many?). When an SLT post is advertised, there is already a lengthy queue forming. By contrast, the number of potential applicants is smaller for headship, just because there are fewer people at SLT level and not all will want to take that step. This means that when the top job becomes vacant, there may not even be one internal candidate. It therefore stands to reason that the toughest gigs to get are assistant headteacher or deputy head, especially once the floodgates have been opened to external candidates, where the same numbers game applies but at a national (or even international) scale.

So the first question to ask yourself is whether this is the role for you. What benefits will it bring to your professional life, and what impact will that have on your personal life? The single biggest leap you make in a leadership role is arguably from middle leader to senior leader. You experience the single greatest falling off in your teaching commitments, and it is the biggest step outside the classroom. It is also a move from a discrete area of school life (like a year group or department) into the realm of all that is whole-school. The stakes get higher too, and you will soon get to know which middle leaders are not good at leading up the way (expect them to pass you all their problems, while simultaneously scapegoating you at their break meetings).

The salary is better, but not to the point where you'll be off to your new villa in the south of France every holiday, not least because more of your holidays will now be taken up by work. Most middle leaders don't think their workload could get any higher, but somehow, at senior level, it does exactly that. The remit seems to defy the laws of time, in ways that only Stephen Hawking could explain. Longer hours at school, and more time spent working at home will definitely have an impact on your personal life, so it's important to prepare the people closest to you for the burden you are taking on.

By this stage you might be thinking that our purpose is to put you off leadership entirely. Far from it – we have loved our leadership roles, and strongly encourage others to take up the challenge. It's just that you need to go into these roles with eyes wide open, and becoming a senior leader is the hardest transition of all (even harder than moving into headship, potentially). It suits a certain type of person, who thrives in a crisis, enjoys the adrenaline-fuelled days, and has the capacity, efficiency and competence to get many things done quickly and effectively.

Which raises the question of when you are ready for this progression. It is a mistake to move past middle leadership too quickly, as many people do. There is so much valuable experience to be gained here, and also diversity. Broadly speaking, middle leadership offers the chance to explore the academic, pastoral, co-curricular and operational aspects of school life. If you have built up some experience in more than one of these areas – and ideally all – then you have a good chance of being ready to progress to senior leadership. The remits at senior level are, more often than not, highly diverse and there is also what we call the 'skip effect'. This is when the newly advertised deputy head post triggers a reshuffle of remits, and the other members of SLT seize the opportunity to dump their rubbish into the skip that is your new job description (which explains why you're now in charge of GDPR). You need to be ready for all this, and you need to have the capacity to take on more work, and more pressure.

Micromanagers drown at this level, because you simply cannot do everything by yourself. You need to be good at delegation, and you need to have that thick skin we mentioned before. Even the lightest days at this level feel like you're taking heat from all sides. You cannot take things personally, and you do need to be able to release pressure without letting it build up inside you. Perhaps one of the things that puts most people off is a curious one; public speaking. Are you comfortable giving assemblies, or presentations to parents at parents' evenings? Many people are put off making the step up because their toes curl at the idea of addressing an audience other than their own classes.

These are all generic qualities, but they are tangible things in the day to day frenzy of senior leadership. As with middle leadership, there is something strangely addictive about it, and also immensely rewarding. It takes a certain type of person, with some of the prerequisite qualities outlined above, to be able to do it. It certainly isn't for everyone – it is only really for a minority – and only you will truly know if you will thrive in these circumstances.

So let's say you are ready for it. We look at the recruitment process in the following chapter, but there are a few things that are particular to senior leadership applications. We've already discussed the 'pool of talent' problem, so you have to be able to outperform the other candidates in the field. This is easier said than done; you may have done everything right, only for one other person to have edged you in a photo finish. Given the level of competition here, you may have to apply for many jobs, and go through many disappointments over several years before landing the role you want.

Do not lose heart, and do keep going. Always ask for specific feedback from interviews, and work on those areas where you know you need either more expertise, or more experience. If time is on your side, taking on a different middle leadership role, or a more advanced level of professional learning, might make the difference you need to be the strongest candidate in the field. From the other side of the fence, the team doing the interviewing has a really tough job. They have to choose the candidate that best fits both the role and the school, and will likely be looking at a huge field of very talented people. It's part professional judgement, part chemistry, and part lottery. To manage your own expectations, it's really valuable to talk to other senior leaders in various different schools, and ask them about their interview experiences and how long it took them to get the role they wanted. You will often find that they went through ten or more unsuccessful applications before finally making the grade. And ask to see their CV from that final successful application; how does it stack up compared to yours?

Are you ready for it? There are many questions to ask yourself. Is it truly for you? Have you built up enough experience? Are you ready for the trial by fire that is the recruitment process? How will it affect you if you do get it? Probably best to take a long walk in the hills to answer all of these.

CASE STUDY: INTERVIEW WITH VICKY MASON – MOVING FROM MIDDLE TO SENIOR LEADERSHIP

Vicky Mason (@LittleMissB76) is an Assistant Rector at Dollar Academy. In 2020 she took the step into Senior Leadership, having previously been Head of Maths, and spent her first year in the role primarily navigating COVID guidance.

As a middle leader you were Head of Maths, which is a big remit. Which skills have been most transferable to your senior role?

Definitely my organisational and people skills. Leading a large department very quickly taught me the equal importance of both. You can be as organised as you like but if you don't listen to people and display empathy, sympathy and a listening ear as needed, then you will find any sort of leadership role to be an uphill battle.

You've just finished your first year as a senior leader. What are the biggest differences you've noticed between middle and senior leadership?

The main difference has been the increased input into strategic whole-school decision making which has been fascinating. The other, slightly more scary, difference is how many people now actively seek my advice. In a senior leadership position you are sometimes expected to have all the answers and this is not always the case. With a healthy dose of imposter syndrome, I am still surprised when people want to hear my opinion or ask my advice. But with a year now under my belt I have learned that it's OK to take time to consider options before giving out advice.

How difficult is it to make the transition into senior leadership?

In fairness the decision to go for it was hugely more difficult than the actual transition. I think I'm lucky because the senior leadership team who I work with are supportive and challenging in just the right measure. The decision to 'make the leap' took much more careful consideration. I felt the time was probably right and I had done my research, but it is a big step. When it came to it, the transition was difficult in that I was leaving my department, who, in hindsight, had come to be something of a comfort blanket for me, and heading out into a new world. The support of colleagues and family has meant a huge amount as well.

What professional learning have you done that was most useful in developing your leadership skills?

Two years ago I was lucky enough to follow Education Scotland's Middle Leaders Leading Change programme. Over three days (the final day was, sadly, virtual) we were encouraged to carry out self-evaluation of our leadership skills and there was a focus on coaching conversations which has proved to be of significant use. I am also a big fan of Andy Buck's Leadership Matters 3.0 and have used this extensively both in my own development and in assisting the development of others keen to move to leadership positions.

What sort of things should middle leaders consider before moving into senior leadership?

It's a very personal decision and I think self-awareness is key. Consider where your strengths currently lie and be honest in your areas for development. Find a mentor; someone who you trust to give you honest advice about making the move. Also think about how you will manage your time. Time is less structured in senior management, and it is difficult to plan a day as you might have been able to do when you were in the classroom. Your to-do list might never get done – in fact I learned to let my list go very early on in this stage!

Thank you to Vicky for answering our questions about her transition to senior leadership.

HEADSHIP

What does it take to be a headteacher? Tom Rees (@TomRees_77), author of the excellent book *Wholesome Leadership*, gave a memorable talk at researchED Blackpool in 2019 in which he looked at the language of various advertisements for headteachers. The same words kept cropping up: 'inspirational', 'transformative', 'dynamic', 'outstanding'. In short, you had to be Wonder Woman or Thor just to have the temerity to submit an application ('So Diana, Princess of the Amazons, how would you prepare the school for an inspection?'). What Tom argued instead is that teachers want three things from their heads: to be calm, competent and kind. See, it's not so hard after all, is it?

CASE STUDY: AN INTERVIEW WITH DR JILL BERRY – MOVING FROM DEPUTY TO HEAD

So now that we've demystified the 'hero leadership' nonsense, let's think about whether headship is right for you, how to go about making the progression, and what you can expect to find once in post. To be perfectly honest, the book has already been written about this by Dr Jill Berry (@jillberry102) who is calmness, kindness and competence personified. An experienced teacher of thirty years and headteacher of ten years herself, she did an EdD studying six deputy heads as they made their way through the recruitment process to eventually becoming headteachers, and then settling into the job. This research provided the basis for her 2016 book *Making the Leap: Moving from Deputy to Head*. The single best piece of advice we can give is to invest in this book, and to give you a flavour of it, Jill kindly agreed to answer some questions here.

You were a headteacher for ten years. What professional learning did you do to prepare for that?

I did attend face-to-face 'preparing for headship' courses, but I actually think you learn about leadership throughout your career, and that is the most useful professional development of all. In some ways, the best preparation for being a successful head is to be an effective middle leader, then a strong senior leader, constantly reflecting, evaluating, adapting and building your capacity and confidence over time. Being a deputy is an especially useful training ground, particularly if you are working with a head who constantly encourages you to consider, 'What would YOU do if...?' and if you have the opportunity to step up and 'be' the head from time to time in your deputy role, that's invaluable. I don't think leadership at different levels is different in kind (it's always about getting the best from those you lead), but it is different in scale, and you have to continue to build your knowledge of the leadership context (role and school) you find yourself in. In many ways you have to learn that in post; building the bridge as you walk on it, as Robert Quinn said.

In what ways do you think school leadership has changed in the time that you've been in education?

I've kept a diary since the 1970s and it's interesting to reread and revisit entries from earlier in my career and to remember what the experience of being a Head of Department, Head of Sixth Form, Deputy and Head was like as the decades passed. I think many elements of leadership are constant. There are specific contextual changes; in the last couple of years, for example, the pandemic, Black Lives Matter and the diversity/inclusion/equity imperative, Everyone's Invited, and the changes to teachers' pension arrangements have presented particular challenges (and opportunities) for schools and those who lead them. But in terms of vision and values, what leaders are trying to do, and how they go about it – finding the right balance of support and challenge, winning hearts and minds, building mutual trust and respect, lifting others rather than grinding them down – I don't think that has changed. And this came out of my doctoral research too; I looked at the transition to headship across time (from the 1980s onwards) and across the world, and the main elements of making the leap from deputy to head were remarkably consistent.

What professional learning would you currently recommend to people interested in moving into middle and senior leadership?

Make the most of every opportunity to develop your leadership skills and strategies in your current role (and every teacher is leading learning in the classroom from their first day in the profession, so think about the leadership behaviours you are employing as you strive to get the best from students, and consider how you can build your capacity to get the best from colleagues, too). As a middle leader, be intentional about considering what you are achieving in your specific domain, and how you could roll that out onto a larger canvas in a whole-school senior leader role. Build and use networks. Use professional development time for observing and shadowing those in the role you aspire to, and enter into discussions (face to face and via social media) which encourage reflection, fresh insights and ongoing learning. Read; there is so much out there (often written by practitioners) about leadership at all levels; blogs, articles and books. There is far more to professional learning than 'going on a course' but, of course, look out for appropriate training opportunities too. For example, we run a four-week online course on leading within the independent sector designed for both aspiring senior leaders and aspiring heads in the sector.

For your EdD you included a range of senior leaders as case studies. What personal qualities do you think they exhibited that helped them progress from deputy to head?

There were six participants, and they were all quite different, and leading schools in different contexts. But the ones who were particularly successful were, I think, clear about their reasons for wanting to be heads, and they were keen to prepare, during the lead-in period and in the early weeks and months, by tuning into the context of their new school (all were externally appointed) and building the most positive relationships (with students, parents, staff, governors, and across the wider school community within which their school sat) from the outset. Crucially, they had chosen carefully the school they wanted to lead, so there was an alignment between their vision and values and what the school stood for; they understood the legacy they were stepping into and were able to navigate the journey from inheriting the role to inhabiting it and making it their own.

You've been a professional mentor to a lot of headteachers. What's the best advice you can give about handling the pressures of the job?

It's all about finding balance, I think, which is easy to say and can be challenging to do. We need to appreciate that headship is a job – it's an important job – but it is a job and not our whole life and the sum total of who and what we are: it shouldn't define us. The best leaders are not those who work to the exclusion of all else. The strongest school leaders, in my experience, are able to keep a sense of proportion and a healthy perspective, and much of that is about being able to rest, refresh and re-energise (however it works for them to do that) so that their leadership is sustainable and they don't burn out. And I say that knowing how incredibly difficult it has been to achieve that since March 2020. Building strong teams and networks, making the most of the support – practical and emotional – which is out there is key. You are never alone, and you have to remember that and know when and how to mobilise that support.

After headship, you moved into research, training and consultancy. What has that been like personally and professionally for you?

I have loved it! I really enjoyed headship – which was the most satisfying, rewarding and joyful of the six leadership roles I had over my thirty year career – but I have no regrets about stepping back from the role after ten years (which had been my plan from the outset). I didn't want a second headship, but I still felt committed to education, so doing research, reading, writing and talking about education in a range of different contexts, supporting aspiring and serving leaders at all levels in a consultancy capacity; all this has been so fascinating and energising. I do touch on this in the final chapter of Making the Leap *– there is life beyond full-time headship, and it can be rich and full. And it's certainly something to look forward to!*

Thank you to Dr Jill Berry for answering our questions. In 2019, Jill gave a TEDx talk *Take a second look: Bring out the best in yourself and others* that can be viewed online. Jill is an advocate for the opportunities presented by social media for networking and professional development, tweeting @jillberry102 and blogging about education at jillberry102.blog. A QR code leading to the four-week online course on leading within the independent sector designed for both aspiring senior leaders and aspiring heads in the sector, can be found at the end of the chapter.

CASE STUDY: INTERVIEW WITH JANE LUNNON – THE LIVED EXPERIENCE OF BEING A HEADTEACHER

Jane (@_JaneLunnon) became the first female Head of Alleyn's School, Dulwich, in January 2021 having been Head of Wimbledon High School from 2014 to 2020. Her first book, *The State of Independence* was published in 2019 and she is currently Chair of the Teenage Mental Health Commission.

What made you want to be a headteacher?

Honestly, it was the fact that I am pathologically competitive and my twin sister had just got a headship which was the catalyst for me to start applying!

Other than that, I think the spur was the sense, after being Deputy Head, that perhaps I actually could do it! Most of my professional life, I'd looked at Heads with a mixture of awe and admiration as a rare breed of truly remarkable people who were some kind of chosen few, with great super-powers, put on earth to do this job.

And then, as I progressed through my career and got closer to the role and to the people doing it, I recognised that, astonishingly, they were in fact human, just like the rest of us, with their own strengths and weaknesses and idiosyncrasies. The only thing that distinguished them from everyone else, was that they were prepared to do it! To step up to the plate and give it a go. And once I realised that, I began to think in a completely different way about it. And think, maybe this could be me.

And finally, I'm an English teacher – so I love stories and the power of narrative – the way narrative can shape experience. As a Headteacher, of course, you get to write the narrative; to shape the story of your school, in the most profound and powerful way. That's incredibly exciting and a great honour and responsibility too. I love the fact that we hold the flame of our schools (like the Olympic torch, it gets passed from Head to Head and from generation to generation), and there is an essence in every school that it is our job to nurture and protect and keep alive. But around that, there is always a new and inspiring story to tell, and I love finding out what that story is – with the kids and the staff – and then getting on and telling it in all sorts of (hopefully innovative and stimulating) ways.

What was the most effective professional learning you did to prepare for headship?

Being a Deputy Head in two very different schools. Without doubt, that was the most important thing in terms of my learning. I was also fortunate to work (as Anthony Seldon's Deputy) for a Head who was very focused on the craft of leadership and who invited us, all the time, to consider what we were doing as leaders and how we were leading our teams and our projects forward. That was critical for me. But I think there is really no substitute for being very close to the role and seeing it play out and seeing what it involves. And if you're lucky enough to be Deputy for a Head who is keen to develop you and nurture you, you hopefully have increasing opportunities to step up and do bits of the Head's role. Properly standing in for him or her on occasions, doing the odd tricky parent talk, the tough sanctions, heading up Open Days. All of those things go into the 'critical experience bank' and all help you to recognise where your own strengths and development points are.

How hard was it to make the progression from being a deputy to being a head?

It's hard to answer that, because the answer is really polarised.

In some ways, it's the most natural thing in the world once you put your mind to it. The key thing is finding the right school to run. Which is why the highly rigorous and extensive selection process is so important. It's not just about them selecting you, it's about you selecting a school that is truly aligned to you and your values. Becoming a Headteacher is a bit like choosing someone to marry! It's a full-on commitment and you have to give your heart and soul to it. So you need to fall in love with your school, and I think the Head selection process is a bit like dating; you're trying to work out, is this the one, could I fall in love with this institution? Assuming you get that right, the transition into the Headship works, because your values, what you care most deeply about, are reflected in the values and assumptions of the school you've joined. And although there's some learning to do, there is also that lovely sense of being just where you ought to be; of coming home.

But all that said, it's also like nothing else. And the step up to Headship – the first time it's you, responsible, with the eyes of all staff and all students and Governors and parents and alumni on you – really is pretty daunting. I remember vividly how self-conscious I was as a new Head. As I stepped into the Head's office, the Head's routines, all the formalities which go with that particular role, I was very conscious for a long time, of how I was presenting myself and how others might see or judge me; that's tiring and takes some getting used to.

I also remember, after about a fortnight of being a new Head, thinking, 'Can someone else in the school please make a decision!' That's about the fact that people always want to cross-reference stuff with the new Head and, as a new Head, I didn't know what should be mine and what shouldn't be. So that was an important thing to learn and to adjust to: the amount of stuff that comes your way that you are required to have a view on!

Above all, the thing that takes time to absorb is the weight of responsibility you carry. The outcomes, the livelihoods, the wellbeing of so many people are dependent on so much of what you do or don't do as a Head. As, of course, is the success of the school you are running. That's monumental. And the only way to cope with all of that, particularly when you just start, is simply to not think about it. The 'don't look down' approach to new Headship. You're on a tightrope, navigating all sorts of things and there's quite a lot of empty space all around you. The thing is then, to simply do what is in front of you and not give too much headspace, right at the beginning, to the enormity of what you have taken on. Or, as my wonderful mother used to say: 'If you want to grow wings, you must do the next things'. That worked quite well for me!

How important was coaching in your journey to headship?

Incredibly important for me. I was fortunate enough, in my first Headship at Wimbledon High School, to have brilliant employers (the Girls' Day School Trust), who recognised the importance of investing in and supporting their new Heads. One of the ways they did this was by ensuring at least a year's worth of professional coaching was made available to all their Heads when they started in a school. It was truly wonderful and made all the difference to me. I met my coach once every three weeks and she was a fantastic, objective and empowering voice, allowing me to talk through problems that I couldn't share with anyone else and find my own solutions to them.

It was also, honestly, brilliant to have my twin sister taking on a new Headship at the same time as me. It meant that I spent a lot of the drive home from work every day, off-loading on to her, and she did the same! Having someone experiencing the same kind of challenges and excitements as you, simultaneously, is inordinately good for your confidence and sense of perspective. Also, it helps you to laugh at the stuff which is just plain ludicrous. And in my experience, there is a fair bit of that!

What impact does your job have on your personal life, and how do you try to manage that?

That's another very good question. The truth is, I don't much recognise the 'work/ life' dichotomy. I think one of the great privileges and benefits of a good education, is that you can perhaps be fortunate enough to do a job which gives you great satisfaction and great fulfilment and which, in effect, is as much your life as anything else. I don't like the idea that work is something that 'gets in the way' of me living my life; it doesn't. It's a powerful stimulation and a real honour and mostly a real pleasure, to do the job I currently do (running Alleyn's School) and I see that as much a part of my personal life as anything else.

All that said, I'm married to a Headteacher and our two wonderful children have grown up in schools and so they are very used to all of that. What is important is to make sure that you carry on doing other things you love (as well as the job that you love) and for me, it's been important to formally carve out time for that. So Friday evenings and Saturdays (apart from fixtures), I try to keep free time for me and my family to do stuff, and I am a massive believer in holidays as a critical time for restoration and fun and the redevelopment of 'brain food'! I guess the key is to do everything wholeheartedly and that means when I'm relaxing or having fun I am really giving my heart and soul to that.

What's the best thing about your job?

Articulating and living the story of my school with the incredible students and staff. Every day, that feels like the most wonderful privilege and I still can't believe I'm paid to do it!

What's the hardest experience you've had to go through as a head?

I suspect most of us will cite the last 18 months; navigating the realities and challenges of a global pandemic has been profoundly demanding for all. I've also taken over a new school in the middle of that; and I have to say, getting to know a new environment and a new community, in the middle of a full social lockdown, has not been easy.

Other than that, the hardest things, always, are the issues relating to individual pupils in crisis of one kind or another, and feeling profoundly unhappy. The mental health of our young people is a massive issue for all of us and, as a Head, you are acutely aware of the individuals who are struggling most and for whom life has become a huge challenge. As adults, teachers, Heads, our instinct – our very profound instinct – is to try to provide the solution. We are desperate to do so and it can be very difficult when the solutions are about time and patience and space, because we want to provide the 'answer' straight away and alleviate unhappiness and suffering immediately. The fact that we can't always do that – that's the hardest thing I've experienced so far.

What advice would you give to anyone considering moving into headship?

Go for it! Laugh a lot! Don't look down!

Thank you to Jane Lunnon for answering our questions about headship.

CASE STUDY: HEAD-HUNTING – HOW DOES IT WORK?

Finally, this is an area which will be a bit of a mystery to many, but it is a crucial area and worth knowing about. Executive search, known commonly as 'head-hunting', might seem like a 'dark art' but as you're about to find out, it is actually a widely used practice that provides schools and trusts with a better range of candidates for their top posts. Freddie Dennis, Partner and Head of the Schools Practice at Odgers Berndtson in London, does exactly this. He kindly agreed to give us a bit of insight into how the process works.

You work for Odgers Berndtson, an executive search and recruitment firm. What exactly does that mean?

Executive search is a specialised form of recruitment aimed at identifying and attracting senior leadership talent to an organisation. It exists to find the best match for both the position and the organisation, regardless of whether that person is actively looking for a new position or not, as is often the case in the education sector. Often an individual school or school group will develop a long-term relationship with Odgers Berndtson and, when a senior leadership position arises, we act as an extension of their business, identifying and engaging suitable candidates on their behalf. It is a research-led approach, meaning Odgers Berndtson will be paid a retainer fee upfront to carry out an extensive search in order to generate a large pool of top talent for a given opportunity.

What roles do you typically do search and recruitment for in education?

Interestingly, the market is maturing and as the competition for talent intensifies and external pressures increase, schools are beginning to use executive search to fill a wider variety of senior leadership roles. In the UK, we advise some of the country's leading HMC and GSA schools as well as working across the state-maintained sector, particularly with state boarding and state selective grammar schools. We are experienced at appointing Chairs, Governors, Heads (of Junior and Senior Schools), Deputy Heads, Bursars (COO's and FD's) and Development Directors. Internationally, we work with leading international schools and groups throughout Europe, the Middle East, Asia, Africa and Latin America.

How do people get on your radar?

Odgers Berndtson is a well-known and respected brand with a strong market presence in the UK and abroad, which means we are often contacted by talent at all levels within the sector for career advice. Having worked on a wide range of roles, and given our personal relationships within the sector, we have the ability to understand the career aspirations of individuals, allowing us to help them make informed decisions on their future. We also know how to reach many of the key people within the sector, and we are experienced in discreet approaches to gain interest in a role, enabling potential candidates to explore the opportunity confidentially. This gives us the chance to provide advice and support to prospective candidates.

What are the trends you are seeing in the education sector in terms of leadership recruitment?

Like many sectors, the schools sector is constantly changing, and the demands and expectations placed upon senior leaders are changing too. This change impacts upon senior leadership recruitment with a number of clear trends emerging in recent years. First, we have seen a higher turnover of heads, with the average length of a first headship significantly reducing in recent years. This has meant more business for executive search firms but has put significant pressure on the talent pool. Second, the internationalisation of education has meant we are increasingly operating in a global market for talent, with many able and experienced UK-based leaders opting to move abroad, which puts further pressure on the UK talent pool. Finally, we have seen the commercialisation of schools with leaders expected to be financially aware and business savvy, along with the more traditional aspects of school leadership.

Are there typical experiences or qualities that you tend to see in successful candidates?

Every executive search mandate is different with each client requiring different experiences and qualities in their successful candidates. In general terms, schools cannot afford to be complacent and must maintain academic excellence and high levels of achievement, often in very challenging circumstances. In terms of headship, today's Head will be an ambitious, globally-minded leader with the ability to shape, articulate and deliver a purposeful vision for a school. The Head must be visible and accessible, with the warmth and charisma to be a genuinely compelling figurehead for the school community. The Head will be innovative and creative, comfortable with technology, and with a leadership style which is collaborative, inclusive and empowering. They will embrace the marketplace while also grasping the commercial realities associated with operating within a competitive context. The Head will embody the values of the school and nurture its sense of community while also bringing a restless ambition to maintain its reputation and market position. They will have first-class communication and influencing skills, a passion for world-class teaching and learning and the determination to harness the school's strengths and build upon them.

How important do you think professional qualifications are in career progression?

Professional qualifications are important in terms of career progression. Our understanding of pedagogy and associated curriculums is constantly evolving and professional qualifications such as the NPQH ensure that one is at the cutting edge of evolutions in teaching and learning. Beyond this, the insight that such qualifications offer into strategy, risk management and operational delivery are looked upon favourably in the eyes of a selection committee, as well as the commitment and dedication demonstrated.

As an experienced recruiter, what advice would you give to candidates who are about to enter the education job market?

The days of schools relying solely on advertisements to recruit senior leaders are long gone. It is more than likely that candidates entering the senior leadership job market in the schools sector will come across executive search firms. My advice would be to get on the front foot and engage with the leading executive search firms, build relationships with their consultants, which will help immensely when making applications. Executive search is not a 'dark art' and should not be viewed with suspicion or reticence. Second, candidates will need to quickly grow a thick skin and learn to deal with rejection and disappointment. It is rare for a candidate to apply for their first senior role through head-hunters and to be appointed. Executive search processes can be very competitive and it can take multiple applications before success. Importantly, always ask for detailed feedback, learn from the application, and come back as a stronger candidate next time.

Thank you to Freddie Dennis for answering our questions and providing unique insight.

We started this chapter looking at how leadership is diversifying, so we are aware that looking broadly at middle, senior and headship levels seems to be reinforcing that hierarchy. That isn't the intention at all, and you should continue to think about the growing diversity available at each level. As the education system becomes ever more complex, so too do the career pathways that will open up. Ultimately, you are taking a further step away from classroom teaching each time and further into a world of managing people and resources, but that, paradoxically, gives you a greater influence over what happens in the classroom. If that's the right thing for you, have a think about the challenge questions posed below.

CHALLENGE QUESTIONS

- What is it about a leadership role that attracts you?
- What sort of leader do you want to be?
- Are you as comfortable leading adults as you are leading children?
- What level of responsibility and pressure would bring out the best in you?
- When do you feel you would be ready to make a change in responsibility, and how can you plan ahead for that?
- What support network do you have that can help you to prepare yourself in terms of learning, experience, and recruitment processes?
- Who are your leadership role models, and why?

QR CODES FOR FURTHER READING AND INFORMATION

Jill Berry TEDx Talk

https://www.youtube.com/
watch?v=Z5TAPmIVGfA

Jill Berry blog

https://jillberry102.blog/

Odgers Berndtson

https://www.odgersberndtson.com/en-gb

Education Development
Trust – Successful School
Leadership

https://www.educationdevelopmenttrust.
com/EducationDevelopmentTrust/files/a3/
a359e571-7033-41c7-8fe7-9ba60730082e.pdf

**Education Support –
Support for teachers and
school leaders**
https://www.educationsupport.org.uk

LIS Online
https://leadinganindependentschool.wordpress.com

CHAPTER 10

THE APPLICATION PROCESS AND INTERVIEW SKILLS

Purpose of this chapter: To equip the reader with the skills, knowledge and confidence to apply for an internal or external teaching or leadership role.

Every teacher will have to go through the application and interview process to secure their first post. Whether you progress internally or decide to move to another school the application and interview process plays a crucial role in career progression and promotion.

Frustratingly, for many that have filled in several application forms and written personalised letters, there currently does not exist a one size fits all duplicate application form. This means time, effort and dedication has to be invested into each application. The application process is an important first hurdle where many can fall, so before interview skills and questions are explored it's essential that we begin with a successful application.

APPLYING FOR AN INTERNAL POST

Think carefully before applying

A time can arise when teachers or leaders are ready to take the next step in their professional career with a new role within their school. Alternatively, it might not be the timing that is opportune but instead the role which has presented itself. If all is well in the current school an internal promotion can be a fantastic opportunity.

When applying internally the candidate often knows the people in the school community well; colleagues, students and families. An internal candidate has a good grasp of the way the school operates and the systems used. An internal candidate also has insight about the strengths, weaknesses and challenges that lie ahead for the school. It makes sense to seek an internal promotion, but it is worth considering it very carefully before applying.

There can be a pressure felt by some teachers to apply for an advertised role. For example, they have been teaching X number of years or served their time at the school, aren't they expected to seek a new opportunity or challenge? We do need to move away from this mindset. If a teacher, middle or senior leader is happy and content in their current role and wishes to remain in that position, this doesn't equate to a lack of ambition or indicate that they have simply given up. This obligation or sense of duty to apply for internal promotions is all too common. Applying for an internal promotion is an important decision not to be taken lightly or heavily influenced by others.

The attitude of 'I'll throw my name into the hat' when a promotion comes up or 'What's the worst that can happen?' doesn't reflect an understanding of the potential different outcomes. The candidate could be successful but then find themselves in a role they aren't prepared for or even enjoy. Or they can go into the process feeling that they have nothing to lose, and then become so invested in it that their perception changes. This can be either a good or a bad thing – it just depends on the person – but if you take this approach, prepare to feel very differently from how you expected to feel afterwards.

A key thing is to make sure that you are being authentic about applying for the right role, not just the status. When a middle leader is desperate for senior leadership, they can be prepared to take any senior leadership role that comes their way. Lots of leaders are flexible, adaptable and successful in a variety of roles, but there are others who will flourish with a teaching and learning responsibility and might sink while trying to manage data and timetabling.

There are various factors to consider. Is it the right role? Do you actually want to stay at the school? Teachers can find themselves staying at a school longer than they planned or expected due to promotion; it can feel like a blessing or a honeytrap. How will the internal promotion change relationships with other colleagues? For example, if you are internally promoted from middle to senior leadership, it can be a challenge to line manage the person who assumes your old post. It's not fair to impose the way you would do things onto another leader or constantly make them feel things were better when you were in charge.

There is also the possibility of not being successful. This isn't pleasant with any position applied for (we have both experienced this with internal applications) as naturally there is a bitter disappointment and range of emotions from sadness and deflation to anger and frustration. This can be made even harder with an internal post. External candidates can leave the school building and never look back. An internal candidate has to come into school the following day and continue to work in that environment alongside those who interviewed them and then decided not to appoint them, and also work alongside the successful candidate. The person appointed, whether they are internal or external, can be a constant reminder of the position you applied for but failed to secure, and relationships might have been altered (or damaged) during the interview process.

An effective senior leadership team will communicate information to candidates in a sensitive manner and ensure bridges aren't burned with kind, specific and helpful feedback being provided. This can be encouraging and provide good guidance for moving forward. Being unsuccessful in an internal post doesn't mean the door is closed forever, if anything the door is now open and advice has been offered as to how you can confidently walk through to the next stage.

The reality is this doesn't always happen. A generic 'You have been unsuccessful' email can be sent with no opportunity to seek feedback. If feedback is provided it might not be kind, specific or of any help, resulting in further confusion, tension and resentment. Again, with internal candidates you also have to keep in mind that the way you approach the feedback offered is really important. It can determine whether you are in the running for the next post that comes up (assuming you are still keen to change roles). Asking for feedback means you want to know what your strengths are, and what your areas for development are. It should never be phrased as 'Why didn't I get the job?' as this will come across as being personal and a deficit approach far removed from reflective practice. In short, approach the post-interview process with humility and magnanimity.

A pros and cons list can be helpful when considering applying for an internal promotion. It is also very important to carefully consider both outcomes. Is this the right school and the right role? What will happen if you are unsuccessful? Are there options to leave if unsuccessful, or is that not possible?

We can't predict the future and we won't know how we feel in a moment of time until that moment presents itself. Talking to someone trustworthy and experienced can also be beneficial, either within or outside of the school. Usually, time is against a candidate when applying for a position as a deadline looms, so time – as with most aspects of education – is not a luxury, but it's essential to take some time before making that decision.

THE APPLICATION LETTER AND CV

If you make the decision to apply for a position then it's likely you have a limited amount of time to write a strong letter of application. For an internal candidate this may only need to be brief as the school has already appointed you before and knows about your background and character. The main focus of this letter of application will be why you are the right applicant and best candidate for the position. It can be an opportunity to share information that isn't well known, for example any professional development undertaken or future goals and aspirations. It is vital that time and effort is invested into an internal application. This is not something to be rushed with the assumption that you're in the building and an interview is guaranteed, as this isn't always the case. This will show you are very serious about the position and take pride in all that you do.

An internal candidate has a lot of advantages at their disposal. Think about time spent at the school; the successes and celebrated triumphs as well as the areas for development for both yourself and across the whole school. What are the strengths you could bring to the role that will help the school? This insider knowledge can be very powerful, but it also works both ways.

The school knows about internal candidates already; from the reputation they have with colleagues and students, to relationships, and contributions to wider school life. Preferably, it would help if it is already known that you are aspiring to a new role and responsibilities. This can be made evident by taking opportunities to lead without a title (or time and pay sometimes) as doing so is valuable experience and demonstrates a range of attributes such as being hard working, enthusiastic and driven. Seeking qualifications such as NPQs (which are also for aspiring leaders) is another way to show a desire to learn and prepare for the role when it arises. It shouldn't be a complete shock to the senior leadership team when an internal candidate applies for a promotion, if anything they should be expecting it.

The letter written by an internal candidate should be both reflective and aspirational, sharing a range of examples of ways the candidate has contributed to the school already. In addition to this, the aspirations should focus on what else the candidate has to offer the school should they be successful. There is less risk with an internal candidate, and this is something to capitalise on while also demonstrating you have the enthusiasm and new ideas that an external candidate can bring.

The following advice can be applied for internal or external letters of application:

- Write a letter from scratch, don't update a previous letter or copy and paste from an example found online. It is a useful activity to read other examples, but the application has to be authentic and original.
- Compare the letter of application against the job description and specification. Is there a clear match between the two? How do previous experiences or skills link to the job description?
- Stick to the instructed limit. If it is one page, then condense to one page. Following basic instructions is essential as this demonstrates all documentation has been read carefully and clearly understood.
- Sometimes certain people are viewed as the 'stronger' or more likely candidates, but the application letter is an opportunity to shine. It is not the time to be humble or modest. Having said that, reflection and self-awareness of areas for development are important too. The weakness of the candidate shouldn't be the elephant in the room. If a candidate has been known for sending abrupt emails in the past then it could be worth acknowledging this with an explanation as to how this has been addressed, improved on and will continue to be something to be mindful of.
- Ask someone trustworthy to read over, sometimes a fresh set of eyes can see errors that the applicant can miss.
- Triple or quadruple check spelling, punctuation and grammar. It is likely in any promoted position that communication will be key; there is no excuse for typos.
- Learning difficulties, such as dyslexia, should not be a barrier for a successful application. Again, it is worth asking for support and although perhaps challenging, it is best to be open and honest about any learning difficulties.

Our key piece of advice is to cover three things:

- What you believe in personally – your educational philosophy.
- Your skills and achievements to date.
- What you will do in the new role and how you will rise to the challenge, for example what new skills you want to learn.

If a CV is required, it is vital that it has been updated since being appointed at the school (unless this was very recent). A CV should be a document we regularly review and update, but often we only do so when considering or applying for a new role or school. As we advised in Chapter 7, it's a good idea to review a CV once a year as a reflection task. If it is a struggle to add something new, this poses the question; how have you developed in the last twelve months?

A standard CV should be two pages. Previous roles in other schools might have provided relevant experience for the advertised role, so that will be worth emphasising. A CV and a letter of application shouldn't replicate each other, they should complement each other. Anything that could not be included in the letter of application can be added to the CV and *vice versa*. Gaps in employment history on a CV need to be addressed as it can look suspicious, and you may not have the opportunity to explain them at interview.

When shortlisting it can be very frustrating to re-read content that is repeated in different places on the same application; the aim should be to impress the reader, not bore them. This is especially true if there is an application form to complete that has questions on it, and the candidate then just repeats everything they say in their letter of application. An internal candidate doesn't need to focus as much on character and personality traits because they are not entering the interview room as a stranger, and there is already a context, history and relationship. If there is too much to include, for both the CV and letter, then simply allude to it and it can be discussed further at the next stage: the interview.

INTERVIEWING AS AN INTERNAL CANDIDATE

The first thing to get right is your attitude to being up against external candidates. It's highly likely there will be external candidates applying, and you can see them as a threat, thus undermining your own confidence. Remember, external candidates often ask if anyone being interviewed is internal. They can automatically feel a sense of disappointment if there are internal candidates because they feel at a disadvantage. Internal candidates will know a huge amount about the school that they simply won't. Internal candidates will already have established relationships, and although external candidates have their own advantages, just remember that you are probably in the stronger position.

Internal candidates can feel disappointed when external candidates are invited to interview; it may appear that the selection panel don't consider anyone currently at the school to be worthy, but that is unlikely to be true. It's a wise decision to advertise externally, to view other candidates and hear from other voices in education, but that doesn't mean internal candidates have been dismissed.

By law in the UK, Headteachers have to advertise all positions, although how they choose to do so can vary, and an advert on a school website will not gain as much attention, or as many applications, as advertising on a national website such as the TES.

External and internal candidates should both seize the opportunity to impress and shine at an interview, regardless of the various advantages or disadvantages they might possess. Something to note here for internal candidates is that there may be a preconceived notion of you that you need to challenge. Do the SLT have a fixed view of you? To paraphrase Robert Burns, you need the gift of being able to see yourself as others see you. If you can get a sense of that, then think about how you can show a different side of yourself in the interview. This is tough, but it is often the most difficult hurdle an internal candidate will face.

At the interview there will be lots of standard questions – safeguarding will always arise – but also some potentially challenging and tricky questions. It's important to prepare for the interview. This can include searching example questions, speaking to others about their interview experiences and perhaps even carrying out a mock interview with someone senior or more experienced.

It is standard practice to ask all candidates the same questions during an interview, to ensure the process is fair, but this can throw some internal candidates. It can seem insulting to be asked about your character or professional development by people you would assume already know this, but instead view this as an opportunity to elaborate or confirm what the panel already know.

Should an internal candidate ask questions at the end of an interview? Ultimately, no one should ask questions just for the sake of it. It is perfectly acceptable to say 'No thankyou I do not have any questions to ask'. Interviewers can become frustrated when people ask questions at an interview which aren't relevant, or to which they could already have found the answer. The interview day can be very demanding for everyone, so no one appreciates time being wasted when there is an important decision to be made.

However, you can probably do better than this by saying that you did have questions, but they have been answered during the interview, which shows you do have curiosity, but that the interview was rigorously done. An internal candidate knows about the school and the role so may feel that they shouldn't ask any questions. However, we would caution against thinking that way, especially if your silence at the end gives the impression that you think you know everything there is to know. This is a great chance to put your interviewers on the spot and show your curiosity, so try to have at least one good question up your sleeve. If there are any questions about the role then it is best to ask them as soon as possible as the answer may shape your decision to apply or not. However, if the chance hasn't arisen or it is something you realised after applying, the end of an interview can be the time to ask. Questions can be asked during the interview, which can shift the interview to a more conversational style, promoting a dialogue between the interviewer and interviewee. And don't forget, a question about support and professional development in the role is always important.

Context is always key but if there is a specific question that needs answering write it down and take it into the interview; an interview is a high stakes situation meaning people can become flustered and forget what they had hoped or planned to ask. A really good piece of advice is to have two or three things in your mind that you really want to get across during the interview; if you manage to say these, you can reflect afterwards feeling that you gave a true account of yourself. It's always frustrating to think after the fact of the things you wished you had said. However, you can't say everything, so have a short mental list of the things that really matter most to you, and if you haven't covered them, try to bring them up at the end.

Finally, although internal it's still a professional courtesy to offer thanks and show gratitude for the opportunity. Any time we apply for a position it forces us to reflect, evaluate and set goals; all of which are very useful. How a candidate reacts to the news – good or bad – is very important. If it's good news with a successful outcome, then emotional intelligence suggests showing sensitivity if other internal candidates have applied and were not successful. Gloating in the staffroom is not advisable but celebrating privately with those around you is well deserved. If unsuccessful it can be tempting to express anger and upset, but this might not bode well if another opportunity for promotion presents itself, and a bad reaction might confirm to others it was the right decision to make. As celebrations should be private so should ranting and venting if needed.

If an internal candidate wants progression and promotion more so than staying at their current school and has been unsuccessful, the next step in the plan is clear; to start looking for a role in a new school. If you've applied several times for a promotion and it has never happened, it is perfectly fair to ask if you are unlikely ever to be successful. It may be painful to hear this being admitted, but it does at least save you time on fruitless applications and can make up your mind to focus your energies on an external application.

APPLYING FOR AN EXTERNAL POSITION

Many teachers can find moving to another school a breath of fresh air. After the initial adjustment to the different systems and routines it can be an opportunity to gain new experiences, teach different content, work with new people, and if needed it can provide a clean slate. The move to another school can be for personal reasons, a new challenge, or a promotion, but whatever the reason there are once again initial hurdles to overcome during the application and interview process.

Moving to a new school is a very important life change and perhaps the grass isn't always greener on the other side! Doug Belshaw, senior leader and author of *#getthatjob – An educator's guide to finding, applying, and interviewing for a teaching-related job* (which can be freely accessed online via a QR code at the end of this chapter) writes about the importance of being selective when applying to schools:

> One of the best things you can do when applying for jobs is to be selective. It's easy to get desperate, either because of money or stress, but it's important to make sure that you've done your homework on what you might be letting yourself in for. Read everything you can online and, if the deadline is far enough away, phone the school and ask them to send you anything (newsletters, for example) that aren't on their website.[39]

While this extra research does involve more time and energy, it is worth it.

The advice about an internal application also applies here, with the caveat that with an external vacancy your application is the only chance you get to make a great first impression, so it's essential to get the basics right. Have you spelled the name of the school correctly? And the name of the person you're corresponding with? Is there a word count stipulated? Are you within it? And if a CV is not requested, then don't send one as it will have been deemed unnecessary for the initial screening process. Our advice here is the same as we would give to students about to sit an exam: take your time, read the question, and make sure you understand what is being asked. And when you've finished, check, check, and check again.

---

39. The Guardian (2013, 9 January) *Job tips for teachers: how to write a winning application.*
https://www.theguardian.com/teacher-network/teacher-blog/2013/jan/09/teacher-job-tips-write-winning-application

The application form tends to cover basic yet important information, but the accompanying letter is what marks the difference between candidates. When writing a letter of application as an external candidate it is useful to remember you are an unknown, so the more that can be gauged from the application the better. It isn't easy to let personality shine through, but it is possible. We have both read applications where the candidates have tried to be funny and it has backfired. We have also both read applications where a candidate has made us laugh and made us want to meet them and find out more. This is the goal of an application letter – not to make someone laugh – but to make the person reviewing your application want to find out more, meet you and consider you for the advertised role.

A SIDEWAYS MOVE?

When teachers apply for the same role they currently perform – whether that be a classroom teacher, middle or senior leader – but in a different school it is often viewed as a sideways move. However, there are many benefits to doing this. A Head of Year role is a good example of this. A Head of Year 7 deals with very different issues to a Head of Year 11. Head of Year 7 will be supporting with transition, induction and helping younger children feel settled, in contrast to a Head of Year 11 who is supporting students dealing with exam pressures, life choices about their future and any other issues young adults face. In a different school environment, the size of the cohort can vary, the level of support and professional development might differ, and it can broaden a leader's repertoire as they adapt to working in a new context.

A Head of Department might move from line managing a small team of staff to a larger department, putting their existing leadership skills to use while having the opportunity to line manage a larger team. In fact, taking on the same role in a totally different context can often be harder than being promoted within the same setting. From an interviewer's perspective, someone taking on a leadership role similar to their current role can provide confidence that they are not learning from scratch but can bring with them a host of skills, experiences and insight as well as learning and developing new ones. The potential downside for the interviewee is that they run the risk of coming across as someone who just wants more of the same or thinks they are the finished article.

During the application process it is important to address the 'sideways' move. What is your motivation behind this decision? Is it time to leave the current school and experience a new environment? Is it due to the reputation of the school that makes it appealing to continue the same leadership role but in a new context? Are there other factors that play a part? If this isn't addressed in the application then it could be asked at interview as people can often be curious as to why someone would leave their current school, if not for a promotion.

AN EXTERNAL PROMOTION

The challenge with an external promotion to leadership is that not only does the school not know you, but they also need to be convinced that you are ready for the next step in your career progression, so there is an element of risk on various levels. There will likely be internal candidates who also lack the leadership experience but already have their foot in the door and are well known in the school community. There could be other external candidates who are applying and making a sideways move – or even taking a step down – which perhaps make them more of a 'safer bet'. However, despite all those possibilities it is important not to become fixated on other people, and instead invest in a stellar and successful application to show that you are the right candidate for the right role in the right school.

Chris Hildrew, Headteacher and author, provides this helpful advice about what he is looking for when reading letters of application:

> *Straight to the top of the pile go those whose letters explain why they are applying for this particular job at this particular school. Also a winner are those who show exactly how they fit the person specification not only through what they've already done but what they'd like to do next. Above all, though, I like to know exactly why the applicant is a teacher in the first place. A good application will get you the interview; a good interview will get you the job.*[40]

This confirms what we said above; try to get a blend of what you believe as a teacher, what you've done and what you will do. That's the holy trinity of the application letter.

---

40. The Guardian (2013, 9 January) *Job tips for teachers: how to write a winning application.* https://www.theguardian.com/teacher-network/teacher-blog/2013/jan/09/teacher-job-tips-write-winning-application

INTERVIEWING AS AN EXTERNAL CANDIDATE

The first thing to emphasise here is that you are being interviewed from the moment you arrive at the school to the moment you leave. It's amazing how many candidates get ruled out because they are impolite to the receptionist when they sign in. If you think that information isn't passed on, think again. Everyone you come into contact with during the interview day might be asked for feedback on you, so don't naively think that the only bit that counts is when you are in the interview room. In fact, Robin remembers one candidate who did themselves no end of harm when the hotel they stayed in sent a complaint to the school about their behaviour and the mess they caused. Golden rule to remember; people within a community talk to each other, and this isn't limited to just the school community. This might make you feel paranoid, but actually all you have to do is be friendly and polite. If you can show that you are a natural fit for the school community, you have answered one of the biggest questions in the mind of your prospective new employer.

All external candidates have one thing in common; they do not work at the school they are applying to. At the interview it is likely an external candidate will be asked a question along the lines of 'Why this school?' or 'What do you know about this school?' It is worth taking time to carefully consider this and think about a range of aspects such as the school values and geographical location.

When Kate was interviewed for a position as a history teacher as an NQT, the Headteacher asked Kate what she knew about the history of the local area. This was not something Kate was prepared for, and her answer simply wasn't very good (what is known as 'blagging' or 'winging it'). On reflection, asking a question about local history to a history graduate and candidate is a good idea. Fortunately, Kate's lack of knowledge about Buckley town didn't go against her and she secured the job! The Headteacher, Rosemary Jones OBE told Kate it wasn't just history teachers she asked that question to but every candidate she interviewed. If they didn't know about the local area it didn't mean they were disregarded, but it did show the candidate that the local town of Buckley and its history were very important to her and the school community.

Common mistakes are things like memorising the school values or motto from the school website but failing to make a real effort to learn about the school community. Explore social media sites, read news articles, try to speak to people who have knowledge of the school, its history and the local area. Anyone can carry out a quick Google search and scan the school website, so you should go beyond that. This will also help you as a candidate because school websites can be misleading or lacking in substance. The more you learn about the school you are applying to the better. Don't wait until you have been shortlisted either, do this research during the application process so that one of the things which shines through in your application letter is that you have an understanding of the school in terms of its history and direction for the future.

Another key piece of advice we would give to external candidates is to prepare a range of examples of different scenarios you have experienced which you can discuss at interview. An external candidate is often an unknown candidate so sharing relevant examples of how situations have been dealt with will help provide the interviewer with further insight as to how you would react in the future and fit in within the school environment.

The team interviewing external candidates will have never seen them on a bad day, so the only weaknesses they will be aware of are the ones the candidates choose to share during the interview process, unwittingly show, or which are discerned from their references.

An external candidate can bring new and innovative ideas and strategies from a different context and environment. Although arguably this shouldn't be a factor, it can be; the external candidate might be working at a school rated 'Outstanding' or one which has gained a wonderful reputation, and can bring their experiences and knowledge of working in that setting and apply it to a different school context.

QUESTIONS FOR EXTERNAL CANDIDATES TO ASK DURING INTERVIEW

We've already covered this, but the final question asked in each interview tends to be 'So, do you have any questions for us?' For the external applicant, this can be a great opportunity to find out more about a potential new employer, the school, your role and what the future may hold. The interview panel will also be assessing you on the questions you ask. As such, you should spend time before the interview carefully considering what questions you will ask and writing them down, as you are in a high stakes situation in an interview and may forget.

During the course of the interview, discussions can take place and your questions might have been addressed and answered. You could ask them to elaborate and extend or you could quite simply say that your questions have been answered, which is much more preferable than asking questions for the sake of it, or asking questions that actually demonstrate a lack of research. Below are some useful questions to ask at the end of your interview.

Ask for information you couldn't find during your research. An error that too many candidates make is asking questions when they could have found out the information themselves. Don't ask about a policy unless you have checked if it is available online or contacted the school in advance and asked to view it. Then, if you haven't had the chance to view the school behaviour policy – for example because it is not available to the public – then asking about it at an interview is perfect timing.

What is the best thing about working at your school? A lovely question to ask and often a lovely question to answer. This can end the interview on a positive note for all. The responses can be very insightful, too. If the answers include the students, staff, professional development or support, then all of those factors create a strong sense of the school culture. If someone answers that the best thing is free car parking on site, then that is very telling, too!

How will you support my professional development? Perhaps, one of the most important questions that can be asked. This information might be available in the job advertisement but you might want to find out more. If there is no reference to professional learning then you should definitely ask about it. This shows that you have an interest and desire to develop and that the support of a school is essential for you to do so. If the response is vague and you are keen to delve deeper you could ask if there is a staff professional learning library and/or how inset days are delivered to gain further insight.

Ask about school/departmental areas of development and priorities. It is very likely that candidates will be asked to talk about their areas for development, in addition to talking about their strengths. A reflective teacher will be aware of their areas of strength and areas of development, and this is something a school should be aware of in terms of whole-school improvement. This information could be public, and if so it is worth exploring it in slightly more depth at the interview. During the recruitment process, schools naturally want to create a positive impression to attract strong candidates, so they may tend to focus on strengths rather than areas of development, but this is important to know.

How do you support teacher wellbeing at your school? Wellbeing is becoming more widely discussed in schools and this is a very good thing. Many teachers can be reluctant or afraid to ask about mental health and wellbeing at interviews in case they give the impression that they are weak and need support, which they fear might put off potential employers. The reality is we all need support at some point in our lives, either professionally or personally. You may not be struggling now but anything can happen in the future. It will be reassuring to know how a school would support you.

THE CLOSER

A 'closer' is where the interview ends on a strong, positive and memorable note thanks to a closing statement from the candidate which is brief and positive about their suitability and potential for the role. The moment to go for this is when the interviewer wraps up by asking if you have any questions or anything else you would like to add. Most people go for the usual 'No, I'm fine thanks', and some give the distinct impression that they are relieved it is finally over and they can escape the room. Instead, the closer provides a quick, positive, confident statement that ends the interview on a high. This can be difficult to master, as it's important to not appear arrogant or forceful but instead keen and confident to leave a lasting positive and memorable impression. The main thing a closer does is show that you would love to do the job and would take it if offered (needless to say, you should only deploy it if you do actually want the job).

Examples of 'closer' statements:

'Thank you for taking the time to interview me for this position. I am excited about the prospect of working in this role/school and being a part of a highly motivated team.' This is an example of gratitude, enthusiasm and confidence without being arrogant, no one should assume they have the job in the bag!

'Thank you for meeting with me. It sounds like a great fit based on my experience and the focus the school has moving forward.' This shows a desire to work at the school, confidence and clear vision for the future, as any candidate must be able to clearly see themselves in that role in that school.

'I carried out extensive research on the school beforehand and was really excited about this interview. This has been reinforced by everything I have heard, observed and learned today. I appreciate the time you have taken with me and I am positive about my ability to perform successfully in this role.' Again, this ends an interview with enthusiasm and shows a desire for the position in that particular school as well as reassuring the panel that you are more than capable of taking on the role.

Avoid closer statements which seem arrogant, for example assuming the job is secured or asking when to sign the contract! Showing that you really want the job is important, but acting like you are not bothered by the outcome isn't playing it cool, instead it shows a sense of apathy and lack of ambition or motivation.

VALUES-BASED INTERVIEWING

Many schools now use values-based interviewing (or values, behaviours and attitudes interviewing). This is totally different to a competency-based interview in that it is not about your CV, but about your values, and whether they align with those of the school community. It started for child protection reasons in the aftermath of the inquiry into the Soham murders, which showed that there were insufficient safeguarding procedures in the interview process for people working with children. This was why police checks (known initially as a CRB, and now DBS) came into effect. However, a specific method of values-based interviewing was developed by the NSPCC and later became widely used in the NHS. You can understand why schools find it useful too, and why it is being increasingly used for teaching jobs (as it is at Robin's school).

You can't prepare for these interviews, and candidates that do by trying to research potential answers online usually end up struggling because they come across as being rehearsed. What it really involves is being asked a question which relates to one of the school's core values, where your answer comes from giving examples from your own life around how you align with that value. The purpose of this is simple; to see if you will be a good fit for the school community. As we all know, there are some schools where we would be perfectly happy, and others where we would not. It doesn't mean that you are not a good person, or that the school isn't a good one, it just means you have a different approach to life, and that's fine. So if you are told that you are being given a values based interview, don't panic. It's just a conversation and it actually benefits you. If you're not aligned with the school's values, you've saved yourself from what would be a very unhappy move.

APPLYING TO TEACH INTERNATIONALLY

If you decide to apply for a teaching position internationally then you need to prepare for the interview as best you can, as you would for any interview. To live and teach internationally is a major life change. The international education scene is much more transient, so it is vital that schools appoint the right candidate. This can sometimes mean a much lengthier process than applying for a position in the UK because a lot of time and money is invested in the candidate, including aspects such as moving allowances, visa processes, induction and more.

When applying for a job overseas for the first time it can be very daunting not knowing what could be asked at an interview. There will be questions that are similar to those asked in the UK but there will be some additional questions unique to the context of the school.

Why do you want to work at this school and in this country?

This is a common interview question, but it is essential in an international context. The answer should focus on both elements; the school and the location. Candidates can sometimes focus their answer on the country, this is important as it shows they have researched the country they want to live in and have a cultural awareness, but that simply isn't enough. There is an ethical element here; are you happy to work in a country that has a problematic human rights record, or isn't free and democratic? Research on this element is highly advised.

Candidates need to know about the school too. If an answer focuses on moving to a country because of the weather and lifestyle, that's great but what about the school? Why that specific school? What do you know about the school? What appeals to you? Why does it stand out? Why do you think it would be the right school for you? Those are questions to consider and prepare for.

International schools invest a lot of money into their school websites as it is a competitive market, but often these websites are not very helpful, focusing on the key strengths rather than providing much realistic insight. If possible, try to find a contact who either works at the school or has knowledge of the school from being part of the local area.

AN ONLINE LESSON SNAPSHOT

It is becoming more common for candidates to deliver an online lesson, although there are a range of variations as to how this can be done. The first option is for a candidate to pre-record a lesson. This shows how a teacher plans, communicates and delivers a lesson. However, a pre-recorded lesson doesn't show how a teacher interacts with students, responds to questions or manages their classroom. An alternative to this is to deliver an online lesson. This can be carried out on platforms such as Zoom, Microsoft Teams or Google Meet, and although not ideal, it can give an overview of how the teacher engages with learners. There are challenges with this, but it helps to have a strong internet connection, a quiet space, and to just ensure that you are thoroughly prepared.

The school will want to know about your classroom practice. Be ready to discuss a lesson that went well and be able to explain why it went well. Make sure you can describe the lesson in detail from beginning to end. Describe a lesson for the subject you are applying for; so if you are applying for a history position the interviewer wants to hear about a history lesson not a politics or geography lesson. You could explain how you would prepare and deal with any potential behaviour issues or questions that arise. Also be willing to describe a lesson that didn't go to plan. This shows reflection and the ability to recognise and learn from mistakes and weaknesses.

What can you offer the school outside of your subject?

International schools pride themselves on the co-curricular provision they provide for their students. All teachers are expected to run co-curricular clubs and events, this is not restricted to the PE department and the arts as academic clubs are also offered to students. You can often find out what co-curricular clubs you could support which are already on offer such as chess, debating, Model United Nations and a wide range of sports, often with high-quality facilities and resources.

What strategies do you use to support EAL (English as additional language) learners?

Most international schools have a diverse student body. There will be local students from the region in addition to students from all corners of the globe. This may or may not be something you have experience with in your current school. If you do, then be ready to share the strategies you use and explain why they work. If you haven't had experience working with many EAL students, then read about this before the interview as it will be something you will be expected to do if appointed. It is worth learning about the student body and curriculum provided so you can be as prepared as possible; at the interview stage and also if appointed.

How would you deal with a safeguarding concern?

This is a standard interview question (it could be phrased differently, or it could potentially be a scenario to respond to). It is a compulsory question schools have to ask in the UK, and that is also the case in many international systems. The answer can be brief as you mainly need to show an awareness that all safeguarding issues must be reported as soon as possible to the Child Protection Officer (CPO) or Designated Safeguarding Lead (DSL). There could be information available on the school website about their policy or you could request this in advance because this is a question not to be taken lightly or to get wrong in any context.

The reason we are focusing on this question for international teaching is that different countries have different rules and even laws when it comes to safeguarding, so this is worth considering and researching prior to the interview. The safeguarding question could also be scenario based, where you are given a situation and asked how you would handle it. You can practise answering this by running through some safeguarding issues that you have come across, and considering how you would explain them. You'll see that it comes down to policy, process, and professional judgement. The most important thing is to show that you are putting the safety of the child at the forefront of your thinking.

FINAL THOUGHTS

Throughout the process, whether applying internally, externally or internationally, keep a positive outlook and attitude. Everyone within the profession has aspects of their job they dislike and it is important to be honest, open and reflective, but a school will not appoint a negative person or someone they perceive to be negative. A classic example is when you are asked 'Why are you leaving your current school?' Don't start ranting about how much you dislike your school, it is a surefire way to rule yourself out of a move.

The interview process, whether in person or online, is a two-way process, where the school learns about the candidate being interviewed and the interviewee can learn more about the school. It has to be a mutual fit.

CHALLENGE QUESTIONS

- How often do you update, review and reflect on your CV?
- What would your ideal role be?
- How are you currently preparing for this ideal role?
- Would you be willing to move school for this role?
- Reflecting on your previous interview experiences, how do you perform under pressure?
- What are your strengths and weaknesses during an interview?

QR CODES FOR FURTHER READING AND INFORMATION

TES Jobs
https://www.tes.com/jobs/

Teaching Vacancies – Gov.uk
https://teaching-vacancies.service.gov.uk/

International School Services
https://www.iss.edu/services/teacher-recruitment

Doug Belshaw – #getthatjob
https://issuu.com/dajbelshaw/docs/getthatjob

CHAPTER 11

THE INTERNATIONAL TEACHING LIFE: TEACHING ABROAD

Purpose of this chapter: To provide an overview of the different elements of teaching abroad for readers who are considering this or simply want to find out more.

Kate and Robin have experience teaching internationally (both in the United Arab Emirates) and have both visited schools around the world. Robin was a teacher of history and Head of History and Theory of Knowledge (TOK) in Dubai from 2008 to 2011. He has also worked with schools across Europe, the Middle East, Australia and New Zealand, and taught at a summer school in Hong Kong. Kate has been a teacher and middle leader at two schools in Abu Dhabi since 2016. She also worked with the British Council for two years, as part of a project for the Connecting Classrooms programme, which involved visiting a school in Sri Lanka and hosting a return visit to Wales for teachers and senior leaders. In addition to this Kate has volunteered at a nursery in Thailand and has visited schools in Hong Kong, Bahrain, Qatar and across the UK and Europe. Hence why we both felt it was important to include a chapter focusing on international teaching as it has enriched both of our lives, professionally and personally.

This could be a book in itself and it is far too broad in terms of countries, schools, and packages to cover in one chapter. However, we do want to provide teachers and leaders considering moving abroad with as much information as possible; so in addition to this chapter we have created and launched a website https://theinternationalteachinglife.com/ which we will regularly update with international case studies and blogs linked to international teaching.

The 2020 COBIS research report *Teacher supply in British International Schools 2020*[41] had the following key findings:

- *Teachers move in both directions between the UK and international school sectors, with many teachers returning to the UK with valuable transferable skills.*
- *Positioning teaching as a global profession would enrich the professional experience of teachers, allow UK schools to benefit from the repatriation of skills developed in an international context, improve teacher retention, and enhance the attractiveness of the profession to increase recruitment to Initial Teacher Training.*
- *More consistent recognition of service overseas is needed to ensure teachers with international experience are welcomed, encouraged and supported to enter or return to the UK school sector.*
- *Teaching in a British international school gives teachers the opportunity to develop personally and professionally and supports teacher retention.*
- *Teachers in the international sector have positive perceptions of their experience including workload and work/life balance.*
- *Teacher supply continues to be a challenge, but the international sector is contributing to the growth of the global teacher workforce, in part by engaging with Initial Teacher Training.*
- *Increasing international training opportunities and growing the workforce in a scalable way could reduce stress on domestic supply if barriers to training new teachers internationally and teacher mobility were removed.*

International teachers have struggled in recent years due to the pandemic as this has meant many flights have been restricted and teachers who may have returned home to the UK often weren't able to do so for a long time. However, despite these challenges, the consequent pandemic 'Zoom Boom' has meant that teachers around the world have been able to engage in live webinars taking place in other countries and stay connected with those back home. If time zones are an issue, there is now a wealth of high-quality professional learning materials available to view online at a time to suit any teacher wherever they are in the world. International teachers have never been more connected to the UK in terms of professional learning and development.

---

41. COBIS (2020) *Teacher supply in British international schools.* https://resources.finalsite.net/images/v1591875549/cobis/sozjbejmrn1fpuigd8ne/COBISTeacherSupplyReport2020FINAL.pdf. Please note that this was compiled between January and March 2020, so doesn't take into account the impact of the pandemic.

THREE INTERNATIONAL TEACHING MYTHS BUSTED

1. International teaching is for the young and single.

It's often believed that most international teachers are young professionals, who, after a few years of experience teaching in the UK, embark on an exciting adventure abroad. As well as looking for adventure, some young teachers go with the aim to save enough money for a property deposit for their return to the UK, and this is arguably true of many teachers abroad. Rising property prices are making it increasingly difficult for teachers early on in their careers to be able to save enough money for a property deposit but with the international teaching package and wage (sometimes tax-free, but more information about the packages below), it becomes more of a reality and therefore very appealing. Young teachers without children, a mortgage and other commitments are able to travel the globe living and teaching in different exotic locations. Places such as Dubai, Madrid, and Bangkok attract young professionals due to the lifestyle, nightlife, culture and more.

Conversely, there are many other teachers with families who are showing that not only is it possible to teach abroad with a family in tow, but it can provide them with a wonderful and enjoyable quality of life. This is especially true of couples where both spouses are teachers. The international teaching package is just as – if not more – attractive for couples with children. Annual flights, accommodation and healthcare are often provided for the whole family. Many international schools offer places for the children of staff, often with a significant or full discount (typically for a maximum of two children, but this does vary considerably). Teachers who have children at the school are often supported with childcare for Inset days, meetings and so on (again this can vary). Their children can access a high-quality education with the British or American curriculum, or the International Baccalaureate (IB) if it is an all-through school. An additional benefit many see is that their children can be part of a multicultural and diverse society and become well-travelled young people. A number of teachers who own properties in the UK rent their house out to pay the mortgage while they live in accommodation provided by their employer. Many chose to buy property in the country they move to as a form of investment.

There are challenges for those with families, as many teachers with young children often miss the support from family that they would receive at home. However, within most expat communities there is a closeness that is more defined and interdependent than school communities in the UK. In the UK teachers are surrounded by their friends and family outside of work, but due to the absence of friends and family when living abroad, colleagues become very close, very quickly. A fair number of expat teachers with families choose to get extra support with a nanny or maid which is possible due to the international package and wage.

Families with children are less likely to travel between different international schools and countries because of the impact this can have on their children. That said, some teachers do, and many children cope well with the change. Some, however, can struggle with culture shock and feel unsettled. If teachers can find the right school in the right setting, they can happily settle for several years. Spending time doing research before accepting a contract can make a huge difference to making sure the move is the right thing for everyone involved.

2. It's difficult to secure a job in the UK on return.

There are some elements of truth to this myth but generally the majority of teachers who return to the UK find positions at schools. The difficulties can occur during the interview process, as an international teacher might be unable to fly to the UK for an interview or it may be too much of a risk to embark on an expensive selection procedure with no certainty of securing the job. As many interviews have switched to online platforms these risks have been somewhat mitigated, which has greatly helped international teachers when applying for jobs in the UK.

Social media, online news platforms and digital professional learning has meant that international teachers are no longer out of touch with educational news, practices and updates in the UK. Many international teachers, especially those who plan to return to the UK, make a conscious effort to regularly stay connected to education back in the UK. They often work at schools that have a healthy CPD budget so they will likely be returning to the UK with a range of experiences, knowledge and even qualifications, making them a very strong candidate when applying for jobs.

3. International teachers have it easy.

International teachers often have an improved standard of living and a more manageable workload, but teaching is a demanding job anywhere in the world. The challenges vary with each context, but it is fair to say that many expat teachers spend their weekends relaxing and this has been a huge draw for many teachers and leaders in the UK who do not feel they have balance in their life. However, the concept of Instagram versus reality should be applied;

an international teacher may post pool and beach photos on social media regularly but that doesn't mean this is a reflection of their day to day working life. International teachers work hard, but what's the point of living abroad if not to embrace all of the perks and surroundings? An international post is worth pursuing if it means high-quality professional development, and the ability to save money and gain wider life experiences. If one of those three is missing then perhaps reconsider.

SO, WHAT IS IT LIKE TO TEACH ABROAD?

Continuing with one of the recurring themes of this book, doing your research is essential when looking to make a change. This probably applies to an international move more than any other career choice a teacher can make. The best advice we can give here is that you should try to speak to someone who is working in the country you are interested in going to, and ideally has knowledge of the school you are thinking of applying to. Even then, experienced testimony is not a guarantee of success, as everyone has different ambitions and needs, but you are at least making an informed decision.

To give you a sense of what is out there, we interviewed eight teachers who were kind enough to give us the benefit of their experiences of the country in which they worked, or are still working. They are:

Anna Peachey – Denmark
Craig Cook – India
Humayun Ahmed – Egypt
Kevin Brennan – Australia
Madeline Churchill – China
Titus Edge – Brazil
Tom Hicks – Hong Kong
Tom Rogers – Spain

Each answered the same set of questions, which explored their motivation for going abroad, the professional development opportunities they had, the highs and lows, and the advice they had for anyone looking to follow in their footsteps. Suffice to say, the interviews were fascinating and as we've mentioned above, fuller content will appear on our website, which we hope will be an invaluable resource for teachers looking to move abroad.

WHY TEACH ABROAD? PERSONAL AND PROFESSIONAL PULL FACTORS

So, let's start with motivation. What prompted our interviewees to pack up and go? There were some common denominators, and it is fair to say that all our interviewees had a desire to experience a different culture, and love to travel. They are certainly not risk averse, and appreciated that the move would entail a major upheaval. A recurring theme was the personal benefit that would come from giving their families a broader life experience (especially if they already had children). Humayun, for example, was very clear about the cultural benefits for his family as he told us that 'I love diversity and inclusivity is a key value of mine. I wanted my children to experience and mix with different cultures and people.' Some of our subjects moved abroad because their partners got a foreign posting and so they moved first and got a job second, so it was not always an automatic choice to teach abroad.

There was also a perception that there would be a better work-life balance abroad. Some of our subjects said that timing was significant, as they had reached a point where they needed a change and fatigue was starting to set in. We imagine many teachers will empathise with Tom Rogers when he hit a point that a change was not just desirable, but essential:

> I'd done nine years in the UK – the workload, pressure and intensity had been crazy. I hit 30 years old and was asking why I was living this life the way I was. I didn't have a partner, kids or a mortgage. Teaching internationally had always been something I'd been interested in. I toyed with the idea of leaving my school in North Wales in 2010 to go off and teach in Tanzania, but didn't feel it was the right time. This time it did. I applied for a job in Ecuador and didn't hear anything, but then I spotted one in Spain and it just felt right straight away. I got the job, packed up all my belongings into my old Corsa and that summer, I drove from Liverpool to Vigo via the car ferry from Portsmouth to Santander. I think it took 36 hours in total, but I felt 'alive' again, you know? I felt as though I was free from this very constrained and scrutinised professional life that I'd had in the UK.

Professional reasons also play a significant role. Tom Hicks is very clear in his view that 'International schools and school groups are the future of education, offering economies of scale in resourcing and collaboration, as well as promoting a global outlook and alternative perspectives.' Titus spoke on a similar theme when he said that 'The international scene provides the additional opportunity to be a part of the hugely successful global brand that is British education. Few countries come anywhere close to having this sort of educational reach.' This is worth emphasising; qualifying as a teacher in the UK has a significant cachet around the world. Robin was told in no uncertain terms by a Jordanian friend and colleague that British people have no idea how lucky they are to have a UK passport. The same might be said of UK teaching qualifications.

PROFESSIONAL LEARNING AND DEVELOPMENT ABROAD

This was a much more variable picture. For those working in a schools group, there was clearly a huge amount on offer. Tom Hicks (Harrow Group) and Madeline (Wellington Group) gave a very similar overview of the collaboration and resources that come from having a network of schools which clearly see professional learning as a main draw for recruitment. Titus, as a headteacher in Brazil, also pointed out that the international sector does offer good opportunities for career advancement: 'There is a healthy turnover of talent and opportunities abound for capable and energetic educators to make a real mark at the school in the time they are with us.' Anna made exactly the same point about promotion, and also cited the additional time that teachers have in Denmark for professional development (note to reader – you should be warned that the following paragraph may reduce you to tears):

> *Most importantly, the much-reduced contact time made the biggest impact. At the school I worked in, contact time made up 55% of a teacher's timetable. While some other time was taken with meetings, it left a huge amount of time for professional development, course development and professional collaboration.*

Given the strength and number of IB schools around the world, this is also an avenue for professional development. Robin moved to an IB school in Dubai and went on residential training courses for Diploma Programme History, and Theory of Knowledge in Athens and Oxford respectively. The best IB schools invest heavily in training up staff, and accept that they will usually have to recruit teachers who will be starting from scratch. It opens up a whole new world of curriculum, pedagogy and assessment. Craig emphasised this point about his school in India, where all teachers have to undergo IB training. There is also a professional development committee which oversees all development proposals, demonstrating a strategic approach to professional learning.

While many teachers are drawn to international and IB schools, remember that a significant number go to schools within national systems. Kevin did that in moving to Australia, where the availability of high-quality professional learning is impressive:

> *The professional development opportunities I have received here have been excellent, both within the school and from external providers. The PD industry is large and diverse, with opportunities both domestically and abroad.*

Online professional learning has clearly been a benefit to the international sector. This has traditionally been cited as a drawback of working abroad – the lack of good quality CPD. However, the 'Zoom Boom' has clearly changed that significantly, and several of our interviewees cited this as a positive trend.

But it isn't all sunshine and roses. Many international schools lack a decent budget for training, and don't have access to wider support networks. When this happens, teachers are left to fend for themselves, which means sourcing your own professional development opportunities, and funding them. Some schools also apply strict policies about any funding they do grant, such as repaying the amount if you leave within two years of completing the training.

It's great because...

This section is not intended to be an advert for teaching abroad, but you could be forgiven for thinking otherwise. In terms of teaching, there is clearly something to be said about the synergy of different cultures that you experience internationally. Anna, Tom and Kevin made very similar comments here, with the latter saying that:

> *The best thing without a doubt has been the opportunity to bring the best parts of the UK system and add them to the best parts of the Australian system. This cross-pollination of experiences has been hugely beneficial for myself personally and has kept my enthusiasm to learn and develop high.*

Or, as Craig so eloquently put it, the highlight is 'Being able to work in a diverse setting where my cross-cultural skills get utilised to maximum effect.'

Humayun's enthusiasm for his students, and Egyptian culture, was wonderfully infectious when we spoke to him.

For me, there isn't just one aspect. Top of the list is the students! Our school has 65 different nationalities of students and they are an absolute delight to teach. You actually get to teach students and not push paperwork around or deal with other issues. Secondly would be the Egyptian people, their culture and language, it's just beautiful.

There is also a very real sense of togetherness that comes from being part of a community going through a shared, and exciting, experience. Madeline and Anna both touched on this. Speaking of her experience in China, Madeline said 'I would also highlight the people and friendships formed while working internationally. The school community can be very supportive especially as you look after each other living away from home.' We both felt that Anna (speaking of Denmark) could easily have been describing our experiences in the UAE:

There was an almost intangible element of 'coming together' in an international school too. The necessarily transient nature of much of the community leads to a camaraderie and collegiality which I have not experienced elsewhere. Put simply, people want and need to make connections quickly and are far more open to doing so.

Unsurprisingly, the ability to travel was frequently cited. We have both explored the Middle East by going on very low-cost flights to places like Oman, Lebanon and Jordan. For Madeline, based in Tianjin, she had easy access to amazing destinations in Asia:

My partner and I travelled to Vietnam, Malaysia and Japan among others, and we have spent time in the great cities of China; Beijing, Shanghai and Hong Kong. The diversity of culture and food across our host country is unbeatable.

Family life was also a common theme, with the standard of living being a significant draw. Anna noted of Denmark that 'The general standard of living, with emphasis on family, health (both physical and mental), happiness and hygge is excellent.' If you don't know what hygge is and are off to Google it, we predict that it will be your new favourite thing.

And just to round it all off, you really can't argue with Titus when he says 'There's something about working at a school with palm trees lining the entrance that always raises the spirits.' Try not to think of that as you head into school tomorrow.

Don't pack your bags just yet...

So before you get on the TES Jobs page and set your filter to 'International', take a moment to consider the down sides. There is no doubt that you will have to adapt to a way of working which will seem at times illogical, frustrating and inefficient. Bureaucracy is definitely an issue, and Titus cautions that 'Brazil is an amazing place to live and work but it has its problems and frustrations. If you think you're coming to paradise, think again.' Kevin found the different approach to compliance for teachers in Australia cumbersome, warning that:

> *As an experienced teacher I was still required to complete a proficiency year, which is more in depth and heavier on the paperwork than the equivalent NQT year in the UK.*

As for academic culture, you need to be able to bend yourself to the climate you find yourself in. It certainly won't work the other way around. Anna eventually got used to the more egalitarian system in Denmark, but it wasn't easy:

> *The challenge was the difference in expectations of behaviour from students. Uniforms are not worn in Denmark, there are few direct 'rules' and young people are expected and encouraged to be independent and speak their minds.*

Exam systems are something else to get used to. As Tom Hicks notes, 'In Hong Kong the pressure for academic results is fierce so the stakes feel very high.' Kevin also found it very different going from the two years of GCSEs and two years of A-Levels to just having the final exams of HSC in Australia. There is a very different feel in terms of pupil focus prior to that final year.

Pedagogy also needs to be adapted. This definitely applies to the use of humour in the classroom; you quickly become aware of the fact that British humour (especially sarcasm) doesn't travel as well as you think it might. The same goes for cultural references, where you have to develop a whole new set to be able to make analogies in lessons. Rigid didactic learning is common in China, and this gave Madeline a real challenge at the start:

> *Teaching Art in China has been quite different to teaching young people in the UK. I have had to adapt my teaching practice to cover a much wider range of ability and nurture personal creative responses from pupils who are used to rote-learning and memorisation. It has been challenging but it has given my teaching a renewed sense of purpose.*

And then, of course, we have the personal side of things. Wherever you are, you will, from time to time, simply miss home, family and friends. Titus hit the nail on the head when he told us:

> Home feels a long way away for expat teachers and is also unhelpful for staff recruitment. Brazil is a wonderful country, but I think we all have days when we feel a longing for Marmite, fish and chips, the local pub and even some good old British drizzle.

Again, Craig put it beautifully when he said that 'Being a global nomad at times has been tiring as one longs for the stability of a home base.'

You also realise that there are many things that are undervalued back at home. Number one on the list is probably the NHS. Humayun cited this when he said that:

> Egypt is beautiful but some things we take for granted in the UK are either not available or not as good. Calling for an ambulance for example; it can take ages to arrive here, so people tend to just go to a local hospital or clinic. Health insurance generally covers it, but you may have to pay first and claim later. Driving in Egypt is crazy and very expensive to buy or rent a car.

It is fair to say that the words 'comfort zone' can feel woefully inadequate when describing many of the situations you may find yourself in.

A final point worth making is that you have to accept the culture and traditions of the country you settle in, and this can often feel uncomfortable. For example, many of the states that teachers head to in their droves are not democracies, and have troubling human rights records. Again, do your homework and know what you are letting yourself in for.

ADVICE FROM THOSE THAT KNOW

Which brings us neatly on to the final section; what advice did our interviewees pass on about their respective host countries, and moving abroad in general? Well, without exception they recommended it (hardly a shock, we know, but the feeling was pretty strong). Titus represented the consensus when he said:

> Go for it; teaching is a profession where it is relatively easy to work around the world and settling back into the UK is much easier than it once was …

But go in with eyes wide open; do your homework and get as realistic an understanding of the country as possible.

Tom Hicks sounded a cautionary note which is absolutely true: if you aren't fully supported by your new school in making the move, you will find it incredibly hard:

We are blessed with a fantastic HR department who made the transition easy, quarantine and all, but trying to work out visas, children's schooling, accommodation, banking, cars, insurance etc. with no help would make for a really stressful experience.

Madeline gave some very useful and practical insight when she said:

Look for schools which are part of an established group as this suggests stability and security. Try to find out about the accommodation offered and how far you may have to commute each day. I would also note the efficiency of communication with the school – it can tell you a lot about how a place operates!

If you ever need an agent, Humayun is your man. He gave a very useful checklist of things to ask about contractually, and how to approach that at the interview stage:

I would say do it only if you have a package which you feel comfortable with and can live with. The packages being offered by some international schools now are very low. You would be able to survive, but maybe not save anything. So always negotiate the package, make sure health insurance is included, schooling, accommodation, additional baggage, flights, visas and documents (as a lot of schools are now getting candidates to notarise their documents themselves, which can run up the bill to around £500). The big thing is to negotiate. If the school wants you, they will pay for you. Do not give in as you will regret it later.

Anna sounded a similar note of caution for Denmark; 'The cost of living is very high and moving without a relocation package could be prohibitively expensive.' That said, the standard of living was something that she really enjoyed and thought teachers were more highly valued than in the UK, due in no small part to the strength of Danish teaching unions.

Touching on how to adapt to a different culture and climate, Craig advised to 'Be flexible and ready to live and thrive in ambiguous situations where one doesn't have the sense of control as they do in their home culture.' This really can't be emphasised enough. If you crave stability, predictability and control, then living abroad – and the wonderful chaos you often get with international schools – is probably not for you.

We should probably add our reflections here. Did we enjoy working abroad? Absolutely. Did it make us better teachers? Without question. Would we do it forever? No. You do miss home and family, so for us it had a shelf life. Some people do move abroad and decide not to return, but that's a personal call and only something you can find out once you've taken the leap. Working abroad isn't for everyone, but we have no qualms in saying that we absolutely loved it.

Finally, some of our general advice if you are moving abroad to teach

Be financially prepared. The transition process overseas is often very costly (there can be a relocation allowance, and it is worth asking about this in advance). In the long-term teachers can reap the financial benefits of teaching internationally but the first six months are often expensive so be prepared and save the pennies in advance. It is worth asking about relocation allowances and to not be shy or hesitant when asking for that money.

The package you are offered is absolutely vital. It's much more complex than the UK, as it has several moving parts. The standard components include:

- annual return flights to your country of origin
- health insurance
- accommodation (or an allowance – make sure this is adequate)
- free or reduced fee education for your children
- relocation support (covering things like flights, shipping costs, and possibly a furniture allowance)
- an annual gratuity, which is typically one month of salary for every year of service, paid at the end of employment (so a nice lump sum when you move on).

With all this factored in, check whether your monthly salary will allow you to live well and save.

Be patient. There will likely be an immigration process to secure a work visa or identity card and the time this can take will vary with different individuals and schools (if you have to go somewhere for official documentation then take a book, as you might be there longer than expected). This process can involve medical testing, the taking of fingerprints, signing different documentation and so on. The process differs with each country but can be very complicated. This can be challenging, and it is easy to blame the human resources staff, but the majority of the time this process is out of their control.

Embrace your colleagues. In the UK, staff in some schools may only socialise at the annual Christmas party but the international scene is very different. Colleagues will become friends quickly and your family away from family. You are bonded by this unique experience, the highs and lows. It is advisable to make friends outside of school, but the school community internationally is very different with less separation. This has pros and cons but the good will likely outweigh the bad.

Be prepared and have an exit strategy. If things suddenly go wrong, you may need to get home quickly. The last thing you want to do is have to make a huge number of arrangements in a short space of time, especially if that means losing out financially. This especially applies in states where teachers can be summarily dismissed (check if trade unions are legal or not in your country of choice), because again this is a massive difference from the UK. Ultimately, there can be a variety of reasons why you may need to leave at short notice, so try to have things set up (including a reserve of cash you can access) so you don't get caught out.

Finally, learn as much as you can prior to moving. Culture shock is real. There is often a lot to adapt to, from missing personal comforts at home to the different weather and climate. Learning about the laws, cultures and traditions helps immensely. It can be useful to learn a few phrases of the language, even if it's just a please and thank you, as this shows respect and locals are more likely to be hospitable, welcoming and friendly.

CHALLENGE QUESTIONS

- If you are interested in moving abroad, what do you want to get out of the experience, both personally and professionally?
- Where would you like to move to and why?
- How would the move help you to progress in career terms?
- What sacrifices or compromises are you willing to make?
- How would you cope without your friends and family being immediately around you?
- What would your exit strategy be?

QR CODES FOR FURTHER READING AND INFORMATION

The International Teaching Life
https://theinternationalteachinglife.com

COBIS – Council of British International Schools
https://www.cobis.org.uk

BSME – British Schools in the Middle East
https://bsme.org.uk

WhichSchoolAdvisor.com
https://whichschooladvisor.com

**FOBISIA –
The Federation of
British International
Schools in Asia**
https://www.fobisia.org/

World-Schools
https://world-schools.com

CHAPTER 12

THE TEACHING LIFE: LONG-TERM CAREER STRATEGY

Purpose of this chapter: To help teachers and leaders plan and prepare a long-term career strategy.

'Life is really simple, but we insist on making it complicated.' – Confucius

By now, we hope you have given some deeper thought to your teaching life. There is no doubt that what we do is demanding, exhilarating, draining, addictive and absorbing. It also goes by very, very quickly. Being in control of your teaching life might seem difficult, but it shouldn't be. We talk a lot about agency in education, and the most significant way in which you should exercise agency is in your career planning. Do not leave it in the lap of the Gods, but take control of it and chart your own course. You have one teaching life – even if it comes in several different instalments – so make it count.

This is the chapter that you either read last, or first, depending on your priorities. We have deliberately structured this book with professional learning coming first, and career development second, because the former is the precursor to progress. However, you may well have purchased this because you are contemplating an imminent move, and need to crack on, and that's fine with us. We thought it was worthwhile concluding with this because we believe it is rarely covered in other books on education, and is a practical process that needs some stimulus material. Teachers are, contrary to popular opinion, very career-minded people and the education sector is diversifying at a rapid rate.

To be a teacher is to work in education, but to work in education does not necessarily mean you are a teacher. There are multiple pathways opening up that challenge the traditional understanding of career progression, and we have touched on many of these already. This chapter is a further prompt to self-reflection, in the hope that you will, by the end, have a better understanding of what you want to achieve and where you want to go with your career. If you are on autopilot, or other people are forcing decisions on you, then you are not in a position of strength. This is really about taking control of your professional life, for the betterment of your personal life too.

Teaching is a unique profession. When we speak with people who work in other sectors, they are confused about how it works, not least from an HR standpoint. Admittedly, the first part of any such conversation is a grumble about how much we get in the way of holidays, but once you get past that you realise just how different education is. Take recruitment, for example. It's not unusual for teachers to secure a new job six to nine months in advance of the start date. In a recent conversation, a finance professional asked if senior leaders are put on gardening leave when that happens. Imagine! You would probably start planning a move every so often based on the need for a 'no-strings-attached' sabbatical. Equally, with references, most other professions are terrified of referees being approached during the recruitment process because they haven't told anyone that they are applying for a move. Teachers typically have a good discussion with their referees before even being called for an interview, because we are very open about our interest in new positions. What seems perfectly normal to us is, to many others, utterly bizarre.

Knowing this is important. It allows you to leverage the unique way that teaching works, and to plan accordingly. If someone goes straight from school to university, and straight into teacher training, and then works to the anticipated retirement age, they are looking at four and a half decades in their teaching life. That is a very, very long career and in truth, not many will actually do that. What it does mean is that you will probably hold many roles, in many different locations, and if you have some degree of control over that career you will make the most of it. When you finish, you should have absolutely no regrets, and be in a very good position to enjoy the rest of your life to the fullest.

Looking after yourself at every stage of your career is vital if you are going to reach this end goal; in her (pre-COVID) book, *Can't Even: How Millennials Became the Burnout Generation*, Anne Petersen shows that millennials are the first generation whose life expectancy is expected to shorten compared to their predecessors, Generation X. One of the key drivers of this is the blurring of work and personal life, and the added pressure that comes from things like student debt. Financial planning and a proactive approach to your own wellbeing, are therefore core elements of career progression. No one goes into teaching to be rich and famous, but neither do we expect to be poor and unloved. Effective career planning will help you to steer a course that allows you to flourish personally and professionally, so it's time to get that notebook ready and scratch down some thoughts as you read on.

A WORD ABOUT WELLBEING

Wellbeing has been an implicit theme of this book, woven through the chapters to ensure that professional learning and career progression are not achieved at its cost. Our simple comment on this is that wellbeing is a bespoke thing that means different things to different people, and your career choices have a significant impact on your sense of self and satisfaction. When devising a career strategy, make sure you factor in wellbeing because it can often fall off the radar when big decisions are being made. We are of the school of thought that believes good wellbeing comes from being challenged in the right way, to the right degree. It is about being personally and professionally fulfilled, and not over – or under – worked. That means being in the right role, in the right setting.

It is all too easy to think that making a drastic change will fix wellbeing concerns, but in truth many of the issues that cause burnout and frustration are system-wide, and not peculiar to any one school. Yes, there are variables, but don't expect changing setting to be a panacea. You will only really know what the difference is likely to be if you do your homework on what a prospective new school is actually like, and what the expectations are of staff. You also need to think very carefully about taking on additional responsibilities, such as moving up the leadership levels. Is it really the right thing for you? Will you thrive or struggle under added pressure?

It is absolutely the case that schools are responsible for the wellbeing of their students and their staff. Yet it is also the case that teachers are responsible for their own wellbeing, and are often their own worst enemies. Yes, workload is a major problem with no easy solutions, but so too is overworking, frequently caused by 'going the extra mile' once too often. Again, devising a career strategy where the roles you are in allow you to maximise your potential without compromising your wellbeing is the real aim. True progression can't be achieved if you burn yourself out.

WHEN AND HOW TO MAKE A CHANGE

This is about taking an Aristotelian approach to life: making the right move, for the right reasons, at the right time, in the right way. Have you ever managed that? Don't feel guilty if you haven't, you are in good, plentiful company. Making a change typically means changing your role, changing your school, or both. If it does involve a new school then it can also mean moving home, and that adds a whole other dimension of stress and effort. It's why many people don't make a change; but change can also be liberating. Remember that teaching can be a very long career, and passing up opportunities time and again will likely lead to regrets later on. Essentially, making the right amount of change across the span of your career will allow you to achieve all you want to, without overburdening yourself.

There are several questions you need to ask yourself on a regular basis.

Are you genuinely happy doing what you are currently doing?

The right job at the right school should be consistently challenging you and developing you professionally, so that you are always progressing, even if – or especially if – you are staying in the same role. If you are not being challenged and finding it hard to articulate what new skills and experiences you are acquiring (think about the CV challenge in Chapter 7), you have to ask if you are continuing to do this just out of convenience. That may be the case, and it may be driven by personal reasons such as family circumstances and wider responsibilities, but you can still try to mix things up a bit by giving yourself a new challenge somehow. What would that look like?

Do you feel you are valued?

Most teachers don't need to be lavished with praise on a daily basis, but you need to feel that your work is recognised and appreciated by the three key constituencies of students, parents and colleagues. Often teachers feel that they love the students they teach, but that the management at their school is lamentable. This leads to loyalty to the students, and by extension the school, but at a personal cost. One of the toughest decisions in making a move is that nagging feeling of betrayal to the children you teach, but remember, they will leave at some point too. Change is a constant in life, and you are not abandoning them. Other very good teachers will come along too, and you are doing them a disservice if you continue to work in a place where you are not fully valued and fulfilled. It prevents you from being the best teacher you can be.

The key metric of any career move is that it should make things better for you. How you define improvement in that sense is entirely up to you. It might be the professional challenge, it might be financially, it might be time (a shorter commute is a great thing). If you weigh up any move and calculate that it is better both professionally and personally, then you are heading in the right direction. There is always an element of risk, in that you might arrive in a new post and realise that you have been totally mis-sold on what it involves, but much career progression is based on assessing the risk involved. Not every move you make will pay off, but staying put and stagnating is also a risk. In short, we live with risk every day. The point of risk assessment is to minimise it, not eliminate it.

That means making a move requires careful research. You should never take a blind leap of faith, or make a major change on a whim. We have both worked with colleagues who snapped at a particular moment and their first reaction was to go online in search of new jobs elsewhere. That led to a series of events that, some months later, leaves a nagging feeling that they didn't make a change for the right reasons. Which leads to the next important question...

What are your reasons for making a change?

After all, it's highly likely to be a direct question at an interview. You don't want your answer to be 'I detest my Head of Department/Headteacher.' You need to have rational, tangible reasons for making a change; not just to get through the interview, but to be able to look yourself in the mirror and know that you did the right thing.

So the 'when' part of making a change comes from asking yourself if you are happy, valued, fulfilled and challenged in what you do. The 'how' part involves planning well in advance, researching fully, and then doing as much as you can to demonstrate that you're the best candidate in the field (that's really what Chapter 10 is all about, in case you skipped it). If it helps, keep in mind the pithy Scottish saying, 'What's for you won't go by you'. If you go about change in the right way, you will, in all probability, end up in the right place.

MATERNITY, PATERNITY AND FLEXIBLE WORKING

Family life should, ideally, always be more important than professional life, and one of the great unknown variables in career planning is when little ones will come on the scene. It might seem blindingly obvious, but the step change that comes with children starts with maternity leave, and lasts until the youngest sibling reaches school age themselves. If you have one child, you're looking at five years of different working patterns, but if you have two or more children it can be longer than a decade. Even then, work and life patterns will be different, and the thing that usually gives way is sleep, because parental time and teacher time have one thing in common: they are zero sum games. If you add one thing in, you probably have to take something out.

Having a family causes a significant recalibration of your priorities and you can never know how you will feel. For some, they can't wait to get back to work, and for others it makes them reassess things and deprioritise the professional side of their life, sometimes permanently. If the mantra of this half of the book has been to plan ahead, this is probably the most significant area where that will fall down. If you are on the threshold of that change in life, it's a good idea to speak to people who have had families and taken very different directions afterwards. Find out what it means to recommit fully to a career after having a family, and also what it means to leave it all behind.

There are two significant trends emerging which will have a real impact for teachers and school leaders. Neither is particularly new, but both are on the increase. The first is shared parental leave, which in the UK means that both parents can share the 50 weeks of entitled leave for birth and adoption. More men are taking advantage of this, but some have found that it doesn't always come with the full support of colleagues that they would hope. This has a lot to do with the lack of uptake previously, and stereotypical projections that parental leave is for the mother rather than the father; views which are outdated and unwelcome. However, there is a lot of support and advice out there. Check that you qualify for the shared leave, ask for policies and also check in with your union to ensure that you are getting all you are legally entitled to. When done properly, it is a brilliant thing, but it is still imperfectly understood so expect there to be obstacles to overcome.

The second trend is towards flexible working requests. These have been around for years, but it is likely that the pandemic will be an accelerator. All industries are seeing greater demand for flexible working requests (FWR) and education is no different. However, not all roles lend themselves to this easily. If it means a job share then that can mean sharing classes with another teacher, or splitting up a leadership role, and that can leave students, parents and even colleagues feeling uneasy. It can be done very well, or very badly, depending on the commitment of everyone involved and the relationships that underpin the job share. Remember, making a request does not mean that it will be accepted; you need to have a good rationale for it, and there are a range of reasons why an employer can turn it down, including affordability, recruitment problems, and reduction of service (meaning, in teaching, the impact on students). If your request is declined you can appeal, but if that is also rejected you have to wait twelve months before making a new request. Given that your employer also has a three-month timeframe to respond to the request, and the appeal, this can be a very long process. Essentially, if you really need to move to flexible working be prepared for a lengthy process; it won't happen within a few weeks. The ACAS website https://www.acas.org.uk/ has excellent guidance, so start there if you are considering making this change.

A final, and very positive, note is that career progression through professional learning while you are taking time off work is much easier to do now. One of the best kept secrets is The Maternity Teacher Paternity Teacher (MTPT) Project. This is an online community and resource hub which recognises that many teachers want to keep up professional learning during a career break. As they state on their website 'Wellbeing means different things for different people: for some, this means maintaining a sense of that 'teacher' identity during the 'break' of parental leave.'[42] Don't feel guilty if you are on parental leave and are missing work; see it as a healthy sign that you gain intellectual stimulation and fulfilment from what you do, and it is ok to want to stay engaged with that on some level. Being a good parent and a good professional are not mutually exclusive, and can actually complement each other beautifully. Teaching and raising children are not wildly different, after all.

FINANCIAL PLANNING – PENSIONS, SAVINGS AND PROPERTY

This section is not about giving you advice; neither of us is a financial advisor. This is more about prompting you to think about your own financial future, because that has a massive impact on your career choices. Despite the significance of this, we rarely talk about these things, but change is very definitely coming and what worked for baby-boomers will not work for millennials.

So, what are those changes? Let's start with pensions, because that affects everyone (unless you've won the lottery, or have an oligarch parent). Our opening questions are these: Do you know much about pensions generally? And do you understand your own pension arrangements? If the answer is no to both, fear not, you are in a sizable majority of teachers. That's not out of ignorance, it's just that teaching comes with a security blanket of a very good pension scheme if

---

42. Maternity Teacher, Paternity Teacher (ND) Homepage. https://www.mtpt.org.uk/

you're in the UK, and that all seems to be taken care of when your contributions are taken at source from your monthly wage. However, the system has seen some significant changes and there will be decisions for you to make that affect how well off you are when you retire.

In 2012, the Teachers' Pension Scheme in England and Wales moved from being a final salary scheme (based on what you earned at or near retirement) to being based on a career average. Most teachers are now on the CARE (Career Average Revalued Earnings) which is based on what you've earned over your entire career. It's a complicated bit of maths, that begins with the mechanism that 1/57th of what you earn each year goes into your pension fund. Your employer, from 2019, also contributes 23% of your salary. When you retire, every month of earnings is put together and that forms the basis of your pension. Inflation is built in, based on the Consumer Price Index (CPI). It is therefore a very good idea to keep track of where you are annually, so that any career decisions you make (such as a move to flexible working) are factored in.

Then, there is the wider picture of the changing education system. The National Education Union has this stark warning:

> *Under career average, every month's pay throughout your career will decide your pension. The growing fragmentation of the school system means a growing number of small employers, and more changes of employer for teachers over their careers. These are perfect conditions for mistakes to be made.*[43]

To make sure that mistakes are rectified, the NEU advises that you keep every payslip and P60, and register for the MyPensionOnline service. If you haven't done this, bump it up to the top of your 'to do' list. If you retire early, that will reduce your overall pension. If you want to move to part-time work later in your career, and withdraw some of your pension, you can, it's called a 'phased retirement'. You can also take a tax-free lump sum at retirement, which can help pay off any outstanding debts such as a mortgage. This all needs to be carefully weighed up, and taking expert advice will help you to maximise your earnings so you don't get short changed.

This also has massive implications for several possible career decisions. If you decide to go abroad to work in an international school you will be very unlikely

---

to have a pension arrangement, so will either go without or have to make your own provisions. If you move to the independent sector, you may find that you are no longer in the Teachers' Pension Scheme, as many independent schools are moving away from it because the employers' contribution is on the rise. In 2019, it jumped from 16.5% to 23%, and within a year one fifth of the independent schools in England had left the TPS. A rise to the 30% mark is predicted in 2023, and that figure only looks set to increase. What are these schools replacing it with? They are moving to a defined benefits scheme (DBS), as opposed to a defined contributions scheme (DCS, which is what the TPS is). This will not suit everyone, but it might be attractive for younger teachers. This is because they can choose what contribution level they make, which gives the option of taking more salary early on in their career, which can help with things like student loan repayments, a deposit for first-time buying, or a wedding. If independent schools are going to avoid a massive recruitment headache, they need to offer an attractive package where such flexibility is seen as a plus.

This brings us on to the two major additional areas where teachers try to safeguard their financial future: property and savings. Again, your career choices might have an impact here. Moving abroad might mean forgoing a pension, but it might also allow you to build up savings to invest elsewhere. This is especially true if you are on a tax-free package or are paid in a currency which is performing strongly against the pound, thus giving you a *de facto* pay rise whenever the exchange rate moves in your favour. The decision to move abroad has already been covered, but again research is essential so that you can put a value on the overall package you receive and decide whether you are going to be better off financially. After all, investing in bricks and mortar, or stocks and shares, might be a better long-term strategy than building up your pension. The only way to know that, of course, is by taking sound financial advice.

FINALLY – PREPARING FOR RETIREMENT

This brings us neatly to the end: retirement. It is our sincere hope that you end on a high, at a time that suits you best and feeling just as valued in that moment as you have ever felt before. This is easier said than done.

It is probably never too early to start thinking about retirement, but things really kick in when you are in what we call the 'final third' of your teaching life. The first third is about establishing yourself and becoming an experienced professional. The middle third is where a lot of the big changes take place, either personally or professionally; it is when things can take an unexpected turn, and the big opportunities often come about. The final third should, ideally, be a period of greater stability and just as highly rewarding – hopefully even more so. Yet finishing well is a challenge, because age discrimination is rife. Older teachers have to fight a perception that they are resistant to change (they've seen it all before) overly critical of the regime, and contribute less to the overall life of the school, than the fresh-faced twenty-somethings who seem to volunteer for everything. How then, can we challenge this perception?

The first point is for all readers to consider: everyone finishes at some point, so helping to create a culture where those in the final third are properly valued in the school community will mean that you can finish well too. The second point is stating what should be very obvious: those who have been in teaching for a quarter of a century or more have a massive bank of expertise that is an invaluable resource. We mentioned earlier that one third of all newly qualified teachers leave the profession within five years, so the pool of highly experienced teachers is likely to get smaller, not larger. Senior leaders should be asking how they can ensure that this experience has a legacy effect. Getting involved in mentoring and coaching is an obvious answer, because it allows them to pass on their expertise to less experienced colleagues.

Of course, it may be that teachers in the final third just want to get on with their job, and do it well, without being encumbered with additional tasks. That's absolutely fine too, though remember that progression applies at every stage of your career, and continuing to work on and refine classroom practice keeps up the level of personal fulfilment that is so essential to good teaching. For those who are in leadership roles in the final third, there is also the consideration as to whether you want to finish at that level. Most do, but it is worth considering the phased approach to retirement, either by dropping down a level or going to a part-time role supplemented by your pension. Would that be better for your overall quality of life, and allow for a more seamless transition into retirement?

We finish then where we began, with Archie Bevan. All he wanted to be remembered for was being a teacher, because that was the pinnacle of his professional life. Our final challenge question is this: what do you want to be remembered for? It may seem self-indulgent, but when someone asks you in retirement 'What did you do?' what will your answer be? We wear many hats throughout our career, so which is the one that matters most to you? You may already have achieved that, but if not, think about what you have left to achieve. Go out on your own terms, with no regrets, holding on to all the good memories. The other memories can be left behind, along with the old marking pens and the deleted emails.

CHALLENGE QUESTIONS

- What do you want to achieve in your career?
- What does good wellbeing look like for you?
- Are you in the best position, at the best school, for you?
- What would you improve if you changed roles, or school?
- How well organised are your finances?
- What financial strategy are you following for retirement?
- How do you want to end your career?

QR CODES FOR FURTHER READING AND INFORMATION

ACAS – Making working life better for everyone in Britain
https://www.acas.org.uk

The Maternity Paternity Project (MTPT)
https://www.mtpt.org.uk

Teacherpensions.co.uk
https://www.teacherspensions.co.uk

CLOSING THANKS

This book has an amazing *dramatis personae*, so thank you to everyone who agreed to give their time and share their experiences with us. The interviews were a joy to do, and we are amazed that people continue to be so willing to support us when they are spinning so many plates at once. The case studies are fascinating and we are very proud to include them in our book. We asked lots of experts in a range of fields to read, check and offer feedback; we are truly grateful for the generosity of those sharing their time and wisdom with us. Thank you to Robert Macmillan and Nathan Gynne for helping us with the cover design. There are simply far too many people to name but we have offered our personal thanks and gratitude, we hope we can return the time and kindness shown to us.

To the team at John Catt Educational, thank you for backing us throughout this. Alex Sharratt and Jonathan Barnes, you have been great as always and very patient. The books published with John Catt Educational have enriched the lives of many educators, as reading and learning plays a very important role in our teaching life.

EVIDENCE-INFORMED TEACHING AND LEARNING GLOSSARY

As the findings from cognitive psychology and academic research are becoming more widely known in education, there are a lot of new key terms and concepts for teachers to be familiar with. We hope you find our glossary below helpful and useful.

Asynchronous instruction – Asynchronous teaching and learning refers to all students learning, but not at the same place or same time. For example, class work set on Google Classroom for students to complete, which they will do at different times and from different locations.

Automacy – This is when we do something so often that it becomes automatic, also known as 'auto-pilot'. There are many scenarios, both inside and outside of the classroom, where this can happen, and it will therefore reduce the cognitive load on working memory.

Blocking – This is when subject content is taught or revised in specific blocks in contrast to interleaving (see below), but is not as effective as interleaving.

Brain dump – This is a low effort, high impact teaching and learning strategy. Students simply have to write down from memory what they can recall about a specific topic/unit as instructed by the teacher.

Blended learning – This is also known as hybrid learning, which can contain elements of live teaching from the classroom and online learning.

Chunking – Grouping information into more manageable sections, categories or chunks to support the limitations of working memory.

Cognitive biases – There are various cognitive biases, also referred to as thinking biases, they are thinking errors people make without realising, based on their perceptions of and assumptions about their own reality.

Cognitive load – If we present our students with too much new information, all at once, this will lead to information overload in working memory. It is important for teachers to be aware of this when planning and delivering lessons.

Cognitive load theory – Professor John Sweller has written extensively about cognitive load and this refers to his work, described by Dylan Wiliam as 'The single most important thing for teachers to know'.

Cognitive science – The scientific study of the human mind.

Cognitive psychology – The study of specific mental processes such as attention, encoding, memory, perception, problem solving, and thinking.

Concrete examples – Using specific examples to help understanding of abstract ideas and concepts.

Confirmation bias – When people search for research, evidence and information to support their own beliefs and ideas, or interpret information to suit and match their beliefs.

Control group – When conducting research, there is a comparison of data from an experimental group and a control group. The two groups aim to be identical in every aspect, except the one key difference between a control group and the experimental group is that the independent variable is changed for the experimental group, unlike the control group which is held constant.

Cramming – This refers to intense and last-minute studying, for example revising for a test the night before. Also, known as massed practice.

Curse of knowledge – This is an example of a cognitive bias, where someone assumes that other people know the things they do or that they have the background to grasp what is being discussed.

Curiosity gap – When there is a gap in our knowledge and we need to seek out the answer or information to close that gap; our curiosity is driving that.

Curriculum – This refers to the subjects, topics, content, skills and experiences that are taught in a school.

Declarative memory – A type of long-term memory, also known as explicit memory. Information recalled from declarative memory involves conscious effort to bring it to mind unlike procedural memory (see below).

Desirable difficulties – This is a term coined by Professor Robert A. Bjork and Professor Elizabeth Bjork. A desirable level of challenge and difficulty must be something that students can overcome with increased effort. The 'Goldilocks principle' is that we don't want the level of challenge for tasks to be too high or too low, but instead desirable!

Distributed practice – When study is spaced out over a period of time. For example, it is better to complete six hours of revision over six days instead of six hours of revision in one day. This is also known as spaced practice. We should encourage our students to do this: little and often.

Direct instruction – In academic literature there have been various definitions and interpretations of direct instruction. To generalise, it is academic instruction that is led by the teacher in the classroom.

Dual coding – Providing information in two different formats, for example visual aids and text, to be transferred through two different channels to memory.

Dunning-Kruger effect – This is a cognitive bias where people with low ability can overestimate their ability, believing themselves to be more intelligent and capable than they actually are!

Effect size – This is most commonly associated with the work of Professor John Hattie and quite simply measures the impact of educational initiatives on achievement and outcomes.

Elaboration/Elaborative interrogation – This is a strategy to further enhance memory by elaborating, which is done by asking further questions such as: How? Why? When?

Encoding – This is the act of processing information, and is the first process of memory when trying to learn new material. Information needs to be transferred so it can be stored, then later retrieved.

Episodic memories – If we think back to our own school days we have distinct personal memories, these can include our first day at school, performing in concerts, participating in sports days or receiving examination results. We can remember who we were with, what happened and how we felt. These are episodic memories.

Evidence-based – This is an approach to practice that focuses attention on sound empirical evidence in professional decision-making and action. Schools and teachers often refer to themselves as evidence-based, as they have based their classroom practice on an evidence base.

Evidence-informed – Similar to evidence-based, but evidence-informed practice recognises that it is more challenging to determine the circumstances and conditions where the evidence works best. It is about applying evidence in the unique context of our classrooms and contexts. For this reason, we consider ourselves to be evidence-informed rather than evidence-based.

Extraneous load – The third type of cognitive load according to Sweller (see intrinsic and germane below). This occurs when students are exposed to irrelevant information that requires extra mental processing. This has a negative impact and is linked to the redundancy effect (see below).

Forgetting curve – Based on the work of German psychologist Hermann Ebbinghaus, who was able to illustrate how memory decays over time. If we learn new information but don't attempt to relearn or refresh that information, it can very quickly be forgotten!

Formative assessment – The aim of formative assessment is to monitor student learning and progress in order to provide ongoing feedback, instructions and support.

Free recall – This is the act of retrieval practice without any scaffolding, support or prompts (see brain dump above).

Germane load – This is the second type of cognitive load according to Sweller (the first is intrinsic, see below). It is the process whereby information becomes stored in long-term memory through tasks designed by the teacher to rehearse and repeat exposure to material.

Hawthorne effect – When people are involved in a study or experiment and attempt to change their behaviour because they are aware that they are being studied and evaluated.

Interleaving – This is a strategy where teachers and/or students interleave – mix up – multiple topics and units being studied. Instead of teaching content or revising in large blocks, material is changed up often.

Intrinsic load – According to Sweller, this is a type of cognitive load; intrinsic refers to the mental effort required to understand any given subject content, and can be influenced by prior knowledge of the topic.

Knowledge organiser – A document that is created to support teachers and students with the essential elements of a unit; this can include key facts, dates, terminology, concepts and more. The aim is that a knowledge organiser provides a condensed but thorough overview.

Learning objective/intention/outcome – These describe and explain what it is we want the learners in our classroom to learn.

Leitner system – This is a method of using flashcards for retrieval practice and spaced learning over a period of time.

Long-term memory – Long-term memory is incredibly powerful in terms of how much information can be stored (we do not know the limitations) and for how long.

Low stakes – This refers to testing that is the opposite of high stakes; no pressure, no formal grading, and not stressful but instead informal, regular and enjoyable.

Matthew effect – This concept refers to the vocabulary gap in schools. Originally, the message derives from the Gospel of Matthew: 'For everyone who has will more be given and he will have an abundance. But from the one who has not, even what he has will be taken away.' In an educational context, Daniel Rigney wrote in his book *The Matthew Effect,* 'The word-rich will get richer and the word-poor will get poorer'.

Massed practice – *See Cramming.*

Memory – How our mind stores and organises information and experiences.

Metacognition – An awareness and ability to critically monitor and evaluate the way we think and the progress we make.

Multi-store model of memory – This is a model of memory set out by Atkinson and Shiffrin where they proposed that memory consisted of three stores. The sensory register, where information is encoded before being passed on to the second store, short-term memory. Finally, if information is rehearsed and retained beyond short-term memory it is then stored in the long-term memory.

Neuroscience – The study of the brain and the nervous system.

Neuromyth – When research and information about the brain or memory is misunderstood or not communicated correctly, such has been the case with learning styles.

New theory of disuse – This refers to the work of Professors R. A. Bjork and E. L. Bjork, which suggests there are two key measures of memory strength; storage strength and retrieval strength (see *Storage strength* and *Retrieval strength*).

Peer review – A rigorous process where literature, such as a research paper, is reviewed by experts in the same field to ensure high quality prior to publication.

Practitioner research – This refers to research carried out by people working in that specific field, so for example teachers conducting research into education in the setting and context of their classroom. This is in contrast to full-time academics who conduct research to then share with others in that field.

Procedural memory – A type of long-term memory we use on a daily basis without consciously realising because we know what is stored there so well. Linked to automacy.

Redundancy effect – Coined by Peter Chandler and John Sweller, this occurs when students are presented with extra information that is not relevant to their learning. This can also occur when students are exposed to the same information in different formats and can overload their memory, for example a PowerPoint slide that contains icons linked to the subject content.

Remote learning – Teaching and learning that takes places out of the physical classroom. This is not in reference to a homework task but instead teaching and learning online in the virtual classroom.

Research summary – This is when a research paper or series of research papers, studies and/or journals are summarised in one shorter, concise document.

Responsive teaching – Linked to formative assessment, responsive teaching involves responding to students by asking questions and providing feedback and support, with the aim being to support students to progress with their learning.

Retrieval practice – The act of recalling information from long-term memory in order to enhance and improve long-term memory. This is a teaching and learning strategy, not an assessment strategy although high stakes testing does involve the act of recall.

Retrieval cues – Cues and prompts to aid retrieval and recall. These prompts can include images, key terms or sentence starters. This makes the act of retrieval easier.

Retrieval strength – Retrieval strength refers to how accessible (or retrievable) information is, this is taken from the work of Bjork and Bjork (see *New theory of disuse*).

Retrieval-induced forgetting – This is a memory phenomenon where remembering specific information can lead to forgetting of other information in the memory. To combat this, we simply ensure that all the essential information we want students to remember and not forget is tested regularly with retrieval practice.

Rosenshine's Principles of Instruction – This is based on the work of Barak Rosenshine who wrote about ten key principles which he argues underpin an effective approach to instruction in lessons. The principles include review, questioning and modelling.

Schema – The mental structures used to organise and categorise knowledge and information in the mind.

Semantic memory – Our knowledge base or our own encyclopaedia of facts, information, words and concepts. Knowledge that Rome is the capital of Italy is semantic, while memories of eating gelato at the Trevi fountain are episodic.

Semmelweis effect – The Semmelweis effect or reflex refers to the notion of rejecting or ignoring new evidence or knowledge because it goes against firmly held beliefs and current practices. Named so after Hungarian doctor Ignaz Semmelweis who insisted doctors wash their hands and become more hygienic before working with patients, but initially some thought this idea was absurd!

Short-term memory – This refers to immediate memory where storage is limited both in terms of capacity and duration. This term was more widely used before the introduction of the 'working memory' concept.

Storage strength – Storage strength is how well learned something is, this is taken from the work of Bjork and Bjork (see *New theory of disuse*).

Spaced practice – See *Distributed practice* above.

Split attention effect – This can occur when students have to refer to two different sources of information simultaneously while learning material. This adds extra load to the already limited working memory.

Spotlight effect – This is another cognitive bias where individuals believe other people notice their behaviour more than they actually do. In the classroom context this can prevent some students from engaging in discussions and answering questions.

Success criteria – The criteria that we use to support students during the teaching and learning process, as well as to evaluate their performance and learning.

Summative assessment – The aim of summative assessment is to evaluate student learning at the end of a unit, term, course or year.

Synchronous instruction – Synchronous teaching and learning refers to students all learning at the same time but not in the same place, for example a Zoom lesson where students are in different locations but learning at the same time.

Testing effect – This is the term referred to in academic literature when referring to the benefits of self-testing/retrieval practice. Due to the negative connotations associated with testing being high stakes, the term retrieval practice is more commonly used as it is intended to be a regular low stakes teaching and learning strategy.

Transfer – This is the application of learned information, concepts or materials to a new/different context, also known as the transfer of learning.

Working memory – Both short-term and working memory refer to immediate memory, which is limited in both duration and capacity. Working memory is a term coined by Baddley and Hitch as they believed the concept of short-term memory was too simplistic.

Zeigarnik effect – Based on the work of Russian psychologist Bluma Zeigarnik, this suggests that people tend to remember unfinished or incomplete tasks better than those completed. Students can be reluctant to begin tasks that may seem overwhelming such as an extended essay or coursework assignment. The Zeigarnik effect suggests that the key to overcoming this dread and procrastination is to simply just get started as it doesn't have to be completed all at once.

ACRONYMS USED IN EDUCATION

There are many acronyms used in education and as we have shown they vary across different countries within the UK! Compiling this list made us realise how many there are in education and not all acronyms are included! Some of the acronyms are more well known than others but hopefully this will be a helpful reference for you.

ADD – Attention Deficit Disorder

ADE – Apple Distinguished Educator

ADHD – Attention Deficit and Hyperactivity Disorder

AFL – Assessment for Learning

ASCL – Association of School and College leaders

ATL – Association of Teachers and Lecturers

CAMHS – Child and Adolescent Mental Health Service

CAT – Cognitive Ability Test

CEO – Chief Executive Officer

CLT – Cognitive Load Theory

CPD – Continuing Professional Development

CRB – Criminal Records Bureau

DFE – Department for Education

DHT – Deputy Headteacher

DI – Direct Instruction

DSL – Designated Safeguarding Lead

EAL – English as an Additional Language

ESOL – English for Speakers of Other Languages

EBacc – English Baccalaureate

EBD – Emotional and Behavioural Difficulties

ECF – Early Careers Framework

ECT – Early Career Teacher

EEF – Education Endowment Foundation

EYDP – Early Years Development Plan

EYFS – Early Years Foundation Stage

FE – Further Education

FSM – Free School Meals

GB – Governing Body/Board

GTC – General Teaching Council

GDPR – General Data Protection Regulation

H&S – Health and Safety

HE – Higher Education

HMI – Her Majesty's Inspector

HoD - Head of Department

HoY – Head of Year

HT – Headteacher

IB – International Baccalaureate

IEP – Individual Educational Plan

ITE – Initial Teacher Education

ITT – Initial Teacher Training

INSET – In-Service Education and Training

JCQ – Joint Council for Qualifications

KS – Key Stage

KO – Knowledge Organiser

LA – Local Authority

LAC – Looked After Children

LTM – Long-Term Memory

LSA – Learning Support Assistant

MAT – Multi-Academy Trust

MFL – Modern Foreign Languages

MLD – Moderate Learning Difficulties

MPS – Main Pay Scale

NC – National Curriculum

NEU – National Education Union

NGA – National Governance Association

NPQ – National Professional Qualification

NQT – Newly Qualified Teacher

NVQ – National Vocational Qualification

OECD – Organisation for Economic Cooperation and Development

OFSTED – Office for Standards in Education, Children's Services and Skills

PD – Professional Development

PDR – Performance Development Review

PGCE – Postgraduate Certificate in Education

PMLD – Profound and Multiple Learning Difficulties

PPA – Planning, Preparation and Assessment

PR – Peer Review

PRU – Pupil Referral Unit

PSHE – Personal, Social and Health Education

QTS – Qualified Teacher Status

RI – Requires Improvement

RQT – Recently Qualified Teacher

SAT – Standardised Assessment Test

SCITT – School-led Initial Teacher Training

SDP – School Development Plan

SEND – Special Educational Needs and Disability

SENCO – Special Educational Needs Coordinator

SEMH – Social Emotional Mental Health

SI – School Improvement

SIMS – Schools Information Management System

SLD – Severe Learning Difficulties

SLT – Senior Leadership Team

SM – Special Measures

SMT – Senior Management Team

SoW – Schemes of Work

SPaG – Spelling, Punctuation and Grammar

SS – Storage Strength

STM – Short-Term Memory

TA – Teaching Assistant

TEFL – Teaching English as a Foreign Language

TLR – Teaching and Learning Responsibility

TP – Teachers Pensions

UCAS – University and Colleges Admissions Services

UPR – Upper Pay Range

VP – Vice Principal

WAGOLL – What A Good One Looks Like

WM – Working Memory

#THETEACHINGLIFE